The gospel in the modern world

The gospel in the modern world

A tribute to John Stott

Saphir P. Athyal
D. W. Bebbington
Michael Cassidy
Timothy Dudley-Smith
Martyn Eden
Michael Green
Os Guinness

James M. Houston
Ernest C. Lucas
Michael Nazir-Ali
J. I. Packer
Elaine Storkey
David F. Wells
Chris Wright

Edited by Martyn Eden and David F. Wells

Inter-Varsity Press
Leicester, England
Downers Grove, Illinois, USA

INTER-VARSITY PRESS
38 De Montfort Street, Leicester LE1 7GP, England
P.O. Box 1400, Downers Grove, Illinois 60515, USA

© Inter-Varsity Press 1991

Unless otherwise stated, Scripture quotations in this publication are from the Holy Bible: New International Version, copyright © 1973, 1978 and 1984 by the International Bible Society. Used in USA by permission of Zondervan Bible Publishers, Grand Rapids, Michigan, and published in Great Britain by Hodder and Stoughton Ltd.

First published 1991

British Library Cataloguing in Publication Data
The gospel in the modern world.
1. Christianity
I. Athyal, Saphir P.   II. Eden, Martyn
III. Wells, David F. (David Falconer) *1939–*
IV. Stott, John R. W. (John Robert Walmsley) *1921–*
230

ISBN 0–85110–644–7

Library of Congress Cataloging-in-Publication Data
The gospel in the modern world: a tribute to John Stott/Saphir P. Athyal . . . [et al.]: edited by Martyn Eden and David F. Wells.
   p. cm.
   Includes bibliographical references.
   ISBN 0–8308–1756–5
   1. Church and the world.   2. Evangelicalism.   3. Evangelistic work.
4. Stott, John R. W.   I. Stott, John R. W.   II. Athyal, Saphir P.
III. Eden, Martyn, 1944– .   IV. Wells, David F.
BR115.W6G67   1991   91–9112
230'.046–dc20   CIP

Set in Linotron Ehrhardt
Typeset in Great Britain by Parker Typesetting Service, Leicester
Printed in Great Britain by Billing & Sons Ltd, Worcester

Inter-Varsity Press, England, is the book-publishing division of the Universities and Colleges Christian Fellowship (formerly the Inter-Varsity Fellowship), a student movement linking Christian Unions in universities and colleges throughout the United Kingdom and the Republic of Ireland, and a member movement of the International Fellowship of Evangelical Students. For information about local and national activities write to UCCF, 38 De Montfort Street, Leicester LE1 7GP.

InterVarsity Press, USA, is the book-publishing division of InterVarsity Christian Fellowship, a student movement active on campus at hundreds of universities, colleges and schools of nursing in the United States of America, and a member movement of the International Fellowship of Evangelical Students. For information about local and regional activities, write Public Relations Dept., InterVarsity Christian Fellowship, 6400 Schroeder Rd., P.O. Box 7895, Madison, WI 53707-7895.

*Distributed in Canada through InterVarsity Press,
860 Denison St., Unit 3, Markham, Ontario L3R 4H1, Canada*

Publisher's foreword

John Stott's association with Inter-Varsity Press as an author extends over thirty years, and we are indebted to him for some of the most lasting and significant titles in our list. The table of his publications shows that, so far, Inter-Varsity Press in England has been the original publisher of more than a dozen of his titles, excluding booklets. Transatlantic arrangements have enabled InterVarsity Press in the USA to publish over twenty of his books.

John Stott is the last person to desire human praise. Greatly daring, we take the liberty of mentioning some of the characteristics which endear him to us as an author.

The first is his *vision of a Christianity that is both biblical and contemporary*. John has inspired his publishers, as he has the contributors to this volume and countless Christians around the world, with a passionate commitment to this shared vision, in our witness to Jesus Christ. Of course other great names, past and present, have also been our mentors, and publishers value every author they publish. We think our other authors will understand if we cite the reviewer of *The Cross of Christ* who spoke of the symbiotic relationship between John Stott and Inter-Varsity Press.

Secondly, we think of his *commitment to books*. We have constantly admired the sense of purpose which guards time for writing, and the industry which has produced so many fine works. As the New Testament editor of *The Bible Speaks Today* series, he has inspired and encouraged others, and helped them with painstaking comments on every manuscript.

The third is his *exemplary thoroughness*. Not for him the quickly dashed-off manuscript, written 'off the top of his head'. Each book is carefully researched, rigorously thought-out, and beautifully polished. (We should add that they are then impeccably presented to us through the tireless skill of his secretary Frances Whitehead.)

Finally, we are thankful for his unfailing *courtesy* and *kindness*, and his *efficiency*. If others also, as we suspect, receive those long letters, many dealing with a dozen or so topics in a way which demands the highest standards of response and action, then many other enterprises must be, as ours is, greatly in debt.

We are privileged to share in this tribute, written, edited and published by a few of his many friends.

Preface

The seventieth birthday of John Stott, which is the occasion for writing this volume, is in a way a pretext. It is true that it offers the essayists in this book a welcome opportunity to express their own very great regard for its recipient. Each has known him as a friend; some have, additionally, worked with him as a colleague; and all have been influenced by him, sometimes perhaps in ways of which they are probably not fully aware. Yet, the warrant for this book is not so much in their friendship, great as that is, as in the appropriateness, at this time, of recognizing the extraordinary ministry that John has exercised, under God, around the world. Those who have contributed essays do so on behalf of the many who stand in John's debt and for whom the chance to write could not be offered. There are those in many countries who first heard of Christ from him; there are many who learned how to think biblically under his ministry; there are many who reaped the benefit of his study from his numerous books; others found in him, additionally, a compassionate counsellor. And what all have seen is how clarity of thought, integrity of character, and courageous leadership can come together in a single person, a person who only wanted to be – and only wanted to be thought of as – Christ's servant. That he has been. And so in this volume we celebrate with John this milestone with gratitude for all that God has accomplished through him.

Our focus, not surprisingly, is the gospel of God and, in particular, the gospel in the modern world. It is this theme that has occupied John for many years and it is our belief that he will be best honoured by our own further reflections upon a theme which has meant so much to him.

Having agreed to do that, the editors were faced with numerous dilemmas. How were we to balance the need for a book of reasonable length with the desire of many who wanted to contribute to it? How were we going to secure a measure of unity to the book, given the fact that the authors were so diverse in age, cultural background, ethnic make-up, experience and expertise? The latter problem was one that, remarkably, resolved itself, and what we have is a set of essays that do, to a large extent, share a common outlook. The former problem was not so easy to resolve and we can only hope that those whom we were not able to include will forgive us!

7

THE GOSPEL IN THE MODERN WORLD

The book opens with a biographical sketch of John Stott by his close friend, Timothy Dudley-Smith. Thereafter, the essays are organized in three parts and we have provided for each part a brief introduction. The focus of Part One is on what constitutes the essence of the gospel itself, that of Part Two on understanding the modern world, and that of Part Three on what it means to be a people of God in the modern world.

MARTYN EDEN
DAVID F. WELLS

Contents

John Stott:
An introduction

Timothy Dudley-Smith

Few clergymen can have been so variously associated with a single church as John Stott with All Souls Church, Langham Place. Conspicuous by Nash's famous spire and circular pillared portico, it stands at the head of Regent Street in the centre of London's West End, 400 yards from Oxford Circus and ten paces from Broadcasting House, the headquarters of the BBC.

As a child, young John and his sisters had been brought to All Souls to attend church and Sunday school from the family home in Harley Street nearby; and he had soon discovered that from his seat in the gallery one could surreptitiously drop paper pellets on the worshippers below. Then, in November 1945, the All Souls parish magazine *Monthly Notes* carried the information that John Stott was to be ordained in St Paul's Cathedral on Friday 21 December at 10.00 a.m. to become their new junior curate. Five years later, in April 1950, *Monthly Notes* gave pride of place to the following brief announcement:

Our New Rector

His Majesty the King has been graciously
pleased to appoint the Reverend J. R. W. Stott, MA,
to the living of All Souls, Langham Place.

The news of this appointment has been received
with joy and thankfulness by the whole Parish.

The Churchwardens

Years afterwards I happened to be talking in a vestry to the then
Bishop of St Albans, Michael Gresford Jones, who had been one of the
suffragan bishops of the London Diocese at the time. We were about
to take part in the institution as vicar of a man who was already curate
of the same parish. Someone remarked that this progression was rare;
and the bishop quoted John Stott and All Souls as the only instance
that came immediately to mind – and added that the Bishop of London
and his staff had not been without some hesitation over that appointment, which was made of course by the Crown (at the urgent request, I
have always understood, of the lay leadership of the church). I asked
the basis of their misgivings, and received the reply, 'We didn't think
he'd stay.' It was not unreasonable. Only a year before, John had
considered two possibilities (no doubt among others) – at Eton College
or in London's East End. But in fact, forty years on from his appointment as rector, and forty-five since his curacy, John Stott has never
left. In 1975 he became (as he remains) Rector Emeritus; and so
continues this lifelong association with the church of his childhood and
of all his settled ministry.

A brief framework of biography

The celebrated Methodist scholar, Henry Bett, wrote of Robert
Southey's *Life of Wesley*:

The final judgment on Southey's book was passed long ago by
one of Wesley's old preachers, who said, when he finished
reading it: 'Sir, thou hast nothing to draw with, and the well is
deep!'[1]

It is in much the same spirit that I approach this Introduction now. It is
not, of course, even a sketch of a biography or an assessment. It is
bound to be partial (Geoffrey Best in writing of Owen Chadwick

makes the point that in such a context 'partial' has to be understood in more senses than one);[2] and it is incorrigibly insular, which I recognize as a serious shortcoming, but can do nothing to remedy. It was a source of some puzzlement among his friends in England to note how for years – for decades – John Stott was seen in the countries he visited overseas as a world figure, and welcomed as such, while beyond specifically evangelical circles this was not the case at home.

I must add, too, that what follows is not only partial and insular, but necessarily personal. Any one among hundreds of John Stott's friends from the Arctic to the Amazon would have written from a different perspective. But I think most of them would have had this in common with me, that I write (as may be seen) not only from long friendship but from a sense of indebtedness and privilege. In what follows, I try to give the necessary biographical framework, at least until the mid-1970s. From that point on the pattern remains more constant – global travel, writing at the Hookses (his cottage in Wales), time in London – though the content differs of course from year to year. But in the nature of things, fewer of those who read these pages will have known John Stott in the earlier days than know him now. I have then outlined what seem to me to be certain distinctive themes which leave their mark on all his thought and work, not least his ministry of writing.

John's early home was in Harley Street because his father, Sir Arnold Stott, was a distinguished physician. He was a keen naturalist, and brought up his son to take an observer's interest in the world around him. John's first collection included – as with many small boys – moths and butterflies (one imagines them as being impeccably mounted, labelled and arranged); but before his schooldays were over this had focused more sharply on the study of birds, which has been his relaxation ever since. When, as their young rector, John sought the advice of the Churchwardens of All Souls about his first invitation to America to conduct a student mission, the Wardens insisted he should accept, subject to three conditions. First, they asked that he should leave behind a curate who could continue the preaching tradition of the church; secondly, that he must be prepared to make a habit of such visits; and thirdly, that he should plan to take a few days off bird-watching before returning home refreshed. Since then no bird in six continents has ever been wholly safe from John's binoculars and camera, about its bath and about its bed, and spying out all its ways.

Rugby School and Trinity College, Cambridge (his father's school and college), must have seemed a very suitable background for a career in the Diplomatic Service for which John's natural gifts, and his talent for languages, fitted him so admirably. There is a photograph of him as head boy at Rugby in which one can discern a certain patrician cast of

countenance, as of one unlikely to suffer fools gladly, before the grace
of Christian humility had been long at work. But God had other plans.
Let John take up the story in his own words:

> My adolescence was typically religious. Though my father, a
> physician, was a scientific secularist, my mother had been
> brought up as a devout Lutheran. She taught my sisters and me
> to go to church on Sundays, and to read the Bible and 'say our
> prayers' daily, which practice I continued throughout my early
> teens, more out of affectionate loyalty to her and out of routine,
> than as a personally meaningful discipline. In fact, I found the
> whole exercise extremely unsatisfying. Convinced that there
> was more to religion than I had so far discovered, I used on
> half-holiday afternoons to creep into the Memorial Chapel by
> myself, in order to read religious books, absorb the atmosphere
> of mystery, and seek for God. But he continued to elude me.[3]

He goes on to describe a meeting of the school Christian Union to
which he had been invited by a friend, John Bridger, a year senior to
him. The Reverend E. J. H. Nash of the Scripture Union had come as
visiting speaker. John wrote:

> He was nothing much to look at and certainly no ambassador
> for muscular Christianity. Yet as he spoke I was riveted. His
> text was Pilate's question: 'What then shall I do with Jesus, who
> is called the Christ?' That I needed to *do* anything with Jesus
> was an entirely novel idea to me, for I had imagined that
> somehow he had done whatever needed to be done, and that
> my part was only to acquiesce. This Mr. Nash, however, was
> quietly but powerfully insisting that everybody had to do some-
> thing about Jesus, and that nobody could remain neutral. Either
> we copy Pilate and weakly reject him, or we accept him per-
> sonally and follow him.[4]

In many mission addresses, and in his book *Basic Christianity*, John
used the third person to describe what followed, his own experience of
conversion to Christ:

> A boy in his later teens knelt at his bedside one Sunday night in
> the dormitory of his school. In a simple, matter-of-fact but
> definite way he told Christ that he had made rather a mess of
> his life so far; he confessed his sins; he thanked Christ for
> dying for him; and he asked him to come into his life. The

following day he wrote in his diary: 'Yesterday really *was* an eventful day! ... Up till now Christ has been on the circumference and I have but asked him to guide me instead of giving him complete control. Behold, he stands at the door and knocks. I have heard him and now he has come into my house. He has cleansed it and now rules in it. . . .' And the day after: 'I really have felt an immense and new joy throughout today. It is the joy of being at peace with the world and of being in touch with God. How well do I know now that he rules me and that I never really knew him before. . . .'

These are extracts from my own diary. I venture to quote them because I did not want you to think that I am recommending to you a step which I have not taken myself.[5]

Before long – even while he was still at school – John found himself drawn into Christian work and witness: helping first at a children's beach mission in Wales, then at a local church evangelistic mission, in both cases as a member of a team led by E. J. H. Nash. From this point on, until his ordination in 1945, John combined the task of secretary-treasurer of Mr Nash's schoolboy houseparties with a senior scholarship and then a double-first at Cambridge and with training at Ridley Hall for the ordained ministry. He was then, as now, able to combine a single-minded attention to the work in hand with a strong pastoral sense towards the individual. I shall never forget bumping into him during my first week in Cambridge as a freshman in October 1944. I had met him before, but hardly expected to be recognized, let alone remembered. We were outside my college, Pembroke, and John was on his bike. He stopped when he saw me, chatted for a moment, and then asked me if I planned to go to the pre-terminal meetings of the CICCU (the Cambridge Inter-Collegiate Christian Union). I told him I knew nothing about them. He explained, and said the first meeting would be that evening in Trinity OCR – the Old Combination Room above Great Court. Perhaps he saw irresolution in my eye: 'Do you know where that is?' he asked. I shook my head. He glanced at his watch, and leaned his bicycle against the wall, saying, 'I'll take you there. It takes just seven and a half minutes.' So we walked together along King's Parade to Trinity, across the Court, up the famous steps, and so to the OCR. John opened the door to show me the gracious high-windowed empty room. Then we walked back (I'm sure it will have taken fifteen minutes precisely) and John retrieved his bike, said, 'See you tonight, then,' and rode off to Ridley Hall. That was forty-five years ago, and a turning-point in my life. It was no surprise to learn, not long since, that the committee of the Christian Union formally decided in John's second or third year that they were not going to invite him to join their number – and sent Oliver Barclay to tell him so – because his gifts were better employed in his personal ministry to younger Christians in the University.

As an ordinand, John Stott was exempt from military service, and in 1945, four days before Christmas, began work as the junior curate at All Souls. I do not think it is fanciful to suppose that, among the fashionable and well-to-do members of the West End congregation, much of his heart was already given to the rougher quarters and back streets of that part of the parish which was really Soho-north-of-Oxford-Street. And those who have seen that side of John Stott which is closer to nature, and freed from urban convention, will have little difficulty in picturing him in that most typical of the new curate's duties, taking the boys' club to camp.

They would set off on bicycles, or in his ex-army pick-up truck known to the parish as his 'old jalopy', crammed with tents, blankets, cooking pots and camping gear. Camp fires, rain and mud, brilliant sun – all the usual ingredients of a camping holiday – would be there in full. But there would be more. Round the camp fire each night there would be an opportunity for these back-street London youngsters to think together, Bible in hand, under John's gentle leadership, of life's serious issues.

John was always determined that boys who found Christ for themselves at camp should be helped and encouraged in every possible way on their return. He wrote in a note to the church congregation:

> It was a good camp. Despite friendly but determined opposition, the message brought to the boys at Prayers each day bore fruit. Few of us have any idea of the struggle our boys have to undergo if they really give their allegiance to Jesus Christ. It takes a real man to stand up for decency and honesty, let alone for real Christianity, in the surroundings in which some of them live and work. Yet a few have boldly taken their stand. Will you pray for them? And when they come to Church on Sunday nights – give them a welcoming smile! J. R. W. S.

When in 1950 John Stott was appointed rector, following the illness and death of the much-loved Harold Earnshaw Smith, All Souls Church was still not fully restored following bomb damage and the congregation was worshipping in St Peter's, Vere Street, now the headquarters of Christian Impact (of which the London Institute of Contemporary Christianity is a part). Here on 26 September the new rector was instituted and inducted.

By that time, however, John had already begun to share with his people his own vision for their church life. His first sermon as rector-designate (on Acts 2:44: 'All who believed were together') had been a five-point manifesto of what he looked to see developing yet more fully among them, a church together in study, in fellowship, in worship, in prayer and in evangelism. All Souls with St Peter's, he reminded them, is a parish church:

> Our first duty is local, and yet our impact on the neighbourhood is small and the percentage of Christians in the population negligible. The multitudes are outside. Are we too respectable to go out and bring them in? Too afraid of public opinion to employ well-tried methods? Too sensitive to convention to devise new means of reaching the unbeliever? The task is beyond the power of the clergy. A staff of ten curates could not do it. There are only two alternatives. Either the task will not be done, or we must do it together, a task force of Ministers and people thoroughly trained and harnessed as a team for evangelism.

He developed this further on a Scottish holiday that summer, writing his letter for the September magazine 'perched precariously at the end of Stranraer Pier' encircled by herring gulls and oyster catchers, and accosted by a small boy enquiring, 'Och, are ye a poet, mon?' He wrote:

> The question which rests most heavily on my heart at present is how to reach the hungry multitudes who are without Christ . . . God has entrusted to us the care of some 10,000 souls living within the parochial boundaries. As Christians living near or worshipping in St. Peter's we have an unmistakable, inescapable responsibility towards our neighbours who are strangers to Christ and His gospel of grace. This responsibility is clearly shared by the whole congregation. The task of evangelism cannot be delegated to the few. Worship and witness go hand in hand. We are all called to worship, and we are all called to witness in some way. I visualise (and hope before next month to be able to explain in detail) the training of a considerable number of Church members for the task of bringing the Gospel of our Saviour Jesus Christ to every house in the parish. We cannot play at this. It will mean real sacrifice in our busy lives to commit ourselves to thorough training once a fortnight for six months, and then to go out two by two to visit from house to house.

This vision was to be worked out in practice in All Souls, and then shared in different ways across the world. When John Stott was asked to address the London Diocesan Conference two years later on 'Parochial Evangelism by the Laity', his address was published at their request, and reprinted four times in as many years. He later expanded the thinking behind the scheme in the Pastoral Theology Lectures given in Durham University and published as his book *One People* (1969).

Parochial Evangelism by the Laity is a pamphlet; but a year later saw John Stott at work on a book commissioned by his bishop, to be the Bishop of London's Lent Book for 1954. Many thought – perhaps including the author – that the rector of All Souls was an unexpected choice for Bishop Wand, not noted for his evangelical sympathies. The book was *Men with a Message*, 'an attempt to introduce the New Testament, its authors and their writings, to the man in the pew'.[6] Few could have foreseen that it would be the first in a long line of books, stretching (to date) over thirty-five years, almost without exception on the message of the Scriptures. It was the advance paid on this book by the publishers that enabled John to buy 'The Hookses', his Pembrokeshire retreat, where so many of these books have been written.

'The Hookses' is a small slate-roofed Welsh farmhouse in a low valley on the Pembrokeshire cliffs commanding superb coastal views and looking across to the island of Skokholm a few miles offshore. John first discovered it and sought to buy it when camping in the area on holiday. It was deserted and semi-derelict, the farmland having been largely concreted over as an airfield during the war. There was a barn, pigsties and other outbuildings (long since converted for human habitation) and a stream flowing down the centre of the smallholding. In the event it was sold to another purchaser: but when he moved from the area soon afterwards, John was able to acquire it. I recall happy visits there in the early days, laying a new floor to make the barn into a dormitory; helping to build a 'hide' on the cliffs from which John could watch at close quarters the disgusting habits of predatory seagulls feasting on a decaying rabbit; and enjoying, by the light of oil-lamps (there is still no electricity), the reading aloud with which we would entertain one another in the evenings. 'O happy days at Hookses ...' as I wrote to him once, lying in my sleeper from Haverfordwest back to London. I guess John is seldom happier (or more industrious) than when with a few friends in this rural retreat.

A widening world

The fifties and sixties saw not only an ever-increasing extension of the work of All Souls (the evangelistic Guest Services; the Family Services at St Peter's; the Chaplaincy to a number of the Oxford Street stores; the International Fellowship; the Clubhouse community centre) but also the development of much student work in and beyond the UK, notably in student missions in Oxford and Cambridge, and in many of the newer universities and colleges. John Pollock concluded his history of the Cambridge Inter-Collegiate Christian Union, *A Cambridge Movement*, with an eye-witness account of John Stott's mission the year before:

> The church was filled each evening, and on the last night, although chairs were placed in the side aisles and people were sitting in the choir stalls and standing wherever there was space, some of the crowd had to be turned away. But it was not so much the numbers attending which marked the mission as its spirit. The controversial atmosphere of previous years had gone. From the very first night, when in response to the missioner's invitation over one hundred men and women asked for a copy of St. John's Gospel as a sign of 'sincere search for the truth,' there was a quiet determination in all parts of the University to face up to the issues of personal faith. The main addresses were plain unhurried Biblical expositions, almost unadorned with illustrations and without any attempt to force decision; the closest attention was given throughout; such was the desire for the truth that assistant missioners, as one of them commented, 'marvelled at the ease with which men and women accepted the claims of Christ, counted the cost and received Him.' 'This mission,' wrote one undergraduate, 'has taught me most of all that the Bible is the living Word of God.'[7]

Looking back, we were all very young: and I recall travelling with John and other friends by car through Cambridge late in the evening, while John Bridger – can it have been him? – pretended to find in the carefully handwritten notes of John Stott's mission address a variant of 'Argument weak here – shout' which read 'Argument weak here: quote William Temple'!

It would be possible, if wearisome, to supply a long list of strategic Christian causes with which John was identified more or less closely over those years. The Scripture Union, the International Fellowship of

Evangelical Students (IFES), the Evangelical Alliance (and its TEAR Fund), the former Inter-Varsity Fellowship (IVF – now UCCF, the Universities and Colleges Christian Fellowship) are only the most obvious examples. At the same time he was energetically forging new structures for his vision of a revived and renewed evangelicalism. The 'Eclectic Society' was among the first, with an invitation to twenty or so younger clergy to join him for a day at the Crown Hotel, Amersham, on 21 June 1955 – following in the steps of John Newton and Richard Cecil who had founded such a society in 1783 'for mutual intercourse and the investigation of spiritual truth'. 'Christian Debate' was another similar group called together three years later 'for discussing social and moral problems with candour and freedom' – a forerunner of the kind of reading and resource groups described in John's later book *I Believe in Preaching* (1982).

John Stott himself has briefly sketched the story of the founding of the Church of England Evangelical Council (1960), and then of the Evangelical Fellowship in the Anglican Communion (1961) in his chapter in *Evangelicals Today* – though in a typically self-effacing manner.[8] In the mid-60s he also devised and inspired the series of twenty-two small books, *Christian Foundations*, which were another indication of a desire among Anglican evangelicals 'to address themselves to themes, theological and practical, which are of vital significance for the Christian Church'.[9] It would be difficult, too, to overestimate his contribution to the two National Evangelical Anglican Congresses, at Keele (1967) and at Nottingham (1977). Following the first of these, David Edwards remarked that if evangelicals were going to take the Church of England seriously, the Church would need to return the compliment; and following the second, Clifford Longley wrote in *The Times* of 'the growing power and influence' of evangelicals in the Church of England. It would be an exaggeration, but not wholly wide of the mark, to see in such growing power and influence the lengthened shadow of one man.

But all this – and much more was to lie ahead in the future with the Langham Trust, the London Lectures in Contemporary Christianity, Care and Counsel, the Evangelical Literature Trust and an important role in the International Congresses on World Evangelisation at Lausanne (1974) and Manila (1989) – all this is only what is most easily recorded. Charles Smyth, the church historian, wrote once:

> Any intelligent atheist could write a perfectly competent, although probably a somewhat biassed history of Popes and Councils and all that sort of thing. But Church History is something other than the record of ecclesiastical statecraft and

diplomacy or even of those great doctrinal controversies by which it is so much conditioned and controlled. And I would go so far as to say that nobody can write Church History who is not either a parish priest or at least a person who has some real understanding of the problems of the parish priest ... for the central theme of Church History – and, as I myself should naturally claim, of all human history – is Sin and Redemption.[10]

That central theme was for John, as it remains, a war in which there is no discharge. In his travels, his evangelistic missions, his association with Dr Billy Graham, and his teaching and writing ministry, this task was being carried steadily forward. By 1975 the time had come, after twenty-five years as rector, to loosen a little the ties of responsibility to a single church by becoming Rector Emeritus, and so to signal in a new sense that the world had become his parish. An observer in these years could have said of him, as was said of Cyril Garbett, 'that he would have found it extremely difficult to fit a wife into his time-table'.[11] It was also becoming clear, after the particular honour of appointment as a Chaplain to the Queen in 1959, that comparable ecclesiastical recognition and responsibility (for example, as a diocesan bishop or overseas archbishop) would now represent a curtailment of these unique and varied ministries. Instead, God began to give him a vision for a new kind of college, the London Institute for Contemporary Christianity, which would unite together most if not all of the varied major themes which could be identified in John's developing ministry: and it is to these themes we must now turn.

Themes of a life

First, as a background to all his life and work, there are the recurring fundamental evangelical distinctives: the uniqueness of Christ and the need of personal conversion; the living word of Holy Scripture; and the centrality of the cross. 'Evangelical distinctives' is hardly, I think, a phrase that John himself would be eager to recognize. In 1982, in the presidential address to the UCCF conference he began by asking the question 'What is the evangelical faith?' and went on to say:

At the risk of oversimplification and of the charge of arrogance, I want to argue that the evangelical faith is nothing other than the historic Christian faith. The evangelical Christian is not a deviationist, but a loyalist who seeks by the grace of God to be faithful to the revelation which God has given of himself in Christ and in Scripture. The evangelical faith is not a peculiar or esoteric version of the Christian faith – it is the Christian faith. It is not a recent innovation. The evangelical faith is original, biblical, apostolic Christianity. At least that is what we believe it to be, and I for one would not hold it if I were not convinced about this. ... Our fundamental desire is to be loyal to the biblical revelation.

It is that 'desire to be loyal to the biblical revelation' that unites the concern for evangelism and world-wide mission (*Basic Christianity*, derived from his early mission addresses, is now available in thirty-six languages) with the patient study, research and scholarship of his thirty or so later books, including the concept of *The Bible Speaks Today* series for which he is both New Testament editor and (for some volumes) a contributor.

This emphasis on Scripture found illuminating expression in an international symposium on the Lausanne Covenant, *The New Face of Evangelicalism*,[12] to which John contributed the chapter on 'The Authority and Power of the Bible'. He began:

Some readers of the Lausanne Covenant will doubtless think it very odd that a statement on evangelism should not only include a paragraph on the Bible but also place it in such a prominent position, second only to God himself and his purpose. 'Those evangelicals are incorrigible,' our critics may say; 'they always insist on dragging the Bible in somewhere. It's a positive obsession with them.'

But our critics do not always understand us. Far from being irrelevant to a declaration on evangelism, biblical authority and power are fundamental. At least three reasons may be given. First, if evangelism means precisely 'spreading the evangel', it is impossible to discuss evangelism as an activity apart from the message which is being communicated. ...

Secondly, if evangelism leads to conversion, the evangelist should be concerned for the nurture of the converts. What teaching shall they be given? ...

Thirdly, there is more than content in God's Word, in God's revealed truth, which instructs us for salvation; there is power. Evangelism is not a merely human enterprise. Men cannot win souls by their own ingenuity or effort. Only God can give life to the dead. And his power is exercised through his Word and Spirit.[13]

For another 'distinctive', I need only point to his study *The Cross of Christ* (1986) – for 'The centrality of the cross' forms the title of the opening chapter, in what is perhaps one of his most lasting works, demonstrating that 'the only authentic Jesus is the Jesus who died on the cross'.

Beside these basic truths, what other threads should we distinguish which run throughout John Stott's ministry and teaching? I would cite next his concern for witness and evangelism as the task of the local church; and their relation to social action. From the early days of the student guest services in the 1940s, to the founding of the London Institute and the drafting of the Manila Manifesto, this has been a recurring theme, finding expression in books such as *Balanced Christianity* (1975), *Christian Mission in the Modern World* (1975), and (pre-eminently, as relating biblical teaching to social problems) in *Issues Facing Christians Today* (1984). Nor is this simply an academic quest.

In his Epilogue to *Essays in Evangelical Social Ethics*,[14] John spoke of the tasks which await us, urging evangelicals to move beyond questions to answers, beyond words to actions, beyond thought and actions to passion and to vision. It is a theme close to his own heart.

Next, I detect a continuing love and concern for the strategic nurturing and training of tomorrow's leaders. This too begins in the 1940s, with John himself a student, and it can be seen in his training of his personal team (curates, student assistants and so on), in the Eclectic Society, in the Third World Research Scholarships of the Langham Trust, the Evangelical Fellowship in the Anglican Communion bursary scheme, and the Evangelical Literature Trust which provides books for Third World pastors and scholars. It appears also in his continuing commitment to student work, through IFES and UCCF. He wrote in 1989:

> I sometimes wonder on which particular scrapheap I would be today, if it had not been for God's providential gift of the UCCF. For I went up to Cambridge a very wobbly and vulnerable young Christian. I could easily have been overwhelmed by the world, the flesh and the devil. But the Christian Union brought me friendships, teaching, books and opportunities for service, which all helped me to stand firm and grow up. I am profoundly grateful.
>
> Since then I have had the privilege of leading university missions and speaking at student conferences on all six continents. And, wherever I have been, I have been moved to further thanksgiving for IFES and its member movements – for

its indigenous principles, for its emphasis on discipling and leadership training as well as evangelism, and for the quality of its personnel.[15]

It would be difficult to over-emphasize this element in John's ministry. It can be said of him, as was said of Charles Simeon (by Bishop Charles Wordsworth), that he had a following 'larger and not less devoted than that which followed Newman – and for a much longer time';[16] and (by Lord Macaulay), 'If you knew what his authority and influence were, and how they extended . . . to the most remote corners of England, you would allow that his real sway in the church was far greater than that of any primate.'[17]

Next, it is beyond question that the importance of preaching has been, and remains, a cornerstone of John's work and thought. The first chapter of his major work *I Believe in Preaching* opens with the words 'Preaching is indispensable to Christianity'.[18] A much earlier book, *The Preacher's Portrait* (1961), had stated his own conviction that 'We need to gain in the Church today a clearer view of God's revealed ideal for the preacher, what he is and how he is to do his work'.[19]

John has often been compared, as I have just compared him, with Charles Simeon. Simeon is also one of John's heroes (his picture hangs on the wall of his home), and this is not only because Simeon was the man who, under God, was 'one of the greatest and most persuasive preachers the Church of England has ever known'.[20] It is also because, through Claude's *Essay*,[21] which was republished in 1837 with one hundred of Simeon's 'skeleton' sermons attached, the craft of preaching began once again to be studied and taken seriously, so setting a new standard of biblical exposition in the English Church. John Stott introduced some of these principles of homiletics, with forty of Simeon's sermons, in *Evangelical Preaching*.[22]

Next, and all-pervading, comes the quest to develop a Christian mind. Harry Blamires' book *The Christian Mind*[23] seems to have served to focus a set of ideas which cluster round this concept. John developed these in his Presidential Address, 1972, to the IVF Annual Conference, later published under the title *Your Mind Matters*. But it features also as one of the four themes of *Balanced Christianity* (1975), and as chapter two of *Issues Facing Christians Today*. The phrase represents an approach to theology and to Christian understanding which lies behind all John's teaching and writing, from his own early days in the theological tripos to his lecturing at the London Institute, his honorary American doctorate, and his Lambeth DD.

I would also want to single out for particular notice John's handling of controversy. There was a time – long ago now – when I feared that he might not see this as part of his particular calling. I need not have been anxious. From *Fundamentalism and Evangelism* (1956), addressing two of the current controversies of the mid-50s, through *Christ the Controversialist* (1970) to the specifically controversial studies in *Issues Facing Christians Today* (1984), and his penetrating critiques of the reports of the two Anglican-Roman Catholic International Commissions, John has been ready when necessary to embrace controversy to defend the gospel. But it has never been long-range warfare from entrenched positions; nor the scoring of mere debating points. Whether in dialogue with charismatics, liberals, Anglo-Catholics or Roman Catholics, John's hallmark has been not only (in his own phrase) a 'balanced Christianity', but also a Christian standard of debate. His aim is always fully to understand and fairly to evaluate a position with which he cannot agree; and then from Scripture to demonstrate cogently, irenically and fearlessly a more excellent way. Perhaps this is nowhere seen more plainly than in his 354-page debate with David Edwards, *Essentials: a liberal-evangelical dialogue* (1988) where truth and grace are neither of them sacrificed, and the 'defence of the gospel' is courteously and firmly maintained without compromise, yet in fellowship and charity.

In the early days of Wycliffe Hall, Oxford, a student made this comment on the Principal: 'It is not what Chavasse says, but that *he* says it.'[24] The man was the message. In the same way, those closest to John Stott would have much to add of the humility, the personal integrity, the pastoral heart, the simple life-style, that help to make John the man he is. These are not themes to which an Introduction of this nature can do justice; but there are two characteristics which cannot escape mention, his sense of history and his sense of humour. As to the first, I cite his love of the Reformers and his understanding of the continuity of evangelicalism and how much we owe to a Wesley, a Simeon, a Clapham Sect – and to the founding fathers of such bodies as the Scripture Union or the UCCF.[25] As to the second, no-one can spend long in his company without becoming aware of an imp of mischief not deeply hidden beneath the urbane exterior. This comes as a surprise to those who know only his reputation for a certain almost-teutonic thoroughness and attention to detail: and have not detected the twinkle in the eye. We all, I guess, have treasured incidents which reveal this side of him: I certainly have mine. But I shall need to know you better before I can be ready to share them!

David Edwards, who can lay some claim to view our own times with the eye of an historian, tells how Winston Churchill was widely reported to have observed that among the bishops William Temple, although a Socialist, was 'a sixpenny article in a penny bazaar'.[26] It makes all the more striking the generous recognition given by David Edwards to John Stott's work and ministry (please God, a life and work with many years still before them). At the beginning of *Essentials*, David Edwards describes John Stott as

> ... a loved and trusted leader, teacher and spokesman of the world-wide Evangelical movement – and apart from William Temple (who died as Archbishop of Canterbury in 1944) the most influential clergyman in the Church of England during the twentieth century.[27]

That phrase 'the most influential clergyman' sounds (until one tries to think of another) like legitimate hyperbole. In the proper perspective of history, it may well be a true judgment. But about the love and trust which begin the quotation there can be no doubt whatever. For many of us John embodies evangelicalism as he himself once described it: 'The hallmark of authentic evangelicalism has always been zeal for the honour and glory of Jesus Christ. With that, I think, we shall be safe.'

Part One
The essential gospel

Introduction to Part One

When the London Institute for Contemporary Christianity, of which John Stott was the founding Director, was launched in 1982, the religious correspondent of *The Times* observed that its aim was to turn biblical Christians into contemporary Christians. He was not known for evangelical sympathies and the negative intentions of this ambiguous phrase were well understood. In one sense, however, he was correct. Through the Institute and through much of his later writing and teaching, John Stott has sought to help evangelical Christians to relate their biblical faith to the modern world. He expressed this in the statement of distinctives of the London Institute:

> God has not called us to live in the first century or in the Middle Ages or even in the first half of the 20th century, but in its last decades. We must therefore struggle to understand the contemporary scene ... We aim to help Christians develop both a Christian critique of its assumptions, values and standards, and a Christian response to its challenges.

But all this is to be without in any way detracting from, or adding to, the historic gospel. As the essays by Chris Wright and David Wells indicate in chapters 1 and 2, there are those in the church who wish to recast the gospel in sympathy with the relativist assumptions of contemporary Western culture. Neither John Stott, nor the contributors to this book, want any part in that. Our wish is both to live under the gospel, and to communicate it in such a way that its meaning and contemporary relevance are made clear. Our business is that of making a modern translation, not that of writing a new version of the gospel.

The three essays in Part One are, in one way or another, concerned with how to remain faithful to the gospel under the pressures of modernity. In the first, Chris Wright examines the meaning of biblical authority in an age of relativism. The belief that the Bible is God's authoritative Word is not well received today in many parts of the world. It is held to be arrogant to advance the claims of one creed over any other. Tolerance and individual freedom are popularly thought to be the cardinal virtues. In a pluralistic society every belief is considered to be of equal value. There is no place for a faith which claims uniqueness or espouses moral absolutes. Yet, as Wright observes, if nothing has authority, what constitutes sufficient grounds for action? The result is a moral paralysis. It is no help in this context to quote the Bible itself, as some evangelicals do. That is like the boxer Muhammad Ali saying that he was the greatest. Sceptics required some objective evidence. Wright picks up a clue from Oliver O'Donovan's *Resurrection and the Moral Order*, and finds a sufficient basis for substantiating the authority of the Bible in general, and the Old Testament in particular, in its 'revelatory witness to the creation order and to the God who stands behind it', and who has acted within history.

David Wells' essay on the alleged obsolescence of the atonement also has contemporary relativism as its starting-point. If religion were a social construct shaped by one's culture, belief in the uniqueness of Jesus would be untenable. It would follow that his crucifixion could not be given the significance attributed to it by the biblical doctrine of the atonement. In his critique of this position, David Wells draws attention to the irony that what is intended as a means of escaping from a so-called cultural arrogance is itself an expression of just that. Those who deny the possibility of biblical absolutes do so on the basis of their own experience of modernity but then promulgate their conclusions as binding on everyone. As Wells makes clear, however, such a humanist approach to understanding God and his dealings with his creatures is bound to be confused. Without biblical absolutes, how can the relativist grasp the nature of God, the true extent of human sin, and our need for an atoning saviour?

It is probable that anyone reading the first two chapters sequentially will come to the third with the presupposition that evangelical Christianity owes nothing to the eighteenth-century Enlightenment, and was probably a reaction against it. If so, David Bebbington's essay will come as a surprise, for his thesis is quite the opposite. After identifying the essential characteristics of evangelicalism, he demonstrates the various ways in which eighteenth-century evangelicals were immersed in, and influenced by, the Enlightenment. Bebbington is not saying that they were mere creatures of the Enlightenment, uncritically absorbing every aspect of it. Nor will he allow, however, that the Enlightenment was necessarily hostile to the Christian faith. Is there a challenge in this conclusion for today's evangelicals? How well do we 'read' contemporary culture in order that we may live in it without being subservient to it? Neither accommodation, nor hiding in a ghetto, serve the cause of the gospel in the modern world.

MARTYN EDEN
DAVID F. WELLS

The authority of Scripture in an age of relativism

Old Testament perspectives

Chris Wright

Introduction

I offer this essay not as an attempt to rewrite a doctrine of Scripture by redefining its authority, but more as a personal testimony to how I see that authority functioning in two areas with which I am professionally concerned. The phrase 'the authority of Scripture' is commonly used in a prescriptive sense, namely that the Scriptures tell us what we must believe, and what we must and must not do. They have an authority over our minds and our actions because they come from the one who is Lord of both.

A somewhat different, though doubtless complementary, perception of authority stimulated my thinking recently through reading Oliver O'Donovan's programmatic survey of evangelical ethics, *Resurrection and Moral Order*. He defined authority as that which constitutes a sufficient ground for acting:

Authority is the objective correlate of freedom. It is what we encounter in the world which makes it meaningful for us to act. An authority, we may say, is something which, by virtue of its kind, constitutes an immediate and sufficient ground for acting. If someone listens to music, joins a club, or reads philosophy, his action requires no explanation. Beauty, community and truth are sufficient grounds for action in themselves. They make action undertaken in relation to them immediately intelligible.[1]

O'Donovan argues that the created order itself, coming from the hand of God, provides that range of authority within which we are free to act in a great variety of ways, for authority is the pre-condition of freedom. The authority of the Scriptures lies, at least in part, therefore, in their revelatory witness to that created order and the God who stands behind it.

I was led, then, to ask myself in what ways the Scripture 'authorizes' my own action in God's world. It happens that I teach the Hebrew Scriptures with particular emphasis on ethics, in a college which specializes in cross-cultural training. Both of those emphases – assessing and evaluating ethical stances, and seeking to understand and critique divergent cultures – raise questions of authority and both of them, I hope to show, find adequate authority in the Old Testament.

In an age of moral relativism

Any course of study on ethics has to spend considerable time on the analysis and critique of the varieties of moral relativism in the air today. From the pop culture's 'If it feels OK and nobody gets hurt, who can say it's wrong?' to the more sophisticated forms of subjectivism, existentalism, situationism and utilitarian consequentialism, the common dogma is that there is no transcendent authority by which absolute right or wrong, good or evil, can be determined a priori. Morality is relative. It all depends on ... (any number of things). Against this climate of moral relativism, the Christian affirms the authority of Scripture. But the simple affirmation by itself will not get him or her very far, since the issue of what the authority of Scripture (especially of the Old Testament) actually means in practical ethical decision-making has dogged the church since its beginnings.

Three hermeneutical traditions

Richard N. Longenecker suggests, in a brief but thought-provoking article, that three major responses of early Christianity have surfaced repeatedly in arguments all through church history. These were the responses to the question of how the Hebrew canon should be used by Christians.[2]

Marcion, in the second century, simply repudiated the Hebrew Scriptures and all things Jewish as of no relevance or authority whatever for Christians, having allegedly come from another source altogether than the revelation of God in Jesus Christ. Though officially rejected by the church, the ghost of Marcion has haunted the hermeneutical house down through the ages, making its appearance in the antinomian tendencies of the radical wing of the Reformation, in the ahistorical existentalism of Bultmann and kindred spirits, and (for very different theological reasons) in modern dispensationalism. And those are only the theological movements. Many churches are in practice Marcionite in their abysmal neglect of the Scriptures that Jesus himself used, refusing to read them in worship even when lectionary provision is made for it.

The Alexandrian school of the late second and early third centuries stressed the unity of the Scriptures and the Christianness of the Old Testament. This led the Alexandrians to develop a highly allegorical and spiritual exegesis of the Old Testament, on the one hand, and a distinction between the ceremonial and moral dimensions of the law, on the other. The former dominated medieval theology while the second went on to be further refined and still survives. Calvin and the Reformed tradition owe much to this school – not in its allegorical treatment of the Hebrew Bible, which Calvin fully rejected in favour of a careful historico-grammatical exegesis, but in the commitment to the unity and continuity of the Testaments, such that the Old Testament is read as unquestionably Christian Scripture, to be interpreted and obeyed in the light of Christ. This influence can be seen in the Puritans' emphasis on the 'third (moral) use' of the law in the Christian's life. The unity is pushed to its ethical extreme in the theonomic school, which asserts that the moral authority of the Old Testament applies with as much force as the law did for Israel, since it is God's law for all time for all humanity.

The Antiochene school of the fourth and fifth centuries opposed the Alexandrian allegorical exegesis and emphasized the historical development within the Scriptures, as well as the importance of redemptive fulfilment of the Old Testament in the New. This led to a less static and more dynamic approach to biblical authority. Here Old

Testament perspectives could be set aside in the light of the 'new thing' of the incarnation and kingdom of God in Christ. Both Alexandria and Antioch believed in the continuity between the Testaments, but whereas Alexandria saw sameness and made the Old Testament say Christian things, Antioch saw development and allowed the New Testament to override the Old where necessary. The Antiochene antipathy to allegory surfaced again in Luther's bold rejection of medieval scholastic theology. Luther was also more Antiochene than Calvin in allowing the new wine of the gospel to dispense with the old wineskins of the Old Testament wherever he sensed a conflict. Where Calvin sought consistency and harmony, Luther was content with a very free and sometimes inconsistent ethical handling of the Old Testament. This arose from his dynamic and ebullient glorying in the primacy of the gospel as over against the law. As for modern examples of the Antiochene spirit, I think I would point to the heirs of the radical Reformation, such as those Mennonites who are concerned and active in social issues. These stress a radical discipleship and have a strongly New Testament, messianic orientation in both theology and ethics, while emphasizing the importance of the distinctiveness of the people of God, which is a value most strongly inculcated in the Hebrew Scriptures.

Of the three representative streams, the Marcionite is the one that must still be resisted. Popular neglect of the Old Testament is deplorable but can at least be corrected by enthusiastic preaching and teaching. Somehow dispensationalism is more dogmatically impervious since its whole scheme requires the demotion of the Old Testament, though it is true to say that serious biblical and ethical scholars in the dispensational schools, such as Norman Geisler, do make effective contributions to Christian ethical reflection and use the Hebrew Scriptures in doing so.[3]

My own commitment is to a combination of the best of the Alexandrian and Antiochene streams. From the former, and through the Reformed tradition, I would strongly defend the unity and continuity of the Testaments. The authority of the Old Testament is derived from its being an integral part of the canon of Christian Scripture. At the same time I would emphasize, from the latter, the centrality of Jesus as the Messiah, and the importance that historical development and fulfilment makes to our understanding and application of his Scriptures. The two emphases are bound together in my mind by seeing the vital place of the people of God. This is the Israel of both Testaments, focused, fulfilled and embodied in the person of Jesus the Messiah, and sent into the world both before and after the incarnation as God's model community, his holy priesthood, in the midst of the nations, with the responsibility of a life-style and a message.

Authority in relation to history

This emphasis on the role of Israel brings us to the importance of history in our assessment of the locus of ethical authority. The Scriptures give us authorized grounds for acting in freedom, not because they tell us what Israel or the early Christians thought, or how they articulated their own moral perceptions, but because they record what God has actually done in history. This is how the Hebrew Scriptures characteristically underwrite the authority of particular laws: 'This is how you must act because this is what Yahweh has done.' The Ten Commandments begin that way – with a historical indicative referring to the deliverance from Egypt. The motive clause, so distinctive a feature of Israelite law, regularly cites historical precedent or model for the particulars of the law.

The point here is not that there are vague moral lessons to be learned from the past (a truth which probably all human cultures would endorse in general). Rather, the point is that certain specific moral distinctions are made between kinds of behaviour which are mandated, and others which are prohibited, on the authority of concrete historical events, which are attributed to the action of Yahweh. If one meaning of authority is that which provides a sufficient ground for acting, then we are right in referring to the authority of history, provided it is interpreted (as of course it is in the Scriptures) within a theological framework which discerns the action of God. Thus the law is not content to remain on the level of moral ideals such as 'You shall be holy, for I Yahweh your God am holy'. Instead it concretely commands, 'You shall love the alien (with all concomitant rights and privileges that flow from that stance) because I Yahweh your God love the alien, and proved it by the historical act of delivering you from Egypt' (*cf.* Lv. 19:33–34; Dt. 10:19ff.). God's action creates the condition in which it is right to behave thus, and so to aliens. Conversely his action is what makes it wrong to behave otherwise to them. In other words, the moral authority of biblical history is not just that it happened (for, as O'Donovan points out, all historical events are unique and would have no compelling moral authority in themselves). Rather, the moral authority of biblical history is that in it God chose to act in a way which gives meaning and purpose to all history (climaxing in the resurrection), and to reveal the meaning and implications of his action for our moral guidance.

The importance of the concrete historical basis of biblical faith and ethics has often been contrasted with abstract, cyclical, or pantheistic religious world-views. For that reason it has become increasingly relevant in facing the challenge of New Age thinking. Recently I was conducting some seminars on the Old Testament theology of the land. The observation was made how apparently similar many of the scriptural assertions and imagery concerning the land were to the way New Age philosophy talks about the earth. Examples abound in the Hebrew Scriptures of the personification of the land. It rejoices, it mourns, it can vomit, it can be addressed and respond, it suffers but can be refreshed and enjoy sabbath rest. But are we dealing here with the personal world spirit, or the divine 'Gaia'? Nothing could be further from the Hebrew conception. The reason why the land could be spoken of in personal terms was neither because it in itself was personal, nor because of any magical or mythological view of it, but because the land was the stage on which the personal relationship between Yahweh and Israel was enacted in specific historical events that took place upon it.

Even the festivals of Israel which were most closely linked to the land and its fruitfulness were consistently given a historical reference or justification. That is, the recurrent cycle of nature was celebrated as it ought to be. However, the cycle was attributed to the God who, more importantly than the harvest he had just given, had at a specific point in the past acted in justice and redemption to give them the land on which they could have harvests of their own at all (Dt. 26). Similarly all the moral requirements which we might broadly label ecological – relating to land use, harvests, concern for animals, trees and resources – were based on the authority of Yahweh's action in history, not on some innate divine properties in the soil itself. In fact, by being rooted in history rather than in the soil, they proved much more morally durable, both in resisting fertility cults which tend to dominate when the religion of the soil is divorced from response to the God of justice in history, and in surviving the loss of particular turf (as Brueggeman calls it).[4]

So the insistence of the Scriptures that God himself has acted in history, and thereby constituted moral criteria for human action in history, is a major feature of biblical ethics. This sets it against the hyper-individualism of existentialism, in which every individual must reinvent the moral wheel for himself in each moment of decision, and the hyper-corporatism of New Age super-consciousness, which virtually dissolves personal morality, as most pantheisms ultimately do.

Authority in relation to creation

At the same time as we stress the centrality of the scriptural affirmation concerning the moral authority of God's action in history, we need to give adequate attention to its portrayal of God as creator, with all its implications for our world-view. An emphasis on history alone, without the safeguards of the biblical creation faith, could deliver us into the kind of historical relativism which puts all things, morality included, at the mercy of the historical process. This is a danger of which O'Donovan also warns us, insisting that the only proper protection from it is the biblical affirmation of a given order of creation. Though disturbed by the fall, it is still the order within which we live. It will finally be restored to its perfection and glory through God's redemptive action, which has already been achieved in the resurrection of Christ and will be complete at his return:

> That which most distinguishes the concept of creation is that it is complete. Creation is the given totality of order which forms the presupposition of historical existence. 'Created order' is that which is not negotiable within the course of history, that which neither the terrors of chance nor the ingenuity of art can overthrow. It defines the scope of our freedom and the limits of our fears. The affirmation of the psalm, sung on the sabbath which celebrates the completion of creation, affords a ground for human activity and human hope: 'the world is established, it shall never be moved'. Within such a world, in which 'the Lord reigns', we are free to act and can have confidence that God will act. Because created order is given, because it is secure, we dare to be certain that God will vindicate it in history. 'He comes to judge the earth. He will judge the world with righteousness and the peoples with his truth' (Ps. 96:10, 13, RSV).[5]

The importance of keeping a firm grasp on the creation base is to be seen first of all in its anchoring of the gospel itself. An immense amount has been written and said in recent years about the need to see how the gospel takes root in different historical and cultural contexts. In fact, the gospel cannot be understood and responded to apart from the context within which it is heard. We cannot escape some context. But while culture and context will assuredly shape our understanding, reception, response and formulation of the gospel, they do not in themselves determine its fundamental content. This is so for two reasons at least:

> First, because the gospel is in essence good news about something which has happened. It is not an ideology or even a theology, but simply the announcing of an event: namely, the birth, life, death and resurrection of Jesus of Nazareth. The

culture and context of the person or group to whom that announcement is made will shape their perception of it and their response to it, but cannot change the factual reality of it. We will discover in ever changing contexts what the good news *means* for specific peoples, but we will not rediscover what actually happened which makes it to be good news in the first place.

Second, because the gospel is in fact the restoration, redemption and reconciliation of *creation* by God and to God. And the creation is something *given*. That is, there is a reality, an order to human life on the earth under God which we did not invent. In our human history we have messed it up by our sin and rebellion. But it is still 'there', and we cannot escape it or change it any more than we can get outside our own createdness. And it is that given reality which is the object of God's restoration (because it has been spoiled), his redemption (because it is enslaved and lost), and his reconciliation (because it is broken, divided and alienated). There is, therefore, a *givenness* about the gospel also, derived from the givenness of creation. Our evangelism and social action together must be culturally and contextually *relevant* in any historical location, but they are not *dependent* on culture, context or history. We did not invent creation, but we are called to live responsibly within it. Neither did we invent the gospel or discover it, but we are called to live obediently to it . . . If there were nothing given and universal about the gospel, we would not be able to recognize it when it impacts a particular context.[6]

What is true of the gospel is true of the ethic which is integral to it. And what is true in New Testament terms was true also in the Old Testament. The levels and dimensions of meaning in the exodus event, for example, could be appreciated in different ways through Israel's history, but nothing could affect the basic historicity of the event itself. Similarly, whatever the culture or whatever the juncture of history, we all have to live in God's created world as his human creatures. There is a basic shape to that world which we did not invent, and therefore a corresponding shape to the moral response required of us if we are to live within it with the kind of freedom which, by God's so ordering, it authorizes. Morality, in biblical terms, therefore, is pre-conditioned by the given shape of creation, which underlies the relativity of cultural responses to it within history.

The heart of our complaint, then, against those who assert that morality is historically and culturally relative *per se* is that they themselves absolutize that which is relative (the historical process), and relativize that which is absolute (the order of creation):

> Classical Christian thought proceeded from a universal order of meaning and value, an order given in creation and fulfilled in the kingdom of God, an order, therefore, which forms a framework for all action and history, to which action is summoned to conform in its making of history. Historicism denies that such a universal order exists. What classical ethics thought of as a transhistorical order is, it maintains, itself a historical phenomenon. Action cannot be conformed to transhistorical values, for there are none, but must respond to the immanent dynamisms of that history to which it finds itself contributing.[7]

The biblical authority, then, for our ethics in a world of moral relativism, is based on its twin affirmation of creation and history: creation as the fundamental order that shapes our existence in history, and which is destined for restoration in the new creation of the kingdom of God; and history as the stage on which we observe the acts of the God whom we are commanded to imitate by 'walking in his ways'.

In an age of cultural relativism

We live in a multi-cultural world. That was always true, of course, but it is now much more a part of modern self-consciousness than before. Our cities are polychrome and polycultural. Television, coffee-table books and travel to more exotic holiday locations, all bring us into contact with cultures previously unknown. The effect on the popular mind has been a greater awareness of the plurality of human culture and a questioning of the assumptions of the superiority of any one culture. True, Western culture still seems determined to flood the world, but the motive is probably more nakedly commercial self-interest than the self-conscious cultural superiority that characterized previous eras. Then, colonial exploitation accompanied the assumption of a duty to spread 'civilization'. The exploitation continues, but our consciences are soothed by a feeling that at least we respect other cultures more now.

Relativizing the relativizers

At least, we have become highly critical of those whom we suspect of not respecting other cultures, or worse, of destroying them – whether by destroying their habitat (as in the current concern for the rain forests and their inhabitants) or by religious conversion. Thus, the 1990 television series 'Missionaries' started out from its opening footage with the unqualified assertion that missionaries ever since Paul have been marked by an arrogance which confidently sees all other cultures than (Western) Christian culture as both sinful and inferior and therefore to be attacked and replaced.

Now if we take the missionary expansion as a test case, we may agree that in many instances missionaries made judgments about other cultures which were based not so much on essential Christian and gospel values as on their own cultural assumptions. But were they mistaken in making judgments at all? Their judgments may have been faulty and laden with unexamined assumptions of Western superiority, but is it illegitimate to criticize any features of a culture on any grounds? The underlying assumption of series like 'Missionaries' seems to be that it is. No culture has the right to criticize another, and to do so in the guise of religion is both arrogant and destructive. However, even before going on to see whether the Bible gives us authority for critical examination of cultures, it is worth pointing out that the stance of those who produce a series like 'Missionaries' is not itself culturally neutral. The critics of the criticizers of other cultures are themselves the children of a particular culture, with hidden and unexamined assumptions. These are the assumptions of post-Enlightenment secular humanism, which, having relegated religion to the realm of the subjective and out of the realm of factual reality, affirms the dogma of religious relativism, and rules out a priori, as arrogant and self-righteous, any claim to ultimate truth. For devotees of *these* enormous assumptions to criticize those who criticized other cultures, on the basis of *their* assumptions of what cultural dress was appropriate for Christianity, is rather like the blind criticizing the blind.

As Reinhold Niebuhr has helpfully clarified, there are a variety of ways in which the relationship between the Christian gospel and human culture may be expressed, in theory and practice.[8] Evangelicals committed to the authority of Scripture will affirm that, in whatever way the relationship is nuanced, the basic order is that it is the gospel which judges the culture. All culture is a human product and therefore manifests both the dignity of the image of God and the depravity of human fallenness. So while we may not be in a position to make judgments upon other human cultures from the horizontal viewpoint of our own (we may at least be grateful to the relativizers for challenging and undermining all forms of cultural or racist superiority), the revelation of God in Scripture and Christ gives us an elevation (which of course is neither of our own creation nor to our own credit), from which such a critique can be made.

At this point, however, we will be told that the Bible itself is culturally contextual. The Scriptures we take as our authority come from not one but several cultures, over a vast span of history, all very remote from ourselves. How then can religious responses, in a remote cultural context, carry the authority for us to stand in judgment on modern cultures? For some scholars, such as D. E. Nineham, the culture gap is too great for even Jesus to have the kind of moral authority traditionally attributed to him.

Our answer has to begin with the same two points that were stressed in the first section. The Scriptures claim that God has acted in history. The faith of Israel, therefore, was not just a cultural feedback but a response to objective events which they witnessed and in which they participated. The Scriptures which grew within their cultural context were therefore not merely (though inevitably) shaped by that culture (in language, background, imagery, *etc.*), but stood in constant dialogue, and often conflict, with it, shaping and moulding it in terms of the values of Yahweh himself. And the God who thus acted within the historical development of that culture was none other than the creator of humanity and the world. Hence, the direction in which he acted to shape or refine the historical culture of his people was in line with the structure of created order underlying his will for all human life in his world.

Israel as a paradigm for evaluating cultures

It is at this point that the relevance of Israel as an actual historical society becomes most apparent. God in his wisdom chose to act through a human community, which from its beginning in the election of Abraham was to be a distinctive people, committed to his own way in the midst of a world going its own way:

> I have chosen him, so that he will direct his children and his household after him to keep the way of the LORD by doing what is right and just, so that the LORD will bring about for Abraham what he has promised him. (Gn. 18:19)

God's purpose of blessing for humanity as a whole is the end (goal or *telos*) of both the election of Abraham and the moral requirement upon Abraham's descendants (and this was said before Isaac was even conceived!). Similarly, at the point of the constitution of Israel as

God's own covenant people, at Sinai, their identity and mission to be a priesthood in the midst of the nations of the whole earth is linked to the moral demand to be a holy (distinct) community through obedience to the covenant law. God chose, therefore, to make a people the locus of his historical revelation and his saving activity. And that people were intentionally and self-consciously to be a light to the nations.

Elsewhere I have used the word 'paradigm' to describe this feature of biblical Israel.[9] It seems to me both to sum up what God intended in creating Israel and in then giving them laws and institutions that shaped their culture, and also to be a fruitful concept in helping us work from the Hebrew Scriptures to our own situation. When I first used the term, I had in mind its usage in grammar. Paradigm verbs or nouns may be used to show how other words behave in different syntactical arrangements within a language. The paradigm then functions to enable the language-learner to achieve grammatical correctness in the use of all the other words he may want to use. The words and contexts will be of infinite variety, but the shape of the paradigms can be seen in each new sentence.

Recently I came across the use of paradigms in a very different context, but one which struck me as helpful in developing further the point I wish to make. Vern Poythress, in his study of *Science and Hermeneutics*,[10] makes use of Thomas Kuhn's seminal work, *The Structure of Scientific Revolutions*,[11] in which he rejected the classic view of the progress of science, the view associated with Baconian scientific method. Kuhn argued that science did not advance merely by a step-by-step inductive method:

> Research on specific problems always took place against the background of assumptions and convictions produced by previously existing science. In mature science, this background took the form of 'paradigms', a cluster of beliefs, theories, values, standards for research, and exemplary research results that provided a framework for scientific advance within a whole field.[12]

Poythress goes on to distinguish two senses in which Kuhn uses the word 'paradigm'. On the one hand it can denote 'the entire constellation of beliefs, values, techniques, and so on shared by the members of a given community'. On the other hand, it designates 'concrete puzzle-solutions', *i.e.* actual results of experimentation that provide models for further research by suggesting ways of problem-solving for a large number of unsolved problems. Poythress prefers to distinguish the two by using 'disciplinary matrix' for the first and 'exemplar' for the second. It seems to me that both senses of the word 'paradigm' can be fruitfully used in understanding how the Old Testament functions authoritatively for us, particularly in the matter of evaluating human cultures.

In the first sense of the word as used by Kuhn, the emergence of Israel introduced a new paradigm of beliefs and values into the ancient Near Eastern world. This is not to suggest that somehow Israel's beliefs and values were exotic, with no religious or cultural links in their own environment. Vast amounts of comparative scholarship have shown the extent of the interaction between Israel and her contemporary world – as one would expect. Nevertheless it is equally apparent that in certain key areas Israel was different, consciously and deliberately. The requirement that they should be a 'holy people' emphasized this distinctiveness. Among the features of this revolutionary new world-view one could include:

• Israel's monotheism, emerging first perhaps as mono-Yahwism, but certainly developing into a fully-fledged commitment not merely to the uniqueness of Yahweh, but also to his sole deity;

• the characteristics of Yahweh as the God described above – *i.e.* one who is Lord of creation and who also acts in history;

• the values expressed through Yahweh's action in history, made explicit through the exodus and then consolidated in Israel's own law (concern for the vulnerable and oppressed, commitment to justice, rejection of idolatry and its associated social evils);

• a covenantal conception of social structure with remarkable effects in the political sphere – especially the way Israel translated their belief that Yahweh was their king (a common enough belief among ancient nations, as Millard Lind has shown)[13] into the practical rejection of human kingship for several centuries and a theoretical limit on its power when it did emerge;

• a belief in the divine ownership of the land which produced a drive towards economic justice and inverted the dominant pattern of land ownership;

• a belief in Yahweh as creator and sustainer of the natural order which desacralized whole areas of life such as sexuality, fertility (of land, herds and wives) and even death.

These are just some of the contours of the paradigm. This was the overall matrix of beliefs, values and assumptions which shaped historical Israel.

In the second sense of Kuhn's use of the word, Israel itself was a paradigm, *i.e.* a concrete model, a practical, experimental exemplar of the beliefs and values they embodied. Now nobody would want to deny what the Hebrew Scriptures themselves make very clear, that Israel failed to be all that they believed themselves called to be in terms of their own covenant, law and social institutions. Nevertheless it is a simple historical fact that in the transition from Bronze to Iron Age in Canaan, a society emerged with some radically different forms of social, economic and political life, integrally linked to a very distinctive form of religious belief. They called themselves 'Israel' and 'the people of Yahweh', and they succeeded for several centuries to prove, for example, that a theocracy could actually work without a human king; that land could be possessed without being bought, sold and owned commercially; that a broad equality of families with built-in mechanisms for the prevention or relief of poverty, debt and slavery could be maintained; that the people's spiritual needs could be met without a highly consumptive, land-owning, cultic élite.[14]

As history progressed, this historical experiment went through a lot of change in itself. As John Goldingay points out so clearly, the people of God from Abraham to the return from exile went through several major metamorphoses, yet in each era there were the constants, the underlying fundamental ideals of what it was to be Israel, of what was or was not 'done' in Israel.[15] In other words, Israel themselves were called to an ongoing self-check against the paradigm of their own 'constitution'. The settlers in the land were no longer pilgrims in the wilderness, but they still had to manifest the paradigm of Sinai in their new context. And the role of the prophets was to point out precisely where they were failing to do so. Indeed, it could be said that the main canonical function of the negative critique of the prophetic word (both the prophetic historical narratives and the books of the prophets) is to throw into clearer relief precisely what the paradigm of Israel was – *i.e.* Israel as God intended. By exposing the failures one highlights the ideals.

Another feature of Kuhn's second use of the term 'paradigm', as described by Poythress, intrigues me. The 'concrete exemplar' provided by a specific piece of research and its results functions as a model of 'puzzle-solving' for attacking other or subsequent puzzles. That is, scientists working within a certain 'disciplinary matrix' (paradigm in the first sense) assume that a model which successfully solves one problem (paradigm in the second sense) is likely to produce results if applied to other problems in the same general field. The exemplar in fact functions as an authority in the field, as long as it demonstrably fits the facts and confirms the wider matrix of perception of the nature of reality. Newton's theory of gravitation served that purpose and held that authority within the overall field of physics until Einstein showed that it no longer could be seen as a true representation of the nature of the universe.

Now the analogy with science becomes inadequate at this point, because the paradigm provided in the Bible is the result not of human enquiry and experiment but of divine revelation and historical redemptive action. Its truth is not provisional but final. On the one hand, the overall matrix of belief that we find in the Scriptures, as regards God himself, the created world, and humanity in relation to both, is God's own revelation of the way things truly are. Cultural world-views, therefore, which incorporate false views of God (some examples are idolatry, polytheism and pantheism), or false views of creation (such as deifying it, or rejecting it as illusory, or destroying it for greed), or false views of humanity (oppressive discriminations, such as by race or caste, reductionism, self-deification) are exposed as untrue (*i.e.* as failing to correspond with reality) when tested against the paradigm of the biblical world-view. On the other hand, the specific, concrete paradigm of Israel as exemplar can also function both negatively and positively in our evaluation of other human societies and cultures. This is on the assumption that the laws and institutions God gave to Israel accurately reflected, within that particular historical and geographical context, his desire and design for human life in the world.

Elsewhere I have tried to analyse the various responses found in Old Testament Israel to different aspects of surrounding culture.[16] Some features were accepted and absorbed, others were tolerated but with criticism and limiting factors, and others were utterly rejected and banned in Israel. If we examine the aspects of contemporary culture which Israel opposed, they fall into several fairly clear categories. These include: idolatry and related social practices; morally perverted practices, including sexual perversion and bestiality; practices which were destructive of persons, such as child-sacrifice and cultic prostitution; the whole realm of the occult, divination, sorcery, mediums and the like (the above feature mainly in the critique of Canaan); and economic or political systems that oppress or neglect the poor (which is the brunt of the critique of imperial cultures such as Egypt, Tyre and Babylon). Israel's rejection of such things provides a paradigm for our evaluation of comparable elements in cultures we encounter in our own day.

Another way of giving content to the paradigm would be to look at Israel's penal system and the values it embodies, in comparison with the surrounding legal systems known to us from that era. Points of interest would include: the valuing of human life above property in the scale of offences and in the forms of punishment; the absence of imprisonment as a legal penalty; the almost total absence of forms of bodily mutilation as punishment, very common in other law codes; strict limits on corporal punishment; particular legislative concern for the protection of the weak and vulnerable, including unparalleled legal rights for slaves. Since in several cases these aspects of Israel's legal system are directly distinct from the common legal conventions of surrounding culture, we can discern a consciously articulated distinctive ethical stance.[17]

To affirm that Israel functions as a paradigm (concrete exemplar) for our task of cultural critique in our own day is not to say that somehow Israel was a 'normative culture'. It has already been noted that even the culture of Israel itself changed and developed over the centuries recorded in the Hebrew Bible. All culture, being human and historical, is fluid. What it is saying is that within the parameters of ancient Near Eastern macro-culture, God brought into being a society through which he both revealed a new paradigm of understanding himself, the world and humanity, and actually modelled a framework of laws, institutions, conventions and customs, which experimentally proved the truth of that revelation. The Old Testament thus provides us with both the matrix of belief and understanding which corresponds to reality (*i.e.* it governs the shape of our world-view) and it shows us a historical exemplar of what that meant in practice for one human community – both through its achievements and in its self-conscious and self-critical failures.

The scientific idea of paradigm as puzzle-solution is stimulating here too. Newton's gravitation theory did not in itself solve all the puzzles in physics, but it set the pattern by which scientists set about the remaining problems, including ones which the original paradigm had not faced. Likewise, historical Israel articulated a comprehensive corporate response to a wide range of economic, social and political issues in her day. We cannot chide Israel for not solving all the problems of the human race. That is not the purpose of a paradigm. The whole point of a 'puzzle-solution' lies in its specificness. It says to us, 'This is how this particular one works out.'[18] The hermeneutical and ethical task, like the scientific one, is to approach the problems we face within the framework of assumptions and actual experimental results that the paradigm of Israel affords us, with the reassurance that, unlike Newtonian physics, both the wider conceptual paradigm and the concrete historical paradigm as recorded in Scripture comes to us with the status of divine revelation, not provisional human theory.

Conclusion

How then does this shape my concept of the authority of Scripture, particularly the Old Testament? I have argued that the Old Testament by its revelatory witness to the creation order, and to the God who has acted within history, provides authority for commitment to definable and abiding moral values in an age of moral relativism. Furthermore, by its provision of a paradigm (both conceptual and practical) in Israel, the Old Testament gives us authority to evaluate and critique contemporary cultures, without succumbing either to the temptation of cultural arrogance or to the paralysis of cultural relativism.

Having, I hope, justified my job in teaching biblical ethics in a cross-cultural context, one final piece of self-defence may perhaps be forgiven as I bring this essay to a close. Frank Anthony Spina, in an otherwise warm review of my book, *Living as the People of God* (entitled *An Eye for an Eye* in N. America), concludes by raising the question whether my paradigmatic approach to the application of Old Testament ethical teaching diverges from the traditional view of the authority of Scripture. 'For many Evangelicals, authority means a specific, final, irrefutable answer to a particular (ethical or theological) problem. Wright seems to advocate a somewhat more open-ended system . . .'.[19]

Well, yes, I do, but it is certainly not in conflict with a full acceptance of the authority of Scripture. My point is rather that I do not think the authority of Scripture can be earthed in quite the way Spina says many evangelicals would like, when it comes to the complex moral issues with which we have to contend in the modern world. Does the Bible give 'specific, final, irrefutable answers' to issues it did not address? If such answers were available, why do Christians, including those fully committed to biblical authority, differ over the moral interpretation of the biblical evidence on many issues? It seems to me the reason is that the authority of the Bible is such as to allow room for divergence of moral conviction on some issues, but within the constraints of a definite paradigm. So, for example, a moral critique of a government's economic policy might give variant responses to actual policy proposals on welfare mechanisms designed to relieve or remedy poverty, *e.g.* by fiscal arrangements, or loan schemes or direct benefits. The Bible may not directly sanction one or another as policy options, but it certainly endorses the intention of doing something designed to assist the poor and preferably to restore them to full participation in the community. On the other hand, certain economic policies would be ruled out, not because some specific, final and irrefutable text in the Bible prohibited then, but because their intention or likely effects would contradict the whole paradigm set before us in Scripture. To use the Hebrew laws, and the whole of Israel's life as based upon them, as our ethical paradigm is far from being so 'open-ended' as to let blank-cheque moral relativism in by the back door. Rather, to use this paradigm is actually immensely demanding, and sharpens one's whole use of the wide range of scriptural texts. For the paradigm is itself very sharp and specific in its own context. Therein lies both its strength (in preventing Old Testament ethics from being little more than vague generalities), and its ever-changing challenge, in facing us with the task of checking all our culture's values, and our own, against the authority of God's given paradigm of how people should live in his world.

2

The obsolescence of the atonement

David F. Wells

his essay is not advocating the position that Christ's atonement is outmoded; it is exploring why others, within the church, believe that this is so. It is my intention, then, to describe the growing belief that Christ's uniqueness – the uniqueness of his incarnate life and substitutionary death on the cross – is naïve, that it is no longer tenable in the modern world, that it should be abandoned because it is an intolerable offence to other religions, that it is an irrelevance to Christian spirituality and an impediment to mature understanding.

This insistence on replacing the christocentric focus in traditional theology by a vaguely theocentric one that is unspecific enough to leave room for non-Christian faiths has been heard with increasing volume for some time. Stephen Neill has noted[1] that when the first representative missionary conference of the modern period was held in 1860 in Liverpool, many of the concerns expressed were identical to those that are voiced today with one important exception: there was no discussion of non-Christian religions. There was, as a matter of fact, little knowledge of these religions and what knowledge existed was often influenced by unflattering stereotypes.

This has now changed. Not only have these religions been meticulously and minutely studied since then, and not only has an entirely new discipline arisen to refine their differences and agreements, but additionally an assumption has worked its way into the discussion which changes greatly what can be said about these other religions. For if it is the case that we can engage in the study of 'comparative religion', the assumption seems to be that there is a generic reality called 'religion', which may be shaped according to local taste and culture, but which is also universal.

In his book, *The Meaning and End of Religion*,[2] Cantwell Smith contends that religions are simply aspects of particular cultures and, to that extent, human creations, the languages we employ to understand life. If this is indeed their nature, then there seems to be a strong presumption against any particular religion, including Christianity itself, arrogating to itself the claim to being alone true and all of the others being false, regardless of whether this claim is bolstered by an appeal to miracles or not. This claim, Smith in fact declares, is a modern aberration and one that is peculiarly Western. The possibility that Western culture might have been determined by Christian truth in this matter, rather than the reverse, is not given serious consideration, for the obvious reason that it is precluded by the definition of religion with which Smith begins. Even where others in the modern consensus depart from Smith in some aspects of his argument, the upshot nevertheless is to see all religions as being culturally conditioned responses to the divine. The result of this is a new awareness of the cultural factors that determine the content of what is believed and therefore of the need to get behind these factors to the God within the religions. We seem 'to be witnessing the slow *awakening of global ecumenical consciousness*', Hans Küng says and he goes on to add that ecumenism 'should not be limited to the *community of the Christian churches*' alone but should include non-Christian religions as well.[3]

This movement towards an inclusion of other religions, not merely within the sphere of our Christian interest, but within the sphere of God's salvation, has been accelerated by numerous factors which can only be touched upon briefly here. Among these, however, would be the new frankness about the church's life, our growing knowledge of the world and the consequent pressures towards relativism, and the breakdown of historical Christian faith.

Church historians, for example, have cast off many of the dogmatic and apologetic interests under which they used to work and the result, for a century or more, has been a picture of the past which has grown in detail and clarity and which, in the process, has exposed an extraordinary set of warts in the church's life. Is it possible that a religion which is uniquely true would have botched its business in a way that is almost uniquely bad, some are now asking. If one only looks at the missionary enterprise, not only have 'conversions' sometimes been forced at the point of the sword, but even in the modern period it was the 'conviction of the decisive superiority of Christianity', John Hick claims, that 'infused the imperial expansion of the West'.[4] This expansion led to the cultural decimation of the peoples whom Western missionaries set out to convert. Not only so, but Rosemary Reuther contends that we can now see that the subjugation of women in the church is the direct product of the belief about the uniqueness of Christianity.[5] Her argument is so convoluted that it is difficult to summarize, and so improbable that it is only kind not to do so, but I allude to it simply as a further expression of the type of disaffection that has now replaced the affection with which Christian uniqueness was once viewed.

This disaffection, as it turns out, gains credibility with almost every published study on the reality and consequences of modern pluralization and of these there have been many. European sociology, from Emile Durkheim to Max Weber to Karl Marx, has blossomed in our time in the work of the sociologists of knowledge such as Peter Berger, Bryan Wilson and David Martin. Their basic assumption is that social environment is at the very least the explanation of private consciousness and perhaps also of its cause. That means that though what we think may be accorded absolute status by others, and though we ourselves may think it is absolute, in fact it is always relative to and reflective of our environment. Our cultural and social location profoundly affects what we think, what we think is important, and why we think that is so. This argument, if it is accepted at face value and without qualification, destroys the objective uniqueness of Christ because it proposes that there are reasons why a person should believe in Christian uniqueness which are not related to Christ at all.[6] He is unique because in the eye of the beholder it is important that he should be so.

In secularized societies, religious claims are not treated hospitably because that divine reality in which their truth value is to be found is treated as irrelevant in the society. Furthermore, modernized societies have also produced a surfeit of pluralization, multiple worlds of meaning in which different values prevail and, even daily, the experience of passing through these worlds militates powerfully against the supposition that any one set of values could alone be true.[7] The result of

51

this is that very often truth claims are judged to be 'true', even by those who hold them, simply on the grounds of their ability to satisfy personal interest and needs.[8] In other words, they are judged true on subjective rather than objective grounds. Christ may be unique to an individual, inasmuch as he satisfies some personal need in that person to believe, but that uniqueness cannot be proclaimed as a truth applicable in the same way to people all over the world.

The argument which is made from the viewpoint of sociology, therefore, coalesces with the way in which modern people generally view religious matters. And the combination, the one theoretical and the other practical, militates strongly against claims to uniqueness, either for Christian truth in general or Christ in particular. Indeed, these claims now seem ignorant because they do not seem to understand the frail, limited, and relative quality of all human knowing. They are also seen to be arrogant because they supposedly take one cultural expression of religion, one that has been predominantly white and Western, and make it the norm by which all other cultures are to be judged, those that are non-Western and inhabited by people who are brown and black. In the name, therefore, of an enlightened modern view of our cognitive relativism as well as an appropriate cultural humility, the argument is being vigorously made that the time has come to abandon what has been so damaging in the past, the belief in Christ's uniqueness, and to fashion a substitute that will meet the modern tastes, criteria and interests.

In the essay which follows, my starting-point is the diminished significance which Christ has among some of those who claim his name; this will be assumed. What I wish to explore is how this attitude works itself out. I will use the case of John Hick and what he has called the Copernican revolution in Roman Catholic theology to illustrate these developments.

Working by analogy

Analogies and models

The key to understanding the new approaches to religion is to understand how they are constructed. What I will argue is that these new approaches are not actually theologies but rather analogies. They do not offer models of reality,[9] but rather what are thought to be illustrations of it. This is a crucial distinction which needs some illustration.

The famed discoverers of the structure of DNA, Watson and Crick, built numerous models of what they thought its structure might be.

These models were made of balls and connecting rods, representing what they knew of the DNA, and these were arranged in different shapes and configurations to enable them to understand what they did not know of the structure of the DNA. Eventually, of course, they stumbled on the solution that there were two spirals that constituted its centre. The models, however, were not themselves the DNA.

In a similar way, architects often construct models of buildings they are designing in order to see how shapes and spaces will relate to each other, or they use a computer to simulate these for them. The models are not, however, the buildings.

In both of these illustrations, the model turns out to be a replica of the thing being examined. In the one case, that of DNA, the model was many times larger than what it represented and in the other case, that of the building, it was many times smaller. The size was not of importance provided there was an exact correspondence of part for part between model and reality. And it is in this sense that theologies have, traditionally, been understood to work. The doctrine of God, for example, is not God himself. It is a model of God in which there is a correspondence to the reality such that if you understand the model, the doctrine, you will understand God or, at least, those aspects of him for which you have the doctrinal replica.

To be sure, there have been differences between Protestants and Catholics at this point for, following Thomas Aquinas, Catholics have held that the model could be built in part from the materials of reason and needed only to be completed by revelation; the Reformers contended that all of the material from which the model was built had to be given by revelation because of human finitude and sin.[10] But even allowing for this difference, the common assumption was that doctrine worked as does a model. The cash value of the doctrine was known.[11]

By contrast, this new approach does not think of itself as building a model. The connection between the reality and its representation is more distant, less like a model and more like an analogy. In an analogy two things are compared, not because they are actually alike – as was the case with the models of DNA and buildings – but because they have some characteristics in common, or produce similar effects. By understanding the characteristics or effects of the one, the characteristics or effects of the other can be inferred. Thus one might argue, for example, that there is an analogy between the way that a manual for a computer works – reducing the use of a machine that is very complex to easy, rational steps – and how many books on spirituality work. They, too, rightly or wrongly, simplify what is complex and reduce it to easy, rational and manageable steps. In both cases, computers and spirituality, the 'user' is always in charge. The computer manual and the book on spirituality will not be the same length, size or colour, but by understanding what the one is doing, one can understand how it is being proposed that the other is working.

The problem which has given theologians so much perplexity in the modern world, of course, is the social and religious location of Christian faith. The old relation of absolute truth, given by divine revelation, to a world whose thought about itself was not only relative, not only finite, but also perverted by sin, seems no longer tenable. In a world of relativity, absolutes seem embarrassingly out of place, and in societies where humanism reigns, talk about sin is liable to be greeted by snickers. Is there a way, then, to rearrange the building-blocks of Christian faith such that the seemingly fallacious claims of traditional theology, Catholic and Protestant, can be disposed of and an alternative established in their place? Can we formulate the relationship between God and the religions, Christian and otherwise, such that, on the one hand, our understanding of our world as relative is not violated and, on the other, we can still speak of God?

This is the need, and to meet it, it is being proposed that we should now think of God as being *in* the world and that we should establish connections with that reality by working inferentially from our own consciousness. Let us construct analogies from our religious consciousness such that we can build a bridgehead of understanding about God from within ourselves and then extend it into the world. It is by this kind of analogy-doing that the work is proceeding because of the base assumption that God has not uniquely revealed himself in Scripture. That being the case, the only alternative left today, given the collapse of neo-orthodoxy, is to look within the self for his revelatory presence.

God, then, is *in* the world, *in* its history, *in* human nature. But in what sense? The picture is not that of a person *in* a room, for in this sense traditional theology has always asserted that God is 'in' the world. He has always been seen as 'in' the world in the sense that as its creator he has also sustained its life, revealed himself in what he has made, declared his moral presence through conscience, and manifest his providential presence in the sending of the rain, in the rhythms of the seasons, and in the setting of boundaries to civilizations. It is not this kind of presence that is being affirmed in the new approach – for the traditional ways in which God has been thought to be present in the world rest on a distinction between the transcendence and immanence of God which the new proposal denies.

No, the new approach sees God as 'in' the world, not as a person is in a room, but as blood is in a person. There is an identity between the blood and the body which is not true of the person in the room.

Correspondingly, that aspect of God which in traditional theology has been distinct from the creation, 'above' it, is now being eliminated in favour of that aspect of God in which he is seen to be at work in the world. The former aspect of God is the *sine qua non* for the doctrines of creation, providence and revelation. And with its elimination a change has intruded which is of major significance. When the old theology spoke of God as being in the world, it was attempting to understand his providential and non-saving relationships to the creation, to human beings, to history. When the new approach speaks of God as being in the world, it is speaking of his saving relationships and, inevitably, of a new understanding of his *being*; it is the infusion of his being in ours that creates a universal salvation. This little prepositional shift, then, from God being 'above' the world to his being wholly or very largely 'in' the world is one that produces, not simply a different emphasis, but an entirely different conception. It represents the demolition of God's transcendence in favour of his immanence, and the conversion of all natural revelation into supernatural, all general revelation into saving. To be sure, this is a move which is also consonant with the shift which many have been making from the one great Western tradition of philosophical thought to the other, from Descartes to Spinoza, from Kant to Hegel, from Kierkegaard to Whitehead, from the idea that God is remote and perhaps unknowable from within this world, to the notion that he is identified with this world, its life and history, and is coming to expression within it. It is, then, a move that is going with the current rather than against it.

Here, however, the characteristics from which we are to infer truths about God are so obscure that their cash value is singularly unclear and that seems to be the reason that God's presence 'in' the world has proved susceptible to an extraordinary array of interpretations. It is this conception, indeed this preposition *in*, which, we are told, will help us to think afresh about how God is active in the world, in ways that do not presume to know too much nor absolutize our own parochialism. Are the truths that we infer from the one situation to the other, from God in ourselves to God in the world, a good way of understanding what he is actually doing there?

Initially, this question was posed primarily for Christians, whether in slick formats like John Robinson's, or the more radical renditions of some of the death-of-Godders, or the appallingly obscure outcroppings of process theology, or more recently in the blatantly politicized programmes of the liberationists. The idea, however, has also been applied to inter-religious dialogues and it is in this location that I wish to pursue it.

It needs to be noted immediately, of course, that what we are about to explore is not a startingly new and original idea, but rather one that is old, that was seen earlier this century to be hopelessly inept, and that was relegated to the rubbish heap where discarded and unworkable ideas tend to end up. In this case, however, the rumours of its death appear to have been exaggerated, for what the liberal Protestants and Catholic modernists proposed, and what Karl Barth and Pope Pius X destroyed, has once again returned.

How the problem emerged

In 1902, Ernst Troeltsch published his *The Absoluteness of Christianity and the History of Religions.*[12] Although it departed a little from typical liberal nostrums, it also capitalized on Schleiermacher's notion that God is to be found beneath, and is revealed through, all human personality. This led Troeltsch to a conclusion that we can speak of absoluteness in two different ways. The one, 'naïve' in his view, sees Christianity as absolute because it is uniquely true; the other, 'scientific' in his opinion, sees it as absolute only in the sense that it is the finest statement of human religiosity, the pinnacle of achievement, different in degree but not in kind from other religions.

This was, we should note immediately, a half-baked proposal because, while the idea of the relativity of all human thought was used to destroy the normative status of traditional Christian truth, Troeltsch stopped short of allowing the full impact of relativity to ruin liberal ideas of how things are: Christianity, liberals still wanted to say, is at the pinnacle of religious development! Relativity, he apparently was thinking, was a single, not a double-edged sword. It was an idea that could be used on others while immunity from its damage could be claimed for the liberal users!

Troeltsch's solution, however, proved to be unsatisfactory, so in 1923, in a lecture intended for an Oxford audience but published posthumously, he modified his earlier stance and produced his third definition of what *absolute* might mean.[13] Each religion, he now proposed, is 'absolute' but *only* within its own confines and to its own adherents. On this basis, Christianity was not even at the apex of development. If it was supreme, it was supreme only to those who thought it was supreme. Its supremacy, in other words, was not intrinsic to it, nor was it a consequence of its essential truthfulness, but rather it was simply the way some people liked to think about it. The nerve of all missionary activity, all apologetics, was thereby cut; all preaching to those of other religions was dismissed as foolish arrogance.

These benign views about the religious character of all peoples, a notion often coupled in the liberal mind with that of the upward, spiritual evolution of all peoples, soon ran headlong into the hard wall of reality: in Europe, the First World War and in America, the Depression of the 1930s. This theology not only advanced a fallacious view of society but it offered an especially fallacious and fatuous view of faith, and Karl Barth thundered against it. He saw, in a way that the liberals never had, that their ideas destroyed all Christian faith, no matter how patronizing they wanted to be about its great spiritual insights. The root fault was the liberal fascination with the religious consciousness and the baleful habit of imagining that if this was examined, if it was crystallized, God would somehow be found contained in it. We will not call 'God', he said, by shouting 'man' in a loud voice. And Albert Schweitzer, though no Barthian, also said much the same thing about the liberal efforts at reconstructing the life of Jesus. What Schweitzer noticed among the dominant New Testament scholars of his day, many of whom tried their hand at writing biographies of Jesus, was the uncanny resemblance of the Jesus figures that emerged to the rationalistic, German academics who were their authors.[14] Jesus seemed to believe as little in miracles as they did! Schweitzer observed that they had looked down the deep well of human history and, unfortunately, seen their own faces reflected at the bottom.

Barth, in fact, then went on to grasp the nettle of relativity which was at the heart of the liberal reconstruction in general and of Troeltsch's in particular. The supposition that all human thought is tinged by relativity is, he said, entirely correct and he turned this assumption against the liberals. Is it not the case, he asked, that by writing their theology around this point they had become no different from Feuerbach? This was an especially scathing comparison because it was Feuerbach who had said that God is nothing more than a projection of human need and longing, that our interest in 'God' is no different from an interest in ourselves, and that therefore our Magnificat should be sung to ourselves.[15] The liberals, too, had allowed their theology to degenerate into anthropology.

In response to this situation, Barth opposed the revelatory Word which came from above to all human religion. The one came from God, the other from human beings. The one was absolute, the other was relative. In the neo-orthodox programme, this was then carried through in the distinction between 'profane' history, which is relative, and 'salvation history', which is absolute. The former (*Historie*) is the network of cause and effect in the natural world and what in English goes by the word 'history', whereas the latter (*Geschichte*), is the saving meaning which cannot be read off the events themselves and can only be given by God himself. The difference that emerged early in the school of neo-orthodox thinkers was that Barth believed that the saving meaning, *Geschichte*, was only given within the network of ordinary, profane history, whereas Bultmann believed that it was given apart from it. Thus, the resurrection could have no saving meaning for Barth unless Christ had actually risen bodily from the dead, whereas for Bultmann the resurrection had saving meaning despite the fact that Christ had not risen physically from the dead. It was this kind of double talk that led Berger to say that the distinction between these two types of history was 'a legerdemain of the Bultmann school that, alas, loses much of its persuasiveness in any language but German'.[16]

The razor-sharp distinction between all that is relative – all human thoughts about God whether these are expressed in formal religion or not – and what is absolute – revelation that comes directly from above to the individual – in time lost much of its persuasiveness in German too. Barthian neo-orthodoxy, as well as the existentialism of the Bult-mannians, alike faltered because each was as one-sided in its theological construction as had been the proposal of the liberals. If the liberals had banished the transcendence of God in favour of his immanence, the neo-orthodox had banished his immanence in favour of his transcendence.[17] Gustav Wingren therefore observed that they were really just mirror images of one another;[18] what the liberals opposed, Barth proposed. The liberals had therefore written the Barthian theology. What seemed like diametrically opposed schemes actually began to look remarkably similar. And Cornelius Van Til[19] went on to charge that there really was very little difference between the liberal religious consciousness that welled up from within, and the Barthian religious consciousness that was created from above. Since neither had an external, objective, biblical authority, neither could speak except from private consciousness. It was this impasse, this collapse of both the liberal and neo-orthodox solutions to the relation between God's transcendence and immanence, that opened the store to a whole new line of products that emerged in the 1960s. Many of them have now coalesced around this idea that the place where our theological reflection should begin is with the idea that God is 'in' the world, and all of them have a common revulsion of historic orthodoxy.

New game, new players

That the old liberalism is alive and well, that it has managed to shrug off the innumerable indignities to which it was subjected during the Barthian years, is evident, for example, in John Hick's and Paul Knitter's recent work, *The Myth of Christian Uniqueness*.[20] Although it contains the work of multiple authors, there seems to be wide consent to an argument that runs through its pages to which there are three components. First, all human knowledge is relative and reflects the particular context and culture from which it arises. Secondly, each religion is unique because each arises from a particular context and therefore is unlike any other religion. Thirdly, no person in one context and religion can pass judgment on another without first illicitly absolutizing their own cultural perspective. From these assertions two conclusions are drawn. First, all religions therefore have an independent validity. They must be appreciated on their own terms and no-one can say that one is true and another is not. Secondly, given the precariousness of modern life, the possibility of nuclear holocaust, all religions should co-operate to make the world more human and more ethical.

This of course states a general perspective that runs through the book and individual authors angle their expressions of it in slightly different ways. Hick's own expression to these ideas is unusual for two reasons. First, he has retained an insistence that religious ideas can be debated with the aim of discerning their truth or falsehood; he refuses to accept the more radical applications of relativity, which insist that religious ideas simply express the needs, emotional preferences, or even culture of the person expressing those ideas. He also rejects the idea, borrowed from Ludwig Wittgenstein, that religion, like every other discipline, has its own language game, which means that its truth or falsehood is determined only within the precincts of that discipline; of these approaches he is quite critical.[21] Secondly, like the old liberals, and unlike many of their contemporary heirs, Hick is concerned with salvation in the afterlife.[22] Today, the afterlife is not a subject that is considered to be relevant to the construction of Christian faith by many and therefore, in its absence, the older liberal idea of an ultimate salvation for all is replaced by the interest now of seeing all religions as being expressive of the divine. While Hick is intent on including all religions, and seeing God's presence in them, he also retains this older liberal interest of seeing an afterlife in which all will be saved, though perhaps after purification,[23] and in this he is unusual among the proponents of this general school of thinkers.

Hick is uncommonly candid about his point of departure. It is his assumption of the salvation of all in the afterlife[24] that is the fulcrum around which all else is turned. But this effort has been made necessary by two other developments. First, for Hick, historic Christian faith has collapsed. He begins his reconstruction, he tells us, on the assumption that there are no good reasons for believing that there is divinely revealed truth, that the biblical account of creation and the fall are true, that Christ was God incarnate, that he died in our place and rose from the dead, and that there is a gospel message whose acceptance leads to salvation and whose rejection leads to death.[25] Secondly, he tells us that the belief in a creation originally good, into which evil has intruded and from which saving deliverance is to be sought, is so self-contradictory as to be unbelievable. He therefore rejects 'the bad news of a divine wrath which can only be satisfied by the eternal torment of most of the human race' in favour of 'the good news of the reality and love of God'.[26] And this 'good news' is worked out, not in terms of doctrine which is believed, but in actions which are lived. The 'essence' of Christianity is doing right by others.[27]

Hick does make a half-hearted effort to try to show that this kind of universalism is what is actually suggested by Paul and Jesus,[28] but the strong impression that his effort leaves is that his desire has been the mother of this invention. It would have been better for him to have said, quite simply, that Jesus and Paul were wrong and then to propose what he believes is the correct way to view this matter. The fall, he tells us, should simply be viewed as an expression of our self-awareness. Its statement 'expresses our sense of distance from the proper fulfillment of the God-given possibilities of our natures' and judgment expresses 'our sense of the unqualified seriousness of the free choices and responses which are all the time inexorably forming our character for good or ill'.[29]

Ideas like these were heard earlier this century, though, during the years when the Barthians were ascendant, their proponents were forced into embarrassed silence. What is new, however, is the involvement of Roman Catholics in this kind of thinking. Indeed, it would be difficult to overestimate the importance both of their involvement and of the change that this represents for them.[30]

Although there had been Catholics who had ventured down the road that Hick and Knitter have recently taken, especially the modernists at the turn of the century in Europe, the Church had always kept its distance and guarded its own prerogatives with some zeal. At the Second Vatican Council in the mid-1960s, however, that changed. This change has opened wide the door for Catholic participation in building this new model of Christian understanding.

The Council was seeking a solution to the problem that while world population is growing, the traditional means for the salvation of people – the Church and its sacraments – has been diminishing. Was there a way, then, in which the means of salvation might be found that did not always require access to the sacraments? It was the work of Karl Rahner, in particular, that proved helpful here in suggesting that within human nature, within all human nature, is to be found grace whose presence is registered in certain appetites which then take religious forms.[31] Although these forms are not equally true, the grace beneath them is the same and it is potentially saving. It was on this basis that he advanced his notion of the 'anonymous Christians'.[32] The Council, he said later, was searching for a way to describe universal spirituality, not simply that part of it which is Christian, and to secure a universal basis on which salvation could be seen to rest.

The Council's solution to this problem, then, was to say that while all religions had some truth, Catholic faith had the most. To be severed from the Church was not to be severed from all truth, but only from truth in its fullest expression.

The Council therefore began by saying that human religion is rooted in the presence of God in humanity which produces among men and women, a 'profound religious sense'.[33] Not only so, but this divine presence was equated with that of Christ, not simply among baptized Christians, but throughout the whole race, among whom he arouses 'a desire for the age to come'[34] and works to make the whole earth submissive to this goal. Accordingly, the Council abandoned its old, and traditional, habit of insisting that only in the Church could Christ be found. Instead, it in effect reworked this position to affirm, as Christopher Butler stated it, that 'Christ is (anonymously) at work, and that in them [non-Christians] also the Church, *extra quam nulla salus*, is transcending her own visible limits'.[35] There is no salvation outside of the Church, but since God's grace is to be found in all human nature, and since the Church is where grace is, all are in the church! Some belong to the visible, Roman Catholic Church; others belong to the church that is hidden and invisible in God's grace. It was an ingenious way of affirming the traditional doctrine that salvation is not to be had outside the Church while also endorsing the reality of a world spirituality.

This perception led to a whole new way of looking at the other religions, a way which seems to resemble a series of concentric circles. At the centre and, as it turns out, at the pinnacle, is the Catholic Church; Catholics are 'incorporated'[36] into Christ but their incorporation no longer means that those outside of the Church are deprived of any relation to Christ. Protestants and the Eastern Orthodox are separated from the Catholic Church and its fullness, but they are nevertheless 'linked' to Christ and to truth.[37] Of the non-Christian religions, the Council could only say good things and it concluded by speaking of their 'relation'[38] to Christ and truth. Not even atheists, who would represent the outer circle, felt the sword of condemnation. To be sure, the Council did not approve of their atheism, but it nevertheless went on to allow that God does not deny salvation to them provided, first, that they are 'without blame' for their atheism and, secondly, that they 'strive to live a good life, thanks to his grace'.[39] Thus, as Butler observed, salvation has become 'radically dependent on subjective good intention [rather] than on external ecclesiastical allegiance'.[40] And this has meant, as Küng has observed, that while the ordinary way of salvation is to be found through the Catholic Church, God has also provided an extraordinary way in the other religions.[41]

Although new Catholics and the revived heirs of liberalism have their own characteristic ways of thinking about religion, there is a striking consensus that is emerging among them, and which is being formulated for them by both the Vatican and the World Council of Churches. The basic assumption is that God is 'in' the world, that he comes to expression within human consciousness, and that no one religion is exclusively true. Catholics generally wish to preserve a place for Catholic Christianity at the summit of human religion, whereas the revived liberals are eager to dispense with any summits. And this leads to another difference. Catholics still think of Christ's death as necessary. From Christ comes God's grace, whether that is dispersed by creation in 'nature' as Rahner proposed, or by the sacraments in the Church as traditional teaching has insisted. The revived liberals, by contrast, are derogatory about any atonement or the need for any grace peculiar to Christ. There are, then, differences but the fact that there are emerging so many agreements is a matter of no small importance.

Some reflections

There is no question that this new approach is extremely well adapted to the consciousness which modernity creates, to its global sense, to its relativity, to its creation of a world culture that belongs to no one place or people. This newly reshaped religion can travel companionably with modernity. It asks of the modern person no sacrifice, no discomfort. If the modern, secular person disbelieves in biblical revelation, in the uniqueness of Christ, in moral absolutes, this religion does not ask that the secular disinclination be changed. It asks only that the deeper, human perceptions of reality be seen as religious, though they may not have been viewed as such before, that common cause be made with the like-minded to produce a better world (which is usually understood to be a more liberal world), and that other religions be accorded authenticity.[42]

The considerable advantages of riding with the modern tide are attended, however, by the very considerable disadvantages of flying in the face of Christian truth. To be sure, this judgment is made on the basis of a belief in the truthfulness of Scripture, arising from its inspiration, which many of the Protestant proponents of this new approach, as well as an increasing number of Catholics, think is untenable. They also claim that a belief in the uniqueness of Christian faith owes as much to Western experience as to Scripture and those who hold such a view are simply absolutizing Western experience. It is, however, commonly agreed that historically Christianity has viewed itself as uniquely true, that Scripture presents this matter in this light, and that it had to do so in the context of extraordinary religious pluralism in the first century. So what is it that today makes it so hard for us to affirm what, in the first century, the apostles declared without equivocation?

The answer, of course, is on the one hand, that biblical orthodoxy is seen to have collapsed and, on the other, that our own ideas, which are all that remain for us out of which to construct a view of God, must be acknowledged to be relative. We must no longer confuse what we see within our own culture with what everyone else must see within their cultures.[43] This argument, however, is a two-edged sword. If it is the case, as sociologists often suppose, that beliefs are the effect of which experience in society is the cause, and if the proponents of this new approach wish to use this sword, then they should understand that they themselves have no immunity from its sharp edges. Could it not be argued that they have simply absolutized the modern experience of pluralism? It is certainly the case that this religion builds upon extrapolations from inner experience because, it is assumed, Scripture does not secure for us the model from which an understanding of God is derived. This process of extrapolation, in the nature of the case, requires that experience be absolutized otherwise it could not be seen to be relevant to anyone other than the person whose experience it is.

At the very least, then, this approach is an attempt to prescribe for the rest of the world the perspective of those who have experienced modernity but, unfortunately, it involves itself in a serious contradiction. The 'truth' which is being absolutized in this way is also declared to be true, relative only to the modern context, for the context always relativizes our understanding. What this means, then, is that the ground on which this understanding is advanced, for those who are not part of the industrialized West, can only be the despised parochialism or, worse still, the cultural arrogance of the West from which this approach supposedly liberates us.

The more compelling critique, however, is still the one that Barth made. Why is it that we think that we will call 'God' if we keep shouting 'man' in a loud voice? Why is it that we assume that there is a correspondence between our private experience and divine reality? Indeed, why do we think that we have even understood our experience aright? In an age which has explored, as intently as ours has, the contradictions between conscious and unconscious life, between actual intent and the rationalizations by which we obscure that intent, it is surely remarkable that we should find those who self-confidently declare that within themselves they have no difficulty in discerning how God is revealing himself. It is a peculiarly antiquated view that has to be asserted against a massive consensus of psychological findings; that those so in awe of modernity would feel obliged to dismiss findings so important to the modern world as are those of modern psychology and sociology, can only be explained on the grounds that the ideology they have embraced simply demands that the self functions in this way.

This ideology, in fact, declares that sin does not spoil or destroy our capacity to experience God savingly within ourselves, to know him apart from external revelation, and therefore the redemption which Christ alone has provided is, on the Protestant side, seen to be irrelevant and, on the Catholic side, transmitted to each person so secretly and unobtrusively as to be unrecognizable for what it is. Although it is the uniqueness of Christ which bears the brunt of the scorn, it is the reality of sin and the moral nature of God which are just as much despised or modified. We thus have a radical application of the modern ideas of cognitive relativity combined with a naïve view of the utter reliability of our religious perceptions. The former allows the advocates of this outlook to cut down historic Christianity, and the latter allows them to erect their own ideas in its place, and to do so in a way that surely leaves the impression that they believe they are in a discussion about universal truth, not simply about whether they have transmitted their own perceptions accurately. In other words, they want us to think that they have a model of reality in which part corresponds to part, a theology, whereas in fact all they have is the stuff of analogy, in which the effects of the divine within them have to be declared unmistakably discernible in order for them to be able to infer from this that they know how God is at work in other religions. If they are demeaning of the religious knowledge of others, they are overly confident of their own.

In the end, of course, a choice has to be made as to whether the biblical teaching is or is not true, but what we are looking at in these various schemes is not only the rejection of Christian faith but the substitution of a fraud in its place. Although there are immediate cultural gains that accrue to such a substitution, there are enormous religious losses. The whole struggle to understand faith aright in the Reformation period was a struggle to understand the cross aright, to understand God aright, to interpret his saving purposes truly. It is this struggle which has now been abandoned. Richard Niebuhr scathingly denounced the old liberal gospel as proclaiming that a God without wrath had brought men and women without sin, into a kingdom without a judgment, through a Christ without a cross. What Niebuhr denounced is now freshly heralded. And it is being embraced to the undoing of the church, the dishonouring of God and his Son, and the mutilation of the gospel.

The root cause of this problem is a deficient view of sin and of God's moral nature. It is of no small interest to note that Brunner made this same critique of the old liberals. With respect to sin, he said:

> Knowledge of sin – genuine horror of sin – is the presupposition of faith in the Mediator. So long as we do not notice this, so long as we think we have no need of a Mediator, so long are we embedded in the pride of human reasoning. We still believe – however rent and seamed the surface of our life may be – that the underlying depths of our existence are untouched, that they are still united with God. So long as we do not see the need for divine intervention we reject every assertion of such an intervention ... Knowledge of sin, in this universal sense, is the presupposition of faith. This is the first point. The second point, however, is this: this presupposition is never produced by anyone save by faith, the divine revelation, the faith in the Mediator ... Only the soul that despairs knows what it means to believe, and faith teaches to despair rightly.[44]

And he went on to say that so long as we reject the biblical idea of divine holiness and of divine wrath the church would continue to decay. It is this decay that we see today and there is no greater evidence of it than the belief that we are in no need of Christ's atonement. The kind of objective atonement of which John Stott has so ably written in his *The Cross of Christ* is becoming *terra incognita* in the church.

There is nothing to being modern that requires us to think that God has changed his nature or his salvation, or that he needs to. It is his nature, his Christ, and his revealed gospel that require us to change some of what is in our modern consciousness, and there is much within our fallen human natures that resist this. But when we believe God, his Christ and his Word, we find that we have lost nothing that is essential to this life; indeed, we find that we have gained everything essential both to this and to the next life.

Evangelical Christianity and the Enlightenment[1]

D. W. Bebbington

The evangelical Christianity of which John Stott is a distinguished leader is that type of Protestantism which is orthodox in belief and evangelistic in practice. It possesses a gospel that it is eager to spread. It is possible, however, to make a closer definition. There are four characteristics that have marked evangelical Christianity over time, and together they form a defining quadrilateral.

Defining evangelical Christianity

The first characteristic is *conversionism*. This is the belief, common to all evangelicals, that people are not naturally Christians. Rather, they have to turn to Christ if they are to become true believers. This has normally been the burning message of the evangelical movement. In the period of its greatest growth in America during the Second Great Awakening of the early nineteenth century, the call for conversion rang out long into the night around the fires of the camp meetings. Equally G. W. McCree, a London Baptist minister of the mid-nineteenth century, put a strong emphasis on the subject. He held, according to his son, 'That conversion was far above, and of greater importance than, any denominational differences of whatever kind'.[2] That is entirely typical of evangelicals.

Conversion, according to evangelicals, is not the result of a person's own efforts. It is the result of justification by faith, that is, a simple trust in Jesus Christ that makes human beings acceptable to God. The message of justification by faith, revived by the evangelical movement after a period of quiescence, was very much the message of the Reformation. It scandalized many of the clergy of the Church of England mainstream in the eighteenth century. There was no need for good works to be done, evangelicals seemed to be saying, for salvation to be received. Therefore, their opponents concluded, there was no incentive to virtue. Why bother doing anything good at all? Evangelicals brought down on themselves denunciation as traducers of the law of God. Justification by faith was insisted on as the only means of conversion, the first typical feature of evangelical Christianity.

Secondly, *activism* is a defining characteristic of evangelicals. Apologists for the movement in the eighteenth century claimed they did not neglect good works. It is certainly true that evangelicals went around performing all sorts of humane works of charity. They stressed that conversion brings a new motivation to do good, and so leads to true holiness. Consequently, they were activists. Their activism consisted primarily in spreading the gospel. In addition evangelicals have normally, though not absolutely consistently, engaged in philanthropy of various kinds. The activism often ran very deep. American Methodist circuit riders rode hundreds of miles in a month to preach several times a day. Wesley himself expected his preachers to be active for more than one hundred hours per week. It is no wonder that the Methodists early in their existence created a 'Worn-Out Ministers' Fund'. 'When we pray for the advancement of this kingdom', wrote Caleb Evans, a leading eighteenth-century Baptist, with reference to the Lord's Prayer, 'if we are not willing to do all we can to advance it, our prayers cannot be genuine . . .'.[3] That sums up a great deal of what evangelicalism is about.

Thirdly, evangelicalism over time has been *biblicist*. The Bible has been the authority for the message, the source of all truth about God. Hence, according to many evangelicals in the past, theology is not a discipline where knowledge advances significantly. Sometimes that view was taken to an extreme. For example, Sir Robert Inglis, an evangelical Anglican MP in the House of Commons, made a memorable pronouncement in 1850. A Unitarian had said in a debate that theological discoveries should be taught in the universities. Inglis' answer was that 'all the truths of religion are to be found in the blessed Bible'. Alleged discoveries in theology were 'worth neither teaching nor hearing'.[4] The wooden attitude of Inglis is not the only attitude that has marked evangelicals. Their respect for the Bible has often encouraged academic study of the Scriptures. A good example would be the late F. F. Bruce, the member of the Brethren who was Rylands Professor of Biblical Exegesis in the University of Manchester, a man of enormous world-wide influence. Popular devotion to the Scriptures is part of this biblicism. There is the tradition, inherited from the Puritan past, of the family Bible with the genealogical tree setting out the members of the family on its flyleaf. Sometimes evangelicals have taken their devotion to Scripture almost beyond the bounds of legitimacy. John Nelson, an early Methodist preacher, was accused of making his Bible his god.[5] Whatever the details of the specific attitude, biblicism must be seen as a characteristic of evangelicals.

Fourthly, evangelicals have been *crucicentric* in their faith. That is to say, they have placed at the centre of their theological scheme the doctrine of the cross – the atoning work of Jesus Christ in his death. The great leader of Anglican evangelicals in the early nineteenth century, Charles Simeon, preached a sermon before the University of Cambridge in 1811 which was entitled 'Christ Crucified, or Evangelical Religion described'.[6] The two parts of the title were equivalent. Why has the cross been central? Because by the atonement, Jesus Christ achieved salvation, rescuing humanity from sin. Other theological emphases are possible even when there is a focus on the person of Christ. For example, Anglo-Catholic theology for much of the twentieth century has dwelt on the incarnation of the Son of God as its central theme. Again, liberal Protestants in the late nineteenth and the early twentieth centuries commonly concentrated on the example and teaching of Christ. So in stressing the atonement, evangelicals have been distinctive. Normally they have held that Jesus Christ died in the place of sinners. So their doctrine has generally been one of substitutionary atonement. Thus the greatest sermon of Robert Hall, the Baptist who was the most powerful of early nineteenth-century English preachers, was a defence of the principle of the substitution of the innocent for the guilty.[7] The cross is central to the theological scheme of evangelicals.

The four characteristics, taken together, form a defining set of categories for evangelicalism. Other major emphases have been held from time to time, and the various elements have had a different balance over time, but nothing has been of consistently equal importance to those four characteristics. Those who displayed these four features were evangelicals.

The Enlightenment

What was the Enlightenment, the second element in the title of this essay? It was the era that emphasized the ability of human reason to discover truth. Earlier academic usage confined the term to later eighteenth-century German thought, but since the 1950s it has become the equivalent of 'the age of reason'. René Descartes prepared the way for the Enlightenment in the seventeenth century, raising the question of how knowledge is obtained – epistemology – as the central issue in philosophy. Certainty, he argued, is possible only when knowledge is obtained on the pattern of mathematics, by deduction. John Locke was even more of a herald. His *Essay concerning Human Understanding* (1690) repudiates the notion of innate ideas, or the supposition that the mind already contains certain ideas before experience begins. Instead Locke puts the stress on experience itself. He holds that since a child is born without any automatic knowledge, everything that is known comes from sense impressions of the external world. The impact of Locke was reinforced by that of Sir Isaac Newton and the whole scientific movement that had been springing up from the seventeenth century. Newton, especially by the discovery of gravity, did much to raise the prestige of natural science. Locke and Newton together exalted the method of induction in philosophy. General laws were to be established from particular cases. In the light of scientific endeavour it was thought perfectly legitimate to apply that technique not just to the natural world, but also to the human world.

The Enlightenment can be seen as adopting that as its programme: the application of scientific method to the study of humanity. It is true that a number of recent studies have shown that within the age of reason there was an irrationalist stream. Freemasonry was popular, for example, with the élite. But when that has been said, irrationalism was only a counter-current. The main thrust of eighteenth-century thought, especially in the second half of the century, was the stress on the ability of reason to discover fresh knowledge.

Was the Enlightenment irreligious in tendency? Certainly some of the Enlightenment thinkers held that human reason should be pitted against divine revelation. Thus Voltaire uttered his famous battle-cry, 'Ecrasez l'infâme'. His target was institutional religion. Voltaire was not an atheist, but a deist. He was one of those eighteenth-century thinkers who believed that God had created the world but had then left it to operate according to its own internal laws. Divine intervention in the world was ruled out. Many other significant figures of the eighteenth century, Benjamin Franklin among them, held that deistic position. Even within the churches there was a similar liberalizing trend in theology. Latitudinarianism was a powerful current within the Church of England. Edmund Law, Bishop of Carlisle, for example, wrote as a disciple of Locke and an advocate of reason in religion. Moderatism existed in the Church of Scotland. William Robertson, Principal of Edinburgh University and a clergyman himself, was among the earliest historians of America. He was a leader of the Moderates, a group that adopted a more liberal doctrinal stance than had been customary. Such men believed in enhancing reason and its associated values. They made much less appeal to Scripture than had previous generations of ministers of religion. Because of the growth of deism, Latitudinarianism, Moderatism and their offspring, the Enlightenment has often, quite plausibly, been seen as irreligious in tendency. At the very least it has been portrayed as liberalizing.

Therefore it has seemed natural to hold that evangelicalism, a mass religious movement displaying intense feeling, was a reaction against the Enlightenment. John Wesley has been seen as an advocate of traditional folkways. He did produce the rather strange book called *Primitive Physic* (1747) in which he recommends various quack medical cures to his followers. If they were afflicted by the plague, for example, they should rush to obtain some marigold flowers. John Wesley appears a champion of the ancients against the moderns, and so not an Enlightenment figure at all. The whole evangelical movement has been located as an expression of the religion of the heart in opposition to the religion of the head, the rational religion of the Enlightenment. Evangelicalism has commonly been depicted in historical literature as an assertion of emotion against reason. Evangelicalism is reduced to a matter of mere feelings.

A new movement

This view rests on a serious misunderstanding. To posit a sharp contrast between evangelicalism on the one hand and the Enlightenment on the other is mistaken. It can be shown that, on the contrary, evangelicalism was actually launched on its way by the Enlightenment. It is true, of course, that in the eighteenth century there was an existing Protestant tradition in the English-speaking world, but it was remodelled under Enlightenment influence to produce evangelicalism as a new movement in the eighteenth century. The issue can best be approached by contrasting the evangelicals of the eighteenth century with the Puritans of the seventeenth century.

The Puritans were the dominant force within English-speaking Protestantism in the century before evangelicalism arose. The Puritans had three of the defining characteristics of the evangelicals. Puritans were conversionist, biblicist and crucicentric. What they lacked was activism. There was, for example, a remarkable absence of Protestant missions in the sixteenth and seventeenth centuries, a matter that has often puzzled historians. Why should Roman Catholics be dedicated to taking the faith to the Far East at a time when Puritans were making very few efforts? It is true that John Eliot did seek to evangelize the Indians of New England in the seventeenth century but he was an isolated instance, subsequently celebrated precisely because such enterprises had been rare. The Puritans concentrated on preaching the gospel where it was already known. Why was this so?

The answer is to be found in the Puritan spirituality of the seventeenth century. Puritans, as Calvinists, believed in predestination. God had chosen some people for salvation, but not others. The individual, however, did not know for sure whether or not he was among the predestined. In the seventeenth century ministers deliberately encouraged people to doubt whether or not they were of the elect. That cultivated an introspective piety, wrestling with fears and anxieties, the type of spirituality depicted by Weber in his statement of the 'Weber-Tawney thesis'.[8] It was expected that hope over one's spiritual state would be followed by gloom. There was a lack of certainty about salvation. It is true that the doctrine of assurance was taught. It was held that people could know whether they were in fact saved, but assurance was expected to come late in the experience of the Christian and to be the fruit of struggle and anguish. Thus the Westminster Confession of 1646 states: 'This infallible assurance doth not so belong to the essence of faith, but that a true believer may wait long, and conflict with many difficulties, before he be partaker of it.'[9] Assurance was expected to be waited for. People looked within to discover whether there were signs of saving grace in their souls. The Puritans abounded in scholarship and godliness, but because of the concentration on the inward life there was no dynamic leading to mission.

Contrast the evangelicals. Assurance, according to the evangelicals, is the normal possession of the believer. When Wesley announced that assurance is given at conversion, he was sharply criticized for it. Evangelical Anglican pioneers such as James Hervey and William Romaine spoke similarly. Not all of them argued that assurance is of the essence of faith, but what they did hold in common was that assurance is normal, indeed normative, for the believer. Hence the Christian was expected to be full of buoyancy, resilience and joy. Spirituality was transformed. Instead of concentrating on their inward lives, looking for marks of grace, Christians turned outward to the world. They assumed their own salvation and took up the task of spreading the gospel to others. Modern Protestant missions, starting with the Baptist Missionary Society in 1792, are the fruit of evangelicalism in this age.

A new certainty of God

Why did Christians become more confident of their salvation? Why was there a transition from Puritanism to evangelicalism? It was because evangelicals believed that they possessed self-evident knowledge. They were conscious of God having touched their lives as much as they were conscious of any other sense experience. They believed that experience is the source of knowledge in exactly the same way as John Locke. They had an Enlightenment preoccupation with epistemology which led them to affirm that God gave them self-evident knowledge of himself. And if they had that knowledge of God, they wished to spread it to others.

The epistemological preoccupation is evident in John Wesley. In the 1730s he was a teacher of philosophy and logic at the University of Oxford, and as the leader of the 'Holy Club' he was also dedicated to piety and good works. What he lacked in the 1730s was certainty. He asked himself, 'Do I know God?' That is a preoccupation that occurs again and again in his writings. 'How can I be sure I am among the saved?' It was not until he encountered the Moravians, German Christians, that he discovered that the knowledge of God comes through faith alone. That was what led on to the experience of 24 May 1738, when his heart was 'strangely warmed'.[10] He knew God by sense experience: 'warmed' is significant. He actually felt the warmth of God's touch. The theme of sense experience is reflected in the hymns of his brother, Charles Wesley. 'How can a sinner know / His sins on earth forgiven?', asks Charles Wesley in one of them. 'What we have felt and seen', runs the answer, 'with confidence we tell . . .'.[11] Christian experience is a matter of feeling or seeing. These images recur again and again. The Wesleys possessed an Enlightenment confidence in knowledge derived from experience.

Jonathan Edwards, the great Reformed theologian who was a Congregationalist minister in New England, expressed an identical conviction in the same decade of the 1730s. In his parish of

Northampton, Massachusetts, revival broke out in 1734–35. What did Edwards do about it? Earlier Puritans would have encouraged those who professed conversion in the revival to doubt if they really were among the elect. Edwards abandoned that advice. His pastoral practice was entirely different. He urged converts to put away fears that they might not be among the saved. If they had enjoyed an experience of God in the revival, they were to have confidence in it and to spread that experience to others. Edwards adopted the new policy because he held that converts had acquired a 'new sense' of God. They possessed self-evidencing knowledge of God. Edwards must not be seen as a traditional Calvinist resisting the Enlightenment. He did not represent the decaying spirit of piety in an atmosphere increasingly conditioned by reason. Rather, he was an Enlightenment thinker adapting the received body of Protestant thought to the new modes of thinking of his day. His achievement was to blend piety with reason. His *Freedom of the Will* (1754), defending Calvinism, rests on John Locke's *Essay concerning Human Understanding*. Edwards' writings remodelled the Calvinist inheritance in accordance with the Enlightenment assumptions of his age. Other Calvinists in Scotland, England and elsewhere followed his example and gained similar confidence about the knowledge of God. Their movement was often given the label 'New Light'. The light was equally that of the gospel and of the Enlightenment.

In summary, it can be said that through Wesley, Edwards and others who thought as they did, the Enlightenment altered the doctrine of assurance by introducing greater certainty about knowledge of God, and the result was a new impulse to Christian mission. But that does not exhaust the bond between evangelicalism and the Enlightenment. The early evangelicals repeatedly showed 'enlightened' characteristics. A number of them can be considered in turn.

Enlightenment characteristics

Early evangelicals believed in *scientific method*. They were concerned with what they called 'experimental religion'. Experiments were to be conducted as much in religion as in science. Evangelicals wrote scientific treatises called *Enquiries*. William Carey's work that launched the Baptist Missionary Society was *An Enquiry into the Obligation of Christians to use Means for the Conversion of the Heathen* (1792). The key word, 'Enquiry', is the one that Adam Smith used in his influential work *An Inquiry into the Nature and Cause of the Wealth of Nations* (1776). Their intellectual method was the same – enquiry, investigation. Theology overlapped with science, broadly understood, for both disciplines used empirical technique. Thus Thomas Chalmers, the leader of the early nineteenth-century evangelicals in the Church of Scotland, delivered his most powerful sermons, not on some subject of central theological concern but on the wonders of the heavens. The *Astronomical Discourses* (1817) illustrate that there was no gulf between science and religion. Likewise Benjamin Rush, a leading physician in post-Revolutionary America and a disciple of Jonathan Edwards, integrated the study of physiology thoroughly with theology. That was absolutely typical of this age. Science and theology were pursued by the Enlightenment mind as branches of a common intellectual enterprise.

Another feature of the period was *optimism*. The later Enlightenment characteristically supposed that the future holds great promise for humanity. It was at this time that the idea of progress came to birth – the idea that humanity is advancing morally towards a better future. The general optimism of the age was equally characteristic of evangelicals. 'More will in the end be saved than will perish', said Thomas Scott, a leading Anglican evangelical, in 1802. 'Diseases, wars, passions, will all be subdued.'[12] That was optimism. Hope for the future commonly took a doctrinal form. Postmillennial belief, the conviction that the second coming of Jesus Christ will take place after a thousand years of beatitude on earth, became widespread among evangelicals. It was held that the present will merge indistinguishably into the blessed future of the millennium. Evangelicals spoke of the peace and harmony of 'the glory of the latter days'.[13] Some of the impetus for overseas missions sprang from the expectation that the spread of the gospel throughout the world would usher in the millennium. Missionary work would accomplish the Christian hope. Postmillennialism was a Christian version of the idea of progress – utterly Christian, but nevertheless a form of the idea of progress. It was a facet of the optimism of the age.

Thirdly there was *moderation*. It was common, as we have seen, for non-evangelical clergy of the eighteenth century to be moderate in doctrine. Equally, however, moderation was a feature of the theology of John Wesley. His Arminianism was recognizably similar to the prevailing Latitudinarianism of the times. In both there was an assertion of human free will, although John Wesley still insisted on divine sovereignty over all. What is less frequently noticed is that the Calvinist tradition amongst evangelicals also became moderate. That very term was sometimes used. 'Moderate Calvinism' was the characteristic theological position of evangelicals both inside the Church of England and outside it. There was no great difference between the convictions of Wesley's Arminians and those of evangelical Calvinists. The Anglican Thomas Haweis, for example, said that he wrote his own biblical commentary as a Calvinist, but that he hoped that it would be entirely acceptable to 'a spiritually minded Arminian'.[14] Moderate Calvinists dropped the elaborate Puritan distinctions that had so marked works of theology of the seventeenth century and adopted a simple form of doctrinal exposition. They adopted the Enlightenment quality of clarity and that aligned them with the Arminians. They cultivated moderation.

Fourthly, *ethics* were stressed. Eighteenth-century churchmen in general preached morality and often very little else. That was not true of evangelicals because they proclaimed justification by faith. Nevertheless they emphasized the duties of morality. George Whitefield, the great revivalist preacher of Britain and America, defined true religion as 'a universal morality founded upon love of God, and faith in the Lord Jesus Christ'.[15] Religion is essentially morality. That ethical thrust is repeated again and again in the teaching of the early evangelicals and marks them as men of their age.

Fifthly there was *pragmatism*. Evangelicals of the pioneering era were prepared to adapt religion to circumstances. A pragmatic temper is sometimes thought to have been a feature of religion in the New World. In America there were fewer hampering traditions to overcome and so experimentation was particularly easy. Yet evangelicalism in Britain as much as evangelicalism in the New World was marked by pragmatic policy decisions. Field preaching outside church buildings, perhaps the most characteristic strategy for spreading the gospel adopted by Whitefield and Wesley, was a pragmatic measure. It was to break with church order, the standard way in which things ought to be done. Again, lay agency, the principle that ministry should not be confined to the ordained, was marked amongst evangelicals. Chalmers, for example, introduced deacons alongside elders in his congregation in Glasgow in 1819. Businessmen were to be church officials. Similarly Baptists abandoned their insistence on believers' baptism as a condition of communion in order to fraternize with other evangelicals. There was a preparedness to break with traditional notions of church order for the sake of preaching the gospel. Evangelical pragmatism was an expression of the Enlightenment temper of practicality.

In the sixth place there were *matters of taste*. Evangelicals were by no means cultural philistines in this period. After all they wrote literature themselves. William Cowper, one of the greatest poets of the later eighteenth century, was an evangelical who lived at the home of John Newton, a leading evangelical Anglican clergyman. Cowper's identification of elegance with simplicity appealed to many others in the movement. Their achievement of writing literature in accordance with the taste that they themselves possessed is evident in the hymns of Charles Wesley. Disciplined emotion, concentrated meaning, classical idiom and terseness are all crowded into such lines as 'impassive he suffers, immortal he dies'.[16] The technique is typical of the Augustan movement in English literature. Evangelicals expressed themselves in the idiom of the age.

Seventhly there was *reform.* The Enlightenment is commonly associated with a reforming impulse. Evangelicals, it must be admitted, were not noted for their overall reforming zeal in politics in the eighteenth and early nineteenth centuries. In particular, in the wake of the French Revolution, they turned in Britain to the defence of the established order. Even Protestant Dissenters who traditionally believed in the ideals of civil and religious liberty became much less warm in the advocacy of those goals when they saw the anarchy and atheism that spread over France after 1789. The spirit of reform was perhaps more obvious among American evangelicals. Thus Isaac Backus, a leader of the Baptists, believed in the separation of church and state and associated radical causes. Yet the devotion to liberty of the American revolution was applauded by evangelicals among English Dissenters and Scottish Presbyterians. Toleration was valued by evangelicals in general, Anglicans as well as Dissenters. They spoke of their admiration for John Locke and his work *On Religious Toleration.* That would not have been the case among the Puritans.

Most remarkable was the way in which evangelicals threw their energies into the cause of anti-slavery. It is not true to say that anti-slavery thought originated amongst evangelicals. On the contrary, it began amongst Quakers and more secular Enlightenment theorists, such as deists of the stamp of Franklin. Nevertheless because evangelicals accepted the common Enlightenment ideals of benevolence, happiness and liberty, all of which pointed to freeing slaves from being mere articles of merchandise, they had a natural affinity for the anti-slavery cause. Their activism put them in the vanguard of the movement that achieved both the abolition of the British slave trade in 1807 and the ending of slavery in British dominions in 1833. It can be established, notwithstanding certain qualifications, that evangelicals joined in the reforming impulse which is a characteristic of the Enlightenment era.

Conclusions

It is extremely hard to resist the conclusion that the early evangelicals were immersed in the Enlightenment. They were participating fully in the progressive thought of their age. At this point there is a need for caution. Evangelical Christianity cannot be reduced to Enlightenment categories of thought. There was no one-to-one fit between the two movements. There was a difference between their balance of values. The contrast was to become evident as Enlightenment thought spread to more and more sections of society, broadly from the élite to the masses, during the nineteenth century. For many people evangelical religion and Enlightenment thought remained thoroughly wedded. One dimension of the Enlightenment legacy that was retained was a belief in free enquiry. The spirit of investigation was to be utterly unfettered. It was held that a condition of progress in scientific knowledge is a total lack of presuppositions. It began to be contended that basic Christian doctrines cannot be assumed in theological exploration. Thus, by 1879, when Alexander Raleigh addressed the Congregational Union in England on 'The Changed Aspects of Evangelical Faith', he argued that evangelicalism had abandoned its belief in authority in favour of free enquiry.[17] What he meant was that preconceptions derived from the Bible were not to override the results of allegedly scientific investigation. The result of the exaltation of free enquiry to which Raleigh points was an erosion of doctrinal conviction and, indeed, of the evangelical message, especially among Congregationalists themselves in the later nineteenth century.

What was going on here? The more liberal evangelicals of the later nineteenth century were committing the error of supposing that it is possible to banish all presuppositions. In reality, a person who abandons some by expelling them from the front door of the mind finds that others crowd in through the back door. Presuppositions, what we assume about our perceptions of the world, will always be there. The belief that it is possible to operate without any presuppositions was a result of exaggerating one element in Enlightenment teaching. An emphasis on free enquiry was exalted above one of the four evangelical characteristics, biblicism. Ultimately Enlightenment thought was a solvent of evangelical conviction. The process took place, however, not in the eighteenth, but in the later nineteenth century. The marriage of evangelicalism with Enlightenment thought undoubtedly entailed risk.

With that caveat, the main lessons of the Evangelical-Enlightenment relationship are clear: the Enlightenment was not necessarily anti-religious; and evangelicalism was not just a matter of feeling opposed to the reason of the Enlightenment. On the contrary, the Enlightenment and evangelicalism were aligned with each other. It is often supposed otherwise. Lesslie Newbigin, the retired Bishop of the Church of South India, for example, has characterized the non-Christian assumptions of the late twentieth century as the baleful result of the Enlightenment.[18] While there is a great deal of truth in this analysis, Newbigin neglects the extent to which the Enlightenment was blended with evangelical Christianity (of which he is himself an adherent) in earlier days. He criticizes the Enlightenment for being intrinsically anti-Christian. It is true that Enlightenment thought can serve anti-Christian ends in leading, for example, to the exaggeration of free enquiry. In itself, however, the movement is not hostile to the faith. The Enlightenment actually gave rise to evangelical Christianity with its sense of mission. The two were entirely compatible with each other.

What may be concluded overall about evangelical Christianity and the Enlightenment? The values of the Enlightenment, insofar as they were admirable, can be continuous with those of evangelicalism. Scientific investigation, hope for the future, humane reform – surely attractive ideals – do not stand opposed to evangelical religion. That is a principle to which the career of John Stott is an enduring monument. Such ideals share common roots with the evangelical expression of the Christian faith. If these are the values of a rational human being, they are also some of the natural values of the evangelical Christian. In its origins, evangelicalism was aligned with progressive thought.

Part Two
Understanding the modern world

Introduction to Part Two

Jesus' injunction that his followers should be 'in the world' but not 'of the world' focuses our attention on the need to understand the world, both that we might be faithful witnesses to it, and that we might resist being squeezed into its mould. Saying this is much easier than doing it, however. The world's models are everywhere: in the schools, in the mass media, at work and in most social interactions. They reward conformity and they punish those who deviate from worldly values. They are very powerful and before we know where we are, we have picked up attitudes and behaviour which belong more to the world than to Christ. Nothing so clearly illustrates how far the world has penetrated the church in recent years as the way in which Western Christians have been adopting relativist positions on moral issues.

It is impossible to resist its pressures to conform, or to penetrate it with the gospel, without first understanding the modern world: what it is like, how it came to be this way, where it is going, and what is a biblical critique of the answers to these three questions. Os Guinness has contributed a lot towards helping this generation of Christians to better understand the world. His *The Dust of Death* (IVP, 1973) interpreted to us the culture of the 'swinging sixties'. Then his *The Gravedigger File* (Hodder & Stoughton, 1983) worked on a broader canvas in analysing modernity, and the ways in which it is embroiling the church in digging her own grave. His contribution to this book, 'Mission in the face of modernity', was one of the outstanding papers presented to the Lausanne II conference in Manila, in 1989.

His purpose is to help those engaged in world mission to exploit the opportunities offered by modernity, whilst reading the signs of the times with sufficient clarity to avoid its pitfalls. The modern world is not necessarily antagonistic to religion, but it prefers that it be restricted to the private sphere. It also encourages a multiplicity of religious options, with the implication that they all lead to God. Secularism and syncretism are the two great rivals to the gospel in the modern world. Os Guinness urges us to engage with modernity in full recognition that culture is both God's gift to us and the arena in which the devil tries to seduce us to worship him and not Christ. The only grounds we have for confidence in wrestling with modernity are: in terms of our part,

81

prayer and fasting; and in terms of God's part, the Word and the Spirit. There is, indeed, only one answer to the all-pervasive influence of modernity, and that is God. Compared with his glory, even the most dazzling achievements of the modern world pale into insignificance.

Like Os Guinness, Elaine Storkey sees opportunities for the gospel in modern society, provided we are faithful in making a whole-hearted biblical response to our contemporary culture. Her essay 'Change and decay in British society?' essentially provides a case study of one society deeply moulded by modernity. Her aim in making this definition is both to highlight the extent of deep-rooted change even in recent years and to sharpen a biblical response.

Elaine Storkey's strategy is first to contrast British life in the 1990s with that of the 1950s, to bring into relief the dramatic surface changes that have taken place. Next, she tries to look critically, from a Christian perspective, at some key underlying world-views or assumptions, particularly individualism, economism, contemporary relativism and New Age thinking, with its restless quest for meaning. Finally, she asks how we might respond to these taken-for-granted assumptions that lie below the surface of modern society. Our strategy for the gospel needs entirely redirecting to meet contemporary people in their human need.

Though Britain today is regarded as a predominantly secular society, Elaine Storkey concludes that the real picture is more complex. The underlying world-views, New Age in particular, reveal the religious direction of Britain's modern society.

Faith in science is an important dimension of modernity. So, if there is to be a missionary encounter with our culture, evangelicals who are well informed about modern science as well as biblical theology have a key role to play. Ernest Lucas is such a person and his essay, 'The "New Science" and the gospel', is a first step towards an encounter. He begins by reminding us that most evangelicals are still preoccupied with the debates of yesteryear concerning evolution and Darwinism. However, non-Christian scientists have mostly moved on to other issues, and if there is to be a genuine missionary encounter it can only take place on the territory of their choosing. The tactical wisdom of being open to this is heightened by a recognition of the links between the new sciences and New Age thinking.

In his own encounter with the 'new sciences', Dr Lucas looks critically at the 'new physics', the 'new biology' and chaos theory. Readers unfamiliar with anything more than elementary science will not find it easy to follow the technical material – but that is unavoidable if the writer is to address seriously the issues raised by the new sciences and not merely make assertions which will cut no ice with those he seeks to encounter.

INTRODUCTION TO PART TWO

In his reflections on the new sciences and the gospel, Ernest Lucas rejects the 'God of the gaps' response to the challenges of science. This is because it ignores biblical teaching about God's immanence within his creation. He exposes common confusions about the meaning of chance, and suggests how it is possible to believe that randomness – properly understood – can have a place in God's creation. He explains the role of reductionism in scientific methodology and why Christians cannot accept the inevitable loss of human dignity that goes with it. Finally, he challenges claims that the new physics validates Eastern mysticism, and poses two questions for Christians who feel called to join this missionary encounter.

Both Chris Wright and David Wells have discussed in Part One the unpopularity, today, of biblical claims regarding the uniqueness of Christ, whilst Os Guinness observes the trend in modernity to pluralization. But the gospel is about what God has done in Christ alone. Moreover, Jesus' final charge to his followers was to go into all the world and make disciples. So our missionary encounter is not only with our science-based culture, but also with those of other faiths. Indeed the two are not wholly unrelated for, as we have noted with Ernest Lucas, the New Age thinking which is so popular in contemporary culture, draws on both the new sciences and Eastern religions. It is highly appropriate, therefore, that Saphir Athyal's contribution, 'The gospel and Hinduism', focuses on dialogue between Hindus and Christians.

After a word of caution about comparing the best of Christianity with the worst of other faiths, Dr Athyal reminds us that what Christians have to commend is a person and not a religion. Whilst recognizing that salvation is not found in every religious tradition, he is conscious that the Bible bears witness to God's general revelation, common grace and the *imago Dei* in everyone. So, he asks, how do we do justice to these two strands of biblical truth?

Those who know little of Hinduism will appreciate Saphir Athyal's explanations of it. As an Indian who has lived most of his life in a Hindu culture, he clearly respects its nobler elements without in any way compromising his commitment to Christ. Thus, when he discusses ways in which Hindus and Christians can usefully enter into dialogue, it is not on the basis of relativist and pluralist assumptions. His examination of the Indian context of dialogue sheds light on those approaches which make dialogue worthwhile and those which do not. In the end it all comes down to Christians loving and understanding the neighbours to whom they want to witness. However, the writer bluntly admits, dialogue is not a painless way to make the gospel acceptable. 'The offence of the gospel will always remain because of the demands it makes.' That is increasingly obvious wherever we seek to penetrate the modern world with the gospel.

The final essay in Part Two is concerned with Christian thinking and action in politics. The writer, Martyn Eden, suggests that this is one of the areas of life in which Christians have most difficulty resisting worldly pressures to conform. This is partly because of the trend, recognized by Os Guinness, to keep faith out of politics and public life. It also follows from the shortage of Christians willing to try to think biblically about current issues in the way that John Stott does in *Issues Facing Christianity Today*. Martyn Eden's thesis is that Christians have too often allowed themselves to be sucked into the left/right political divide, instead of recognizing that both sides owe more to the Enlightenment than to the gospel. Each reflects one element of the gospel but exaggerates its significance. Proponents of both sides sometimes try to hijack the gospel in support of their partisan causes. The purpose of the essay, 'Agreed in principle?', is to persuade Christians to operate within a distinctively Christian framework, rather than one defined by secular ideologies. Christians in politics are encouraged to work better together to identify and articulate principles from Scripture. The writer is frank about the difficulties of doing this, and recognizes that there would still be disagreements between Christians about the implementation of these principles at the level of public policy. Nevertheless, he holds that such an approach would be more consistently Christian, and would not discredit the gospel in the way Christians do at present when they adopt secular ideologies and sanctify them with a Christian veneer.

MARTYN EDEN
DAVID F. WELLS

Mission in the face of modernity

Six checkpoints on mission without worldliness in the modern world[1]

Os Guinness

Introduction: the promise and the threat

Modernity, or the world civilization now being produced by the forces of modernization, represents perhaps the greatest single opportunity and the greatest single threat the Christian church has faced since apostolic times. Yet no great theme in the Manila Congress has been more overlooked by more Christians with more consequences than this one. For evangelicals at large, modernity is still an unconfronted problem.

Let me open this momentous subject in a simple way with a story, an observation, a thesis and a quotation.

First, the story. Soviet leader Nikita Khrushchev used to tell of a time when there was a wave of petty thefts in the USSR, and the authorities put guards at all the factories. At one of the timberworks in Leningrad the guard knew the workers well. The first evening, out came Pyotr Petrovich with a wheelbarrow and, on the wheelbarrow, a great bulky sack with a suspicious-looking shape.

'Come on, Petrovich,' said the guard. 'What have you got there?'

'Just sawdust and shavings,' Petrovich replied.

'Come on,' the guard said, 'I wasn't born yesterday. Tip it out.'

And out it came – nothing but sawdust and shavings. So he was allowed to put it all back again and go home.

The same thing happened every night all week, and the guard was getting extremely frustrated. Finally, his curiosity overcame his frustration.

'Petrovich,' he said, 'I know you. Tell me what you're smuggling out of here, and I'll let you go.'

'Wheelbarrows, my friend,' said Petrovich. 'Wheelbarrows.'

We may laugh, but we must remember that in the area where the church and modernity meet, the laugh is on us. Modernity is a new kind of worldliness that has sneaked up on us without our realizing it. We have tried to use the forces of modernization to serve us, but unwittingly we ourselves have been shaped by them. We have set up endless patrols to detect the dangers of the world in our societies, but the devil has trundled this new worldliness right past our eyes and into the church. As Peter Berger warns, whoever sups with the devil of modernity had better have a very long spoon.

Second, the observation. Back in the early 1970s, a renowned social scientist at Oxford University turned to me, knowing I was a Christian, and said, 'By the end of the 1970s, who will be the worldliest Christians in America?' I must have looked a little puzzled, and he went on, 'I guarantee it will be the fundamentalists.'

At the time such an idea was startling. Worldliest? Fundamentalism had always been world-denying by definition. But now, nearly two decades later, as we meet to discuss the task of world mission and look at the impact of modernization, that impact confronts us bluntly: World-denying conservatism has become virtually impossible. And Christendom's ultimate worldling today is not the Christian liberal but the Christian conservative. The contemporary church's prototypical charlatan is not the medieval priest but the modern evangelist. The Tetzels of history and the Elmer Gantrys of fiction pale beside the real-life examples of evangelical and evangelistic worldliness in our own time. In its sweatless, disincarnate, electronic form, modern evangelism has created the ultimate parody of the incarnation.

Third, the thesis. A full account of the relationship of modernity and the church is probably beyond any of us, and certainly beyond the scope of this paper. But just compare the church's position in 1989 with her prospects in AD 989 on the eve of the first millennium. In 989 she held only a tiny segment of the globe and had made only a limited impact on the deep paganism that underlay the official layer of

'Christian civilization'. A millennium later she is the world's leading faith, and lays the strongest claim to be a truly global religion. And while the Christian faith is currently in recession in Europe, which was once its heartland, it is still experiencing the most massive world-wide expansion in its history.

At first sight, then, the close relationship between the church and modernity appears to have been overwhelmingly advantageous. The Christian faith has been tied intimately to the most successful, the most nearly global, the most consciously copied of all civilizations in history. Once due allowance has been made for 'Western imperialism' and 'Eurocentrism', the balance sheet from the church's partnership with modernity seems unquestionably positive.

But to anyone who looks more closely, and who examines the contrast between the state of the church in the more modernized and the less modernized parts of the world, a far more sober interpretation is suggested. No persecutor or foe in 2,000 years has wreaked such havoc on the church as has modernity. And the strongest theory that explains this analysis is one which was used as a tool by Marx and Engels but which is rooted in Puritanism and the Bible – the 'grave-digger thesis'. Its argument may be stated briefly: *The Christian church contributed to the rise of the modern world; the modern world, in turn, has undermined the Christian church. Thus, to the degree that the church enters, engages and employs the modern world uncritically, the church becomes her own gravedigger.*

This theme of the church, in her own worldliness, warring against herself becomes most focused in the discussion of mission and modernity. For if modernity represents the most powerful, the most all-embracing and the most seductive setting in human history, then 'contextualization' in the setting of modernity is both amplified promise and amplified threat. The desire to witness and the danger of worldliness are enhanced simultaneously and exponentially.

Lastly, the quotation. One hundred years ago, the German philosopher and self-styled anti-Christ, Friedrich Nietzsche remarked that when there was 'the death of God' in a culture, that culture became increasingly hollowed out, or 'weightless'. Karl Marx, in his *Communist Manifesto*, had noted the same effect earlier: 'All that is solid melts into air, all that is holy is profaned.' But he blamed it on the corrosive acid of modern capitalism, which dissolved the ties and bonds of traditional society.

Today we would place both their insights into the wider framework of modernization, for modern unbelief and modern market economics are simply two related aspects of modernity. But Nietzsche's insight into 'weightlessness' is a telling description of the hollowing-out of reality which is characteristic of modernity – even upon truths as powerful and precious as the gospel. And it also points in the direction of the sole, ultimate answer to modernity, for the biblical opposite of, and antidote to, 'weightlessness' is 'glory'.

Far more than his renown or radiance, God's glory is his own inexpressible reality, a reality so real that it alone has gravity and weight – the only 'really real reality' in the entire universe. Therefore, when things move away from God, they become hollow and weightless. It can accurately be said of them, 'Ichabod' ('The glory has departed', 1 Sa. 4:21) or 'Mene, mene, tekel, upharsin' ('You have been weighed in the balances and found wanting [or weightless]', Dn. 5:27, RSV). That is why idols, by contrast with God, are literally 'nothing'. That is why revival is the refilling of a nation with 'the knowledge of the glory of the LORD, as the waters cover the sea' (Hab. 2:14).

In sum, the civilization of modernity is a world system and spirit that today both encompasses us as individuals and encircles the globe. It therefore raises ultimate questions and requires ultimate responses. We cannot tackle the character and predicament of modernization if we simply summarize trends, marshall statistics, devise strategies and assess prospects. To do that is to limit things to 'technique', and thus to fall victim to the mesmerizing spell of modernity itself, and to fail to see that modernity's real questions and impact go far deeper. Modernity is a profound challenge to the church precisely because its menace is not merely to how we communicate, but to what we communicate and who we are – to the very character of the gospel and the church itself. At a time when the church is on the threshold of 'reaching the world', modernity calls into question what it means to reach anyone. We may indeed 'win the whole world, but lose our own soul'. As Jacques Ellul says, those who understand modernity know that it raises the ultimate question – Christ's: 'When the Son of Man comes, will he find faith on the earth?'

This essay is therefore deliberately different. (1) It is unashamedly theoretical, but only so that mission can be truly practical and effective in the end. (2) It is undoubtedly difficult because of the sociological terms, but partly because some people have not experienced modernity, many who have have not reflected on it, and even for those who have it is notoriously difficult. And (3) its chief focus is a critical view of the character of modernity, but simply because modernity represents a danger of worldliness as strong as any desire to witness. In tempting us with its distinctive secularity, modernity becomes a test of what we believe is ultimately real. Its challenge is to our character and integrity, not simply to our communication and cultural adaptability.

This essay, then, is a call to repentance, prayer, spiritual warfare and hard thinking as much as to planning and new enterprise. It is a call to a deeper, tougher response to a challenge far greater than most Christians have realized. If we are to engage modernity and 'plunder the Egyptians' without 'setting up a golden calf', we shall have to understand more deeply both modernity and an incarnational theology that alone can overcome it.

Definition and description

But what exactly is 'modernization' or 'modernity'? At a rudimentary level, we all have answers to that question, because all of us are to some extent accustomed to many of the components of 'modern society'. For example, think of the fact that those of us born before the end of World War II (1945) actually have preceded many of the advances modern people take for granted: television, penicillin, credit cards, frozen foods, satellites, copying machines, contact lenses, word processors, artificial hearts, tape decks, split atoms, ballpoint pens, fax machines, men walking on the moon and so on. Such discoveries underscore how far and fast we have come. But this view of modernity remains impressionistic. A far harder and more important task is to move beyond impressions to define what modernization is, and to describe how it arose and what its consequences are.

The term 'modernization' is derived from the Latin word *modo* ('contemporary' or 'just now'). But it was coined specially to refer to the fact that modern civilization is the product of at least three revolutions in human experience: (1) the economic revolution, centring especially on the development of market capitalism since the thirteenth century; (2) the industrial revolution, centring especially on the technical innovations since the eighteenth century; and (3) the political revolution, centring especially on the ideological movements of the nineteenth and twentieth centuries. Modernity, in this sense, did not happen yesterday. Yet it has not always been there. It is a unique and specific constellation of things that creates a decisive difference. It must not be dismissed simply as either a fancy word for 'change' or as a philosophical development which can be superseded easily (as in the very different architectural term, 'post-modern').

This general statement can be made a little sharper by underscoring some of the features important to it.

Modernity and its 'carriers'. There is no single cause of modernity, and an infinite number of components comprising modernization. But the best way to grasp and assess modernity is to trace the development and spread of its carriers (in the sense of medical carriers of disease). 'Seven deadly carriers' are of paramount importance: the capitalist market economy, the centralized bureaucratic state, the new industrial technology, rapid population growth, urbanization, the mass media and (as soon as a critical stage is reached) globalization.

Modernity and its 'comprehensiveness'. The carriers of modernization are global in their reach and consequences, though modernization is neither universal nor uniform. It does not affect things everywhere in the same way. Cultures are different, individuals within those cultures are different, and different effects can be seen at different times.

Yet globalization is still real. So Christians cannot simultaneously welcome the arrival of the 'global church' and attack modernity as 'Western' or presume on the immunity of the 'Third World'. Modernization has sprung from Western (and partly Christian) origins, but it is different from 'Westernness' and it is fast making terms such as 'Third World' obsolete. Therefore, to think that anyone can escape modernity through being 'anti-Western', 'anti-American' or 'pro-Two-thirds-world' is an illusion Christians cannot afford. Soon the issue in almost every country will not be 'Modernized or not?' but 'How far modernized?' And, the real test of modernity's effect is not the first generation but the third.

Modernity and its 'consciousness'. It is a mistake to see modernity simply as a matter of objective institutions and technologies. But it is also a mistake to view it as simply a matter of ideas and ideologies (such as liberalism, socialism, modernism). Modernity includes the overall mind-set and broad, subjective awareness which is bred by living with modern institutions (such as bureaucracies) and with modern technologies (such as the tools of the pop-cultural revolution, from 'boom boxes' and headsets to colour television). This consciousness is just as influential as formal philosophies in the modern world, and it is carried and spread by teenagers, as much as by adults and practical thinkers such as business people and engineers (and missionaries), and even more than by philosophers.

Modernity and its 'costs'. Naturally, the popular view of modernity focuses primarily on its benefits and conveniences. Modernity brings a promise not only of the obvious 'bigger, better, richer, faster' but also of the less obvious liberations – freedom from the confines of tradition, poverty and the bonds of clan, tribe and caste. But a complete picture of modernity must include its high price too – the sacrifices and dislocations (in the destruction of traditional life), the economic and social dislocations (including the family crisis as well as exploitation and oppression in the new modern conditions), the cultural and psychological dislocations (such as loneliness, anomy and homelessness) and – especially important here – the religious dislocations.

Modernization is therefore not something simple, local, transient or inconsequential. At its most developed, it confronts us with such relentless power and pervasiveness that it has been aptly described as an 'iron cage' around human life (Max Weber), 'a gigantic steel hammer' that smashes traditional institutions and traditional communities of faith (Peter Berger). This darker side of modernity raises two fundamental questions to us. The first is the human question: How can human beings live in a tolerably human way in a world created by modernization? The second is the religious question: How can religion in the modern world retain its traditional authority and integrity and remain the deepest source of a sense of human meaning and belonging? The answers to both questions are vital, of course, to the church in itself as well as to the church in mission, and we turn now to a series of fundamental checkpoints that help us to engage critically with the opportunity and challenge of modernity to our mission for Christ.

1. Exploiting modernity: two opportunities

The main accent in this essay is on the challenge of modernity, its threat to the Christian faith and to the humanness of life as traditionally understood. But that of course is only half of the picture, if the most neglected half, and I would like to begin more positively. The fact is that even the sternest critics of modernity would be reluctant to return to the pre-modern world. And even beyond the undoubtedly positive aspects of modernity, such as its freedoms and conveniences, there are still aspects of modernization which represent extraordinary opportunities for mission.

Cultural openness

The first, and most obvious, opportunity grows from the fact that certain features of modernity prompt *cultural openness*. As modernization spreads further and further, particularly in the form of decentralized modern media, the totally closed society is made more and more difficult. Mikhail Gorbachev's self-proclaimed 'revolution without bullets' and Deng Xiaoping's pre-Tiananmen Square talk of 'China's second revolution' are dramatic signs that this is true not only of traditional closed societies, but even of centralized totalitarian states.

No societies are finally immune to modernization. And to any society that would hope to benefit from modernization, centralization is a recognized handicap. Thus, for example, when the decision comes down to a choice between Marxist equality and modern efficiency, death by obsolescence or freedom for new ideas, modernity is hard to resist. So the modernizing trend moves inevitably, if unevenly and against considerable resistance, towards societies and nations being open to a myriad of outside influences to which they would once have been impervious. American Express cards are used by Raisa Gorbachev, and 'Big Macs' have entered the world of the 'Big Brother'.

The point needs to be guarded against distortion, partly because all sin and all sinful cultures are in part a form of 'closure' designed to exclude God, and partly because we should never forget those countries still closed and those 300,000 brothers and sisters who each year seal their witness to Christ with their own blood. Yet the point itself requires little elaboration. This dramatic cultural openness is partly why the most explosive missionary growth has been outside the influence of mission-aries – such as the indigenous working-class movements among people feeling their 'homelessness' in the face of the gale-force winds of modernization (for example, Latin American Pentecostalism in its self-supporting, self-propagating form).

In addition, this extraordinary openness is behind the fact that in the last century and a half, Christians have used every last means, medium and methodology to reach the unreached in an enterprise in creative ingenuity unrivalled in history. And no Christian tradition has been richer in such ingenuity, enterprise and pragmatic organization than evangelicalism. What Greek and Roman roads were to the explosion of the gospel in the first century, and the printing presses were to the Reformation in the sixteenth century, everything from steamships in the nineteenth century to radio, television and satellites are to missionary enterprise in the openness of the modern world. What this openness means overall, then, is that the church faces the greatest opportunity for missionary expansion since the days of the Apostles.

Cultural rebounds

The second opportunity is less obvious and only becomes apparent on the far side of the dislocations of modernity. This opportunity stems from the fact that modernization breeds its own distinctive *cultural rebounds*.

The general possibility of these rebounds is grounded in the dynamics of human sin, and no-one should have a better appreciation of irony, comedy and unintended consequences than the Christian. Theologically speaking, sin means holding 'the truth in unright-eousness', which means in turn that neither sin nor its philosophies and institutions is ever stable. But our concern here is with the practical consequence. For modernity reinforces the instability so that every rebound contains some speeded-up disillusionment with some false faith or idol, and therefore presents a moment of spiritual openness – that moment which forms the 'today' in which the gospel addresses every human being.

The list of such cultural rebounds and their ironies is unending. 'God is dead', it is said. 'The modern world has come of age and outgrown the tutelage of faith.' But its prodigal descent has been swift. Modern cities make people closer yet more alienated at once; powerful modern weapons bring their makers to the point of impotence and destruction simultaneously; modern media promise facts but deliver fantasies; modern education introduces mass schooling but fosters sub-literacy; modern technologies of communication encourage people to speak more and say less and to hear more and listen less; modern life-styles offer do-it-yourself freedom but slavishly follow fads and end often in addictions; modern conveniences, being dispos-able and ephemeral, bring people closer to happiness but further from joy; modern styles of communication make people hungry for intimacy and authenticity but more fearful than ever of being prey to phoniness, manipulation and power games. And so on.

Prior to modernity, the corruptions of Christendom tended to rebound into anti-Christian hostility. 'I am not a Christian,' Voltaire is supposed to have prayed to Christ, 'but that is so that I can love thee the better.' Today, the shoe is on the other foot. 'Modern man has come of age,' did someone say? Hardly. Modern man (and woman) is less often a humanist, but that is so that he and she can be more human. The very *reductio ad absurdum* of modernity is the open door for orthodoxy. The ultimate homelessness of our modernized exist-ence is broken into by the way to the ultimate home. The very openness of modernity is a destroyer even of its own unbeliefs.

2. Reading the signs of the times: two pitfalls

Raymond Aron's remark that very few people are contemporaries of their own generation has been made even more apt by the modern explosion of knowledge and the capacity-cum-anxiety that comes with it. As more and more is known and communication becomes faster and better, the lag between information and comprehension grows greater and more frustrating at once. The result does more than divide people between the 'knows and the know-nots'. It lures even those who do know towards two pitfalls that are deepened by the knowledge explosion.

The unknowing

One pitfall of the information age is summed up in the common mentality, 'Happiness is a small circle.' Life is more tolerable, it suggests, if we know as little as we need and care as little as we can. Yet this attitude is the result of knowing too much rather than too little, and in particular it is the result of an avalanche of 'news' which leaves people blindingly aware of the last twenty-four hours, but ignorant of the last twenty-four years, let alone of history.

The resulting state of mind is a form of information without wisdom and of knowing severed from doing. Christians who react to the knowledge explosion by saying, in effect, 'I'm happy with my small world,' grow irresponsible, and their attitude becomes a serious factor in undermining the missionary initiative of the modernized sectors of the church. From that point on, instead of the whole church reaching the whole world, mission becomes a specialized concern of a dedicated minority.

The all-knowing

The other pitfall is not found in society at large, but in those for whom thinking is a profession. Summed up in an attitude which David Boorstin mocks as 'Homo-up-to-datum', this pitfall grows from the belief that harnessing the knowledge explosion offers the key to instant, total information. Its goal is to know everything in order to predict everything in order to control everything. If the first pitfall ends in irresponsibility, the second can end in an idolatry of information which becomes more of a handicap than a help to mission. It pushes mission and mission studies in the direction of the modern specialization and 'professionalization' of knowledge, and eventually towards the creation of a missionary version of the new 'knowledge class'.

The growing numbers and importance of a 'new thinking class' is one of the most distinctive features of the information society, and some of its unhappy consequences for Christians can be noted: (1) Christian thinkers often become closer to the 'cultured despisers' of the faith than to their fellow Christians; (2) expert knowledge is pursued as an end in itself; (3) specialized knowledge (which can be understood only by other specialists) creates a gap between experts and ordinary people; (4) originality and development are so prized that a fallacy is fostered that the newer-is-the-truer and the latest-is-the-greatest; (5) specialization fosters an expertise and professionalism that creates dependency and becomes disabling for anyone but the professional; (6) it is forgotten that ignorance is a constant in human affairs, and the capacity to act is often greatest when the clarity of understanding is smallest (and vice versa); and (7) members of the new 'knowledge class' become slowly adapted to the language and logic of the expanding world of seminars, forums, consultations and congresses (like Lausanne II) and thus further and further from other (Christianly more important) styles of discourse such as preaching and prayer.

Advocates of modern mission studies who scoff at such a caution should ponder the fate of most university disciplines today and especially the fate of Christian apologetics, liberal theology, evangelical higher education and seminary training over the past century. Similarly, we can be sure that sophisticated missiology and 'evangelology' without the love of Christ, compassion for the lost, concern for our neighbour, and utter reliance on the Holy Spirit, could quickly develop its own élitism, arrogance and impracticability. If you asked me to search my own heart and choose between the 'simplicity' of mission as I have seen it lived out by my own missionary parents and the 'sophistication' of much of its equivalent today, I would choose my parents' way without hesitating.

Perhaps the most telling evidence for this point is the style of discourse at Lausanne II itself compared with that of Lausanne I. Under the influence of the 'terrible trio' (advertising, television and pop-culture), modernization has caused profound changes in public discourse: above all in the shift from word to image, action to spectacle, exposition to entertainment, truth to feeling, conviction to sentiment and authoritative utterance to discussion and sharing. Most of these wider cultural shifts have been well exemplified here, and the general diminishing of any sense of 'Thus saith the Lord' has been marked.

If we are to be unriddlers of our time and, like David's followers, to be 'skilled in reading the signs of the times', we need to immerse our studies and strategic thinking in humility, responsibility and a deep sense of the sovereignty of God and the sinfulness and smallness of our human projects. Just because we are modern does not mean that we have modernity by the scruff of the neck or that any of us knows definitively what our modern context is. We are all always more short-sighted than we realize. Modern culture can never be an exotic subject studied by outside observers like a group of anthropologists on a South Sea Island. It is the mould in which we are all cast and which we can only recognize, resist and change by God's outside perspective in the midst of our ignorance – an ignorance in some ways deepened by the overload of modern information.

3. Assessing the damage to persisting religion: two trends

In earlier days, when secularization was exaggerated as progressive and irreversible, religion was widely thought to have no future. It was pronounced fated to disappear. So today's revised assessment of secularization means a revised prognosis for religion. Religion, it is now said more humbly and more accurately, has not so much disappeared in modern society as changed its character and location. What then are the trends which have effected this change, and continue to shape the religion that still persists in the modern world?

Privatization

The first trend, which in many ways is the reverse side of secularization, is *privatization*. By privatization is meant *the process by which modernization produces a cleavage between the public and private spheres of life and focuses the private sphere as the special area for the expression of individual freedom and fulfillment.* There has always been a distinction between the more personal and the more public areas of life, but until recently the relationship between them was marked by a continuum rather than a cleavage. Today in many modern cities it might as well be the Pacific Ocean. On one side of the cleavage is the public sphere, the macroworld of giant institutions (government departments such as Britain's Whitehall, large corporations such as Japan's Mitsubishi and Korea's Hyundai and military complexes such as America's Pentagon). On the other side of the cleavage is the private sphere, the microworld of the family and private associations, the world of personal tastes, sports, hobbies, clubs and leisure pursuits.

Privatization has its undoubted benefits – supremely because it does ensure authentic freedom in the private sphere. Compared with the situation in the past, it permits more people to do more, buy more and travel more than ever before – free of the constraints of community, tradition and other people. But for religions such as the Christian faith, the disadvantages outweigh the advantages. Above all, privatization is limited and limiting. Modern society spells freedom for religion, but only so long as it is confined to the private sphere. Far from being an area of true choice and creativity, the modern private sphere is all too often a sort of harmless play area, a sort of spiritual 'Indian reservation' or 'Bantustan', a homeland for separated spiritual development set up obligingly by the architects of secular society's apartheid.

A classic illustration of privatization came in an interview with the founder of McDonald's hamburgers by the New York Times. Asked what he (a Christian) believed in, he replied: 'I speak of faith in McDonald's as if it were a religion. I believe in God, family and McDonald's – and in the office that order is reversed.' The record of the interview gave no indication whether the reply was facetious or not. But whatever the case, the response was a perfect expression of privatized faith that millions of modern Christians practice daily without realizing it.

Pluralization

The second modernizing trend which shapes all persisting religion is *pluralization*. By pluralization is meant *the process by which the number of options in the private sphere rapidly multiplies at all levels, especially at the level of world-views, faiths and ideologies*.

Unlike secularism, pluralism is by no means new. The church was born in a period of similar pluralism, and modern pluralism even has its roots partly in the Protestant conviction of freedom of conscience. But modernization represents a stupendous enhancement of pluralism that in turn has set off a tidal wave of choice and change. Urban crowding, the knowledge explosion, modern travel, mass media, enormous dispersions of Third World people across the modern West . . . these are only the most obvious of the factors behind the heightened modern sense of 'all those others' and 'all those options'. We have now reached the stage where it can almost be said that 'everyone is now everywhere' and choice is not just a state of affairs, but a state of mind. Choice has become a value in itself, even a priority. Choice and change have become the very essence of modern life.

The side effects of pluralization on religion have been varied. One is that pluralization creates in modern believers a high degree of self-consciousness. Confronted constantly by 'all those others', modern people are constant question marks to each other, and modern faith is rarely as assured as it sounds.

Another effect is that religious believers in the modern world have become conversion-prone. Whereas faith was once rock-like and the turn-around of conversion was radical, complete and lasting, modern believers are prone to being reconverted – and reconverted – and reconverted (or 'born again and again . . . and again'). Multiple conversions are now common, being 'born again' is easily trivialized and even testimonies are reduced to the status of a spiritual visiting card in constant need of updating in a spiritually mobile society.

Yet another effect is that pluralism reduces the necessity of choosing at all. The very extension of choice increases the likelihood of the evasion of choice. But the overall direction is clear. Pluralization means an increase in choice and change that is almost automatically a decrease in commitment, continuity and conviction. Pluralization now creates as many tensions within each church, denomination or religion as there once were between them. With picking, choosing and selectiveness the order of the day, the result of pluralization is a general increase in shallowness, transience and heresy. Few challenges to Christian discipleship and mission are so subtle yet so corrosive.

4. Sizing up the competition: two rivals

A common consequence of exaggerating secularization is to jump to the conclusion that modernity is hostile to religion as religion. Nothing could be further from the truth. Modernity is directly opposed to two defining features of some traditional religions which the Christian faith shares with only a few others – the absoluteness of its notion of *transcendence* and its notion of *totality*. But partly for that reason, modernity is very welcoming to religions without such angular features and such ornery insistence. Indeed, modernity provides an almost perfect setting for reinforcing two potent rivals to the Christian faith. What is common to both rivals, and in strong contrast with the Christian faith, is the implicit relativism in their truth claims and the evolutionary optimism in their view of history, though one tends to be in favour of modernity and the other, at least quietly, against it.

Generalized secularism

The first rival to the Christian faith is a *generalized secularism*, which combines relativism and evolutionary optimism in various types of naturalism that are favourable to modernity. The leading examples today are liberal humanism and Marxism, both being Western in origin, though ironically the second has outgrown its origins and appeals especially to those repudiating the 'West'.

What needs underscoring is that 'secularism' is not the same thing as 'secularization'. 'Secularism' is a philosophy, with all the strengths and weaknesses of one, not least that it is commonly unemotional and that to subscribe to it demands a considerable effort of mind or will. 'Secularization', by contrast (as we defined it earlier), is not a philosophy; it's a process. Its roots are not in an intellectual concept but in institutional change. It's a process which has actually taken place in the structures of society and cannot be avoided or simply wished away.

Secularization (the process) therefore provides the perfect setting for secularism (the philosophy). Modernity is the new context which enhances the old concept, making the latter seem natural, even necessary. Secularization, therefore, has a double thrust: *It constricts religion, thereby decreasing its power, but it also reinforces secularism thereby increasing its power.*

Modernity's reinforcement of secularism is the context for a sobering fact. Since 1900, the percentage of the world's atheistic and non-religious peoples (agnostics, secularists, communists and so on) has grown from 0.2% to 21.3% – in other words from less than one-fifth of one percent to over one-fifth of the world's population. This is the most dramatic change on the entire religious map of the twentieth century. Secularists, or people with no religious commitment, now form the second largest bloc in the world, second only to Christians and catching up fast (at the rate of 8.5 million 'converts' a year).

Generalized syncretism

But this is only half the story. Modernization also provides natural reinforcement to a second potent rival to the Christian faith: *generalized syncretism.* Like secularism, modern syncretism in its varied forms often pivots on a relativism and evolutionary optimism that is conducive to modernity. But it takes them in a religious or semi-religious (rather than naturalistic) direction, and one that is often counter-modernizing (rather than pro-modern) in tendency, and collectivist (rather than purely individualistic) in concern.

The leading examples in the West are the science-based mysticisms, such as the New Age movement, as well as socialism and environmentalism in their more mythic form. But elsewhere in the developing world, where resistance to modernization and resistance to Westernization often overlap, the appeal of, and potential for, such syncretisms is even greater. Such are the blandishments of modernity that few religious leaders will have the obstinacy of an Ayatollah Khomeini to reject it outright. Far more are likely to seek to control modernity and cushion its full impact on their society by some variety of local, national or religious syncretism. Its religion then becomes a key part of any society's selective adaptation to modernity.

Among examples of this trend are the Umbanda movement in Brazil (with its Christian rites and pagan content) and the recent movement in Japan to revitalize State Shinto as a conscious civil religion that will replace 'post-war democratic Japan' and fill the vacuum of values created by modernity. Similar syncretistic movements were Japan's way of adapting to earlier waves of outside influence, such as the introduction of Confucianism from China, Buddhism from India and, in the nineteenth century, the Christian faith from the West.

And, of course, this reinforcement of syncretism by modernity is one reason for the persistence of certain kinds of religion even in highly 'secular' societies. Because of their substratum of magic, superstition and fatalism at a popular level, modern nations like France and Britain are not so much 'post-Christian' as pre-Christian and pagan. Similarly in Japan, animistic worship – of sun, mountains, trees and rocks – was always just below the surface of official State Shinto, so the revitalization of State Shinto will mean a reinforcement of popular animism.

5. Engaging modernity: two master principles

All engagement in the modern world requires or reveals an answer to the question, How do we view modernity theologically? Modernity is only one more form of human culture, and the view of culture we find in the Scriptures is a bifocal vision. Always and everywhere at once, human culture – and therefore modernity – is two things: God's gift to us, and the devil's challenge to us to worship him and not Christ.

Two great master principles have characterized the church at its most penetrating, and both are essential today.

Protagonist principle

The first is the *Protagonist principle* which flows from the theme 'Christ *over* all' and has as its key word, *total*. The story of the exodus provides an Old Testament example. The whole issue with the Egyptian Pharaoh was lordship. He who can liberate is he who is lord. As the bargaining went on, Pharaoh relented enough to let the Israelite men go, at least for worship. Moses said, 'No.' 'Let my people go' meant not just the men and not just for worship. Men, women and children must go, and go for good. Then a remarkable little phrase is added: 'Not a hoof is to be left behind.'

A New Testament example can be found in Luke. Peter, as a

fisherman, was glad to allow Jesus to preach from his boat. But Jesus said to Peter, 'Put out into the deep water, and let down the nets for a catch.' And we can almost hear Peter reply, 'Look, Lord, I'll listen to you as my teacher all day long, but when it comes to fishing, that's my job.'

We know the result. Peter found that Jesus was Lord of nature, too, and he could only respond, 'Go away from me, Lord; I am a sinful man!' Christ was Lord of nature as well as truth. He is the Alpha and the Omega. He is the source, guide and goal of all there is. That is why every eye will one day see him, every tongue will be stopped, and every knee will bow. After all, as Abraham Kuyper said, expressing the Protagonist principle perfectly, 'There is not an inch of any sphere of life of which Jesus Christ the Lord does not say, "Mine".'

This Protagonist principle is indispensable today because modernity renders earlier forms of Christian separatism impossible and many newer forms of activism ineffective. So our engagement – whether in work, politics, art, voluntary action, recreation or mission – will only be faithful and effective to the degree that Christ remains Lord of every part of our lives.

Antagonist principle

The second master principle is the *Antagonist principle*. It flows from the theme 'Christ *over against* all that which does not bow to him', and the key word here is *tension*. The Lord himself puts the point unmistakably in Exodus 20: 'I am the LORD your God . . . You shall have no other gods before [to set against] me' (Ex. 20:2–3). Over forty times in Leviticus 18 and the following chapters, there is the recurring assertion, 'I am the LORD . . .'. Each time it accompanies a strict instruction not to do as the Egyptians or the Canaanites did, neither worshipping their idols nor copying their ideas and institutions.

The reason? The Lord is the jealous one, the one who brooks no rivals. Since he is our 'decisive Other', he demands of us a decisive contrast with everything that is over against him and his ways, his ideals and his institutions. Most wonderful of all, the deepest reason is personal. It is 'that you may belong to me'.

In short, God and the world stand crosswise. We are in the world but not of it. To be faithful to him we have to be foreign to the world. We are not to be conformed but transformed by the renewing of our minds (*cf.* Rom. 12:2). Even the much-vaunted critical analysis of Marxists should pale beside the obedience-rooted critical commitment of Christians. But Marxist hardliners and Muslim fundamentalists are often wiser than we are in their deep suspicion of modernity. It *is* the

'Great Satan' to their cause. It *does* contain 'spiritual pollution', as they say, and Christians should be wary too.

Modernity, in other words, is not 'the holy ground' some urban theologians proclaim. Modernity is the devil's challenge to us. But that is not because we are the innocents and the modern world is so tempting. Rather, it is because we are the temptable ones. The modern world is simply our hearts writ large. Our hearts are simply the modern world writ small. So our view of modernity needs to be theologically realistic. God pronounces the 'No' of his judgment over all our human works before he pronounces the 'Yes' of his grace. But while his 'Yes' transcends his 'No', that is not because his 'No' is merely temporary or apparent. God's 'No' is his total, radical, continual and final judgment of all our works that are born of sin and are moving towards death.

Of course, the Protagonist principle and the Antagonist principle must never be separated. They go hand in hand. Without the former, the latter would create a 'we/they' division which is Manichean and not biblical. The Protagonist principle means there must be no hatred of the world or false asceticism with us. Yes, the world is passing away, and we are passing through the world. But the responsible realism of that bifocal vision should shape our perspective. Holding these two truths together, we are to be, in Peter Berger's memorable phrase, 'against the world for the world'.

6. Overcoming modernity: two points of reliance

Additional checkpoints that might be included here are legion. But let me conclude with one last checkpoint which concerns our practical faith and two grounds of our confidence as we seek to wrestle with and overcome modernity.

Prayer and fasting

First, looking at things in terms of our part, we must acknowledge that modernity poses a challenge that can be overcome '*only by prayer and fasting*' (Mk. 9:29). This, for me, is not something that comes naturally. It would be far easier to speak of requirements such as 'thinking Christianly'. For at the very least, modernity requires a degree of thoughtful wrestling that is on the level of the prophet Daniel – 'Though this word was true, it cost him much toil to understand it' (Dn. 10:1, NEB). But precisely because it is even more difficult, commitment to prayer and fasting is more than a pious truism. It is an emphatic repudiation of modern technique and an open acknowledgment that when we wrestle with modernity, we do not wrestle with flesh and blood. And to link fasting with prayer is even to press beyond the admirable emphasis on prayer demonstrated in modern missions since the Moravian movement (I think of heroic exemplars from Count von Zinzendorf down through Hudson Taylor to the Dorothea Mission and national movements for intercession in our own time such as Intercessors for Britain).

Not only therefore do we have the example and the teaching of our Lord himself as he engaged with the enemy at his deadliest, and taught us how to do the same. We can see that prayer and fasting are singularly appropriate for unmasking modernity because the heart of their spiritual purpose is a direct challenge to the heart of the grand lie of modernity.

Modernity, of course, tries to turn even fasting into a technique. Thus for modern people, fasting has lost its spiritual purpose and become a form of weight control or political protest (such as 'hunger strikes'). Even for many Christians it is either neglected or left at the level of the ascetic, the legalistic or the purely nominal. All of which are a form of reductionism precisely because they have lost their spiritual point.

But when the spiritual is restored and prayer and fasting are rejoined, they form an indispensable weapon without which we could not unmask or disarm modernity. The reason is theological and can be seen in the contrast between Adam and Jesus. Adam, in eating the forbidden fruit, disobeyed God's Word and 'broke his fast'; whereas the second Adam, overcoming the temptation, sustained both his obedience and his fast and thus demonstrated his repudiation of living on bread alone and his dependency on every word that proceeds out of the mouth of God.

Prayer with fasting is therefore both a statement and a stand – a statement about the ultimate meaning of life and a stand against the ultimate lie and its source. What does life mean? In creating 'a world without windows' (Peter Berger), modernity is history's greatest reinforcement of sin's cosmic lie about life-as-bread-alone (purely biological, naturalistic, secular). But, like Adam, modern people who live their lives eating, working, playing, sleeping 'autonomously' – for the sake of these things alone, apart from God – find out that such autonomous life is impossible and such an autonomous culture turns out to be death-producing.

How are prayer and fasting an effective stand against this lie? Fasting quickly brings us to the point of hunger, which is the state when our dependency on something outside ourselves is inescapable.

In knowing how much we need food, we know we do not have life in ourselves. But then we encounter the test which only prayer and fasting overcomes: On what, then, do we depend? Bread alone, says the evil one, so Adam believed him and ate. God and his Word alone, said Jesus, so he refused the devil's lie and shifted the principle of life back to its source.

This pivotal victory in the war against evil and its lie shows that prayer and fasting are practical rather than theoretical, yet profound spiritual warfare rather than a facile 'how-to' technique. Decisive victory comes only through severe testing. It was in praying and fasting that Christ met and overcome Satan. He later told his disciples that Satan can be overcome only by prayer and fasting. Do we think modernity, with all its strengths and seductions, will be different? Unless we recover the practice of prayer and fasting, our best-intentioned use of modern media and methods will end only in assisting the triumph of technique and hastening a new Babylonian captivity, albeit with air-conditioned cells and spiritual Muzak to divert us.

Word and Spirit

Secondly, looking at things in terms of God's part, we must acknowledge that modernity poses a challenge that can be overcome *only by God's Word and Spirit*. This reminder, too, is more than a truism, because once again it addresses the heart of the challenge of modernity. In producing Nietzsche's 'last men', Weber's 'iron cage', and Berger's 'world without windows', modernity does more than spawn a crowd of problems. It is a deliberate locking-out of genuine transcendence that constructs a suffocating, air-tight world filled with problems that admit of no internal solution.

Nietzsche saw clearly what this loss of transcendence would mean. 'Alas,' he wrote, 'the time of the most despicable man is coming, he that is no longer able to despise himself. Behold, I show you the *last man.*'

But modernity's repression of transcendence explains not only the triumph of triviality in the 'last men' of Western consumer societies, but the flawed enterprise of spurious forms of transcendence such as Promethean Marxism. Anyone prepared to believe with Karl Marx that the revolutionary will of history can be incarnate in any human political party is bound to be disillusioned. Addressing this lack of transcendence in Marxism, David Martin points out, 'It is a paradox that a system which claimed that the beginning of all criticism was the criticism of religion should have ended up with a form of religion which was the end of criticism.'

But how is the Christian faith different? As we survey the deepening captivity of the church, is there any lasting escape from modernity? What are the grounds for our confidence? After all, is not our very understanding of God and our listening to his Word dependent on the closed circle of our modern context?

No! A thousand times 'No!' the church cries, because the gospel itself contains the secret of why the Christian faith can survive repeated periods of cultural containment and contamination. On the one hand, it has in God's Word and Spirit an authority that stands higher than history, a judgment that is irreducible to any generation and culture. Which is why, when God speaks, not even the worst – or best – of our hermeneutics can hold him down. On the other hand, the gospel has in its notion of sin and repentance a doctrine of the church's failure which can be the wellspring of its ongoing self-criticism and renewal.

Like an eternal jack-in-the-box, Christian truth will always spring back. No power on earth can finally keep it down, not even modernity's power of Babylonian confusion and captivity. 'At least five times,' noted G. K. Chesterton, 'the faith has to all appearances gone to the dogs. In each of these five cases, it was the dog that died.'

To write these things is not to whistle in the dark, but to grapple with modernity with hope and direction. We do not 'put our trust in princes' (*cf.* Ps. 146:3), nor in management-streamlined missions, television evangelism and computer-planned church growth. Even as we use the best modern media, our reliance from beginning to end must be on God's Word and Spirit and on their grave-opening, jail-breaking power in preaching, revival, reformation and mission. Only so will modernity be restrained and overcome.

Conclusion: the reality and the glory

It should be encouraging to us all that many of the most penetrating observers of modernity are Christians – for example, Peter Berger, Jacques Ellul and George Grant. But when all is said and done, we would be foolish to pretend that modernization and modernity are easy either to understand or to engage. Little wonder that first reactions to the 'big picture' are often pessimistic. We feel overwhelmed. Which of us is equal to the challenge? 'Winning the World by 2000', like John R. Mott's earlier 'The Evangelization of the World in This Generation', is easier to handle as a rhetorical rallying cry than as a job actually to be accomplished before the clock strikes twelve on a certain day in a certain year.

What are my objectives in presenting this burden? Some of the simplest are as follows: As followers of Christ concerned to know him and make him known, we need (1) to put the topic of modernity high on our agendas for our concern, study and prayer; (2) to analyse the local and specific impact of modernization on our own country, region, city, church, ministry and audience; (3) to reform those areas of the church's doctrine and life that modernity has rendered weak or non-existent (for example, the place of truth and the importance of the incarnation in a day of electronic evangelism); (4) to forswear facile excuses and false evasions (modernization may have hit the West first and worst, but modernity is now a world problem and not simply 'a Western problem'. Besides, the real test of 'Third World spiritual vitality' is not the first modernized generation but the third); and (5) to deepen the 'reality' of our own faith in both knowledge and experience in order to be able to combat modernity.

The extraordinary burden of 'Mission in the face of modernity' makes me think of two men under titanic pressure. One was the great German thinker, Max Weber. He never shut his eyes to the modern world. He wrestled with it, but the more he wrestled, the more pessimistic he became. One day, a friend saw him pacing up and down, nearing the verge of a second breakdown. 'Max,' he said, 'why do you go on thinking like this when your conclusions leave you so depressed?' Weber's reply has become a classic of intellectual commitment and courage. 'I want to know how much I can stand.'

Admirable in many respects, that is not the way for followers of Christ. If we are not called to be Promethean entrepreneurs of the gospel, we are certainly not called to be stoics or tragic heroes.

A very different response under pressure was that of Moses. Faced with enemies behind, around and ahead, and finding discontent not only among his own people but within his own family, he suddenly met the ultimate threat to his people and to his task as their leader: God himself. The Lord declared that, because of their sin, he would destroy the Israelites.

His very life and trust in God called into question, Moses countered the challenge daringly by putting God on the line (arguing the covenant), the people on the line (calling for a consecration to the Lord even against families and friends), and finally himself on the line (asking to be blotted out himself, rather than the people).

Then, when the Lord had listened to his prayers, agreeing first to forgive the people and then to come with them in person rather than by an angel, Moses made his supreme request, surely the most audacious prayer in all the Scriptures: 'Show me your glory' (Ex. 33:18). He wanted to know all of God that a fallen sinner could be allowed to know, for nothing less would be enough to see him through the crisis of his calling.

In that prayer, we have our ultimate answer to modernity and to its keenest observers such as Nietzsche and Weber. When 'God is dead' for a nation, a church, a movement or an individual, a weightlessness results for which there is only one remedy – ultimate reality, the glory of God refilling them as the waters fill the sea. Wasn't that Jeremiah's message to his generation? To a people who had exchanged their glory for a god altogether nothing, he warned, 'Ascribe glory to the LORD your God before the darkness falls' (Je. 13:16, NEB).

If in mission today we stress the spiritual aspects of the gospel without the social, we lose all relevance in modern society. But if we stress the social without the spiritual, we lose our reality altogether. The ultimate factor in the church's engagement with modernity is the church's engagement with God.

Are we still tempted today to believe that we or anyone else can pull off the task of evangelizing the world? We must forget it. On the other hand, are we overwhelmed by the thought of the task, overburdened by the state of modernity and the world? Let us forget modernity and ourselves and turn from the what and where of our calling to the Whom. Then we can follow Moses to the source of the only reality that counts, the one power sufficient for facing up to the colossus of modernity.

'Lord, show me your glory.'

Change and decay in British society?

Elaine Storkey

In the 1990s we scarcely know any longer what to make of the farewell Sir Harry Smith's mother gave to her son: 'If you ever meet your enemy remember you are born a true Englishman.' A welter of images come to mind, fuzzied by the years; faded photographs, families large and solemn, centred round an unsmiling patriarch; white-aproned girls in grand houses; horses and ploughs in rustic tranquillity; regiments of soldiers going off to quell the heathens in far-flung outposts of Empire; every man doing his duty.

There are barely any alive now who can share those old memories. Our country and its concerns have changed. So what is it to be British in the 1990s? And what kind of society will be evidenced here as the curtains go down on the twentieth century? These kinds of questions are vital for Christians, for we need to know how we as a Christian church should live out the good news of the gospel in this changing, contemporary setting.

In this short tribute to one who shares these concerns deeply, and who has encouraged so many of us to grapple with them, there is not the space to do this subject justice. So I know John Stott will forgive me if I interpret my task in modest vein, and tackle it in three brief sections. First, to try to assess our contemporary society, I want to focus on social change between generations, and highlight life today against the relief of about thirty-five years ago. Next, my task will be to look Christianly and critically at some of the underlying perspectives, assumptions, ideologies – call them what we will – which are now taken for granted in British thinking, but which may not have been so pronounced at an earlier stage of our social history. Finally, I want us all to ask how we might then respond, as those who are committed to Jesus Christ and to the service of his kingdom.

Social change in our own time

Although the period of the early 1950s is familiar and close to some of us, for many others there is already that feeling of another age about it. We live now in a society where millions have never ridden on a tram, or waved at a steam train chugging through the countryside, or worn a Sunday suit, or received communion. When we read what British society was like thirty-five years ago, therefore, we may be amazed at how far we have travelled, and at how much has changed.

Britain in the 1950s

The 1950s was an era of low geographical mobility. This had many effects. It reinforced the clear regional demarcations within the country, and placed great emphasis on the local area, with its own local government, local policing, local entertainment, local transport. Networks of railways were still linking small towns, providing people with access to their employment and their relatives. In fact, the locality and neighbourhood were central for work, shopping and leisure, with the local cinema given central place in many small towns. Family relationships, too, echoed this local pattern. Many studies on traditional communities have described the importance of extended family living, with jobs being passed down from father to son, and mothers 'speaking for' their married children to the local landlord who could provide them with accommodation. There were fairly fixed gender rôles within the family, and leisure time was often spent indoors with relatives of the same sex across the generations. This was possible partly because of the relatively low percentage of working mothers (although here again there were strong regional differences), and partly due to the fact that sisters, cousins and grandmothers were often only a street away.

Along with low geographical mobility went low social mobility. By and large, people lived within fixed and distinct class positions. Powerful private ownership and hereditary wealth co-existed alongside widespread patterns of non-ownership and very low income. For most workers, two weeks' annual paid holiday was a very recent benefit. Class lines were also reflected in education and voting patterns, with the Labour Party claiming the allegiance of the urban working class. At the same time, intense poverty and hardship were often ameliorated by public provisions, especially in the area of welfare, council housing and health care. Post-war babies were fed on state-provided orange juice, castor oil and dried milk. In fact, for the most part, the 1950s were a period of national optimism, with almost full employment, and the flourishing of traditional heavy industries – iron, coal, steel, textiles, shipbuilding. Post-war nationalization promised increased prosperity, and recruitment of workers from parts of Europe and from Britain's former colonies seemed set to provide the labour force which would help usher the country into a new era.

Yet change is hardly ever as planned. The problems of race relations were already beginning, and policies of redevelopment, slum clearance, along with 'rationalization', epitomized by Dr Beeching's 'axe' on the railway network, were to have a massive impact on all areas of life. The juxtaposition of tradition and change was an uneasy one also, not least in areas of morality and religion. There was no abortion law, a low divorce rate, and homosexual acts were still illegal. Yet backstreet abortions took the lives of many women, and domestic disputes and violence were 'resolved' in the home rather than in the courts. Protestant Christianity was still largely accepted as the national religion (although not necessarily reflected in high church attendance). But the churches had difficulty in coming to terms with an influx of immigrant Christians from the Caribbean, many of whom were equally traditional Anglicans. Indeed the sense that they had been unwelcome in the English churches was to reverberate in the Afro-Caribbean community for decades to come. In fact, many underlying assumptions, which were as yet unquestioned in the 1950s, were to come under substantial attack from the radicals of the 60s and early 70s: assumptions now described as 'class-bound, patriarchal and white'.

Britain in the 1990s

It does not need a social scientist to suggest that there have been some fundamental changes over this last generation. We have seen massive shifts in the areas of demography, mobility, family, work, media, politics, technology, the church and public morality. Under the heading of 'mobility', for example, we could mention the growth of motorways, car-ownership, holidays abroad, new towns, inner-city depopulation; the growth of non-local work and the movement of the labour force; the influence of technology on the location of work; the increase in multi-national firms, supermarket chains, Sunday markets, and out-of-town shopping areas and leisure activities. With geographical mobility, there has also been social mobility: a blurring of class lines and traditional political allegiances. This in itself has been influenced by changing work patterns: the decline of heavy industries, a decreasing power of the unions, the boom in the service sector, the influence of computer technology and the growth in small businesses, agencies and consultancies. At the same time the demarcations between poor and rich remain as strong as ever, but the lines are drawn differently. Still under the heading of 'mobility' we could include the decline of the 'traditional' neighbourhood, and the politically directed decline in public services and amenities. With greater mobility too has come a greater global awareness, as the mass media connects us immediately with disasters and political events going on in every part of the globe. In fact, in many areas of Britain, people are more likely to know what is going on in Iraq, Ethiopia or Berlin than in the home of the widowed old woman living down the street. This global awareness has fed into the growing concern over environmental and conservation issues, for we can see the effects of acid rain and deforestation without looking wider than our television sets. The notion that we are a global village is no longer a remote one with the increase of Third World debt and the growing economic power and political integration of Europe.

If we consider the area of the family we see further changes linked in with many of those already outlined. There has been a blurring of gender rôles, with more autonomy for women, and a greater movement of married women into the workforce. This has gone along with an emphasis away from the extended family to the 'nuclear family', with its accompanying privatization of the home. The 1980s saw a greater emphasis throughout the country on home ownership, and a further growth in DIY activities. Meanwhile, television, video and other forms of home-based leisure have for a long time been seen as a normal and essential part of household consumption. Conventional family living patterns have undergone considerable change, with a decline in the number of first-time marriages, a rise in co-habitation, one-parent families, legal abortions and an increasingly high divorce rate. Children have become more of a commercial and a family focus, with a distinct growth in children-centred activities: sports, music, competitions. Yet there has also been a marked increase in reported violence and sexual abuse towards children, as well as an apparent rise in child pornography and prostitution.

Demographic changes too have been very marked. It is sometimes surprising to realize what we can learn from population figures. In the 1990s, for example, we have an increasingly ageing population and a lower birth rate. Mortality statistics in particular tell some fascinating stories. People have a longer life expectancy, but they also die of different causes and diseases from those of the mid-century. Lung cancer and smoking-related mortality patterns were very much 'male diseases' in the 50s. Since then they have grown far more rapidly amongst women than amongst men. The 'killer epidemics' are now no longer TB, smallpox, polio and London smog, but AIDS, asthma and legionnaires' disease. Deaths too from road accidents, train, boat and plane crashes, as well as from violent attack and domestic assault, have greatly outstripped similar categories forty years ago, and would be greater still if medical expertise in dealing with such areas had not also similarly increased. In other areas of demography there has been a change in the gender ratio of the population. There are now more males than females under the age of twenty-five, and this continues to be the case each year. Finally, we are a much more ethnically mixed population, especially in some of our larger cities, where migrant worker patterns of the 1950s have become settled multi-cultural community patterns. Yet ethnic minorities remain under-represented in many areas of decision-making, and in professions such as the police force.

The nature of religious affiliation has changed also. Although Christianity is still the 'official' religion of the UK, as epitomized by the continuing existence of an Established Church, there has been a movement away from the traditional mainstream denominations, towards new churches, which exist in semi-independence or clustered in what is often called the house church movement. But there has also been a massive growth in non-Christian religions, in Hinduism, and most specifically in Islam. Muslims outnumber British Jews, for example, by about five to one, and they are also numerically stronger than Methodists. With an increase in numbers, and a growth in Islamic fundamentalism, has come an increase in the demands of the Islamic community for their own state-supported schools, their own political party, and their own Muslim power base. The Salman Rushdie affair of 1988 both acted as a catalyst to draw distinct and disparate Islamic groups together, and also separated Muslims from the sympathy of many others in the country who were outraged at their constant calls for murder.

So although Britain is generally regarded as a predominantly secular society, the real picture is a more complex one. The rise of cults, the country-wide fascination with astrology, and the occult, the rise of na_ire worship, and the New Age movement as a whole, are all significant in understanding the religious direction of our country. They are all part of the changes in perception and outlook which have occurred in Britain during this last generation.

Reasons for social change

The problem with this description of a changing Britain is that it is simply that – only a description. As such it does not get at the root issues. We need some explanations of why these changes have taken place. We need too to be able to pin-point the underlying perspectives and ideologies beneath the changes, for they help us to understand what is behind some of our modern-day patterns of living.

Social change is brought about by a mixture of factors: technological, economic, demographic, political and social. Some change occurs directly as a result of new technology, for example, the speed of communications, or the decrease in agricultural workers. Some changes come about through demographic shifts, *e.g.* more men may remain unmarried in the 1990s because there will be fewer women than men in age groups under 30. Similarly, more medical research will focus on illnesses of old age, as the population becomes increasingly older over the next two decades.

Other changes are brought about as a bi-product of decisions made in quite different areas. The decline of the extended family in the late 50s was in many regions directly as a result of planned population shifts, of slum clearance and redevelopment. The rise in Hinduism and Islam in Britain is a bi-product of encouraging immigration from the New Commonwealth to act as a 'reserve army of labour'.

There are also changes which occur as the result of economic factors, often on a global as well as a local scale. A drop in profits may encourage a powerful multi-national firm to pull out of a specific local area and seek a higher profit margin by taking the plant to some cheaper part of the world. As well as bringing mass unemployment and depression to the town, it may have other social knock-on effects: a rise in alcoholism or gambling, or domestic violence. These are different in type, though not always different in short-term effect, from those changes which are deliberately planned and brought about through political policies, and those that are caused incidentally by them.

Finally, there are the changes which occur through a large combination of factors: women's entry to the paid labour force in such large

113

numbers since the 1950s can be seen as the combination of technological, demographic, social, economic and political contributions. A
decrease in family size due to efficient birth control, a growing flexibility
in the perception of gender rôles, a desire of women for greater
economic autonomy, the requirements for a higher family income, and
the needs of contemporary capitalism to have a casual workforce of low
wage-earners, all result in the growth of the number of women working
outside the home. What is clear, then, is that wherever we start, an
assessment of any society, and of how it arrived at a given point, is
certainly a complex task and not to be undertaken lightly.

I am going to make my own task more simple, however, and move
away from trying to offer an in-depth analysis of the ways in which we
might explain the changes that have occurred. More appropriately, in
the context of this book I want to suggest that much change has a
number of underlying perspectives or ideologies which consciously or
unconsciously direct it. The problem for most of us is that, over the
years, these perspectives become largely unchallenged, and obtain a
taken-for-granted status in our society. My aim in the rest of this
chapter is to uncover this taken-for-grantedness, and examine what
lies beneath it.

Underlying perspectives

I want to argue centrally that most of these perspectives are incompatible with a Christian framework of knowledge. Yet they are not
always perceived to be so by those in the church, and indeed can even
be brought into the church and affect the way we live, think and make
our decisions. I think that is because Christians are often trapped
within a moralist view of society, so that they frequently focus on
certain aspects – crime, divorce, drugs, abortion – without seeing them
in the wider economic, political and philosophical context in which
they derive their social meaning. We need to move away from filling
the cavities, and look at the deeper reasons for decay if we are ever to
be good dentists.

In outlining some of these underlying ideologies, I could focus on
any one of five or six. It would be tempting to go over some of the
arguments about 'scientism' – about the faith in science which has
permeated much of our culture since the nineteenth century. However, that has been done adequately elsewhere, and many of my
readers will be familiar with these arguments. Another fruitful area
would be to examine 'romanticism' – particularly the idealization of the
past, and the attempt to recreate the past as some sort of golden age.
But because of limitation of space, I have decided to focus on just four

aspects of a contemporary world-view, and to relate them to some of the factors we have identified as part of our social life today.

The collapse of collectivism and the rise of individualism. It is from the eighteenth-century Enlightenment that Western culture inherited the contest between collectivism and individualism. Both positions have their root in the humanist departure from a world-view which sees God as central, and revelation as a means to understanding both God, ourselves and the world we live in. Instead, the faith is in the fundamental trustworthiness of human rationality. Yet whether that rationality is essentially individual or collective has been the dilemma ushered in by the Enlightenment. It is a dilemma which has moved a long way beyond the Christian recognition that we need to acknowledge the importance of both communities and persons, and yet need to see neither of them as in any sense ultimate. Instead, the humanist legacy has been to vest sovereignty in either the collective, or in the autonomous individual, and for two centuries these two positions have battled for pre-eminence in the ideologies of the West.

Collectivism was dealt a massive blow by the atrocities which Hitler committed because of his faith in an Aryan collective. The alleged collectivist states of Eastern Europe, especially under Stalin, made the option very unattractive to most Western observers. Yet gentler forms of collectivism continued to persist, and tempered our British way of life in the 1950s. The creation of public amenities, nationalization, the Welfare State, the activities of trade unions, were all embodied collectivist ideals, carried out in policies designed to benefit the weaker members. The struggle was against all forms of *laissez-faire*, and against the emphasis on self-interest.

What is so interesting about this last decade is that the battle has now been decided. Individualism has won. It has long been the prevailing political philosophy in the USA, and in Britain throughout the Thatcher years, and has been heralded as the hope for the future. From this perspective the dismantling of the Berlin Wall was hailed as the most dramatic illustration of victory for the idea of the free individual, and the echo of falling stone reverberated throughout the whole of Eastern Europe.

The growing importance of individualism as a prism through which people see reality has many examples. It is widely recognized as being behind the shifts in political and economic philosophy, but there are other more mundane areas which are also revealing. I believe that we will find a deep-seated commitment to individualism behind more than the shifts in taxation and community thinking. It is there in the changing nature of trade unionism, in the movement from a commitment to the solidarity of the working classes to the question of how there will be improvement in my standard of living, my working conditions and my rights and pay. The question now is how unionism will benefit the individual, and the old collectivist mentality, associated with people like Arthur Scargill, Tony Benn, Ken Livingstone and Eric Heffer, is now dismissed as outmoded, belonging to another age.

There has been a similar change in the area of the family, both in the way it is understood, and the way many families live. Very often the prevailing concept is a now-familiar one – that there is no such thing as society, only individuals, and the collection of individuals which we call a family. But we could argue that a living-out of this spirit of individualism, more than any other factor, lies behind the increasing family break-up and divorce rate in the country. The need to be committed to oneself is stressed more than a person's commitment to a marriage or family unit. A sense of autonomy within marriage has been growing throughout the last few decades, and the notion of marriage being about mutual giving and sacrificing has been slowly ebbing away. For something to 'work' as a relationship means above all that it must work for me. The idea that marriage is the coming-together of separate individuals who must retain a large measure of their independence is the view passed on most conclusively by soap operas, and by the media in general.

What has sustained the concept of individualism so strongly is the appeal to freedom. Individual freedom, freedom of choice, of movement, of decision-making, has penetrated our culture so totally that anyone who wants to place restrictions on such freedom is regarded as a blasphemer. The freedom of women to 'do what they like with their own bodies' has become the central plank of the pro-abortion movement, and the question of what constitutes one's own body is relegated to the realms of speculation. The freedom of individuals to spend their money as they wish, to read whatever literature they wish, to see whatever videos they wish, to consume whatever goods they wish, has become deeply entrenched in our thinking by the 1990s.

One of the biggest problems with this notion of freedom is the problem underlying individualism as a whole. We are not individuals. Each of our lives touches and involves the lives of many other people. We live in families, we cluster in neighbourhoods, we teach one another, we drive on roads together, buy at the same shops, use the same drainage and sewage systems, breathe the same atmosphere, drink the same water, suffer the same pollution, die of the same diseases. We are part of a common economic, environmental, political nexus, and the needs of the whole community impinge on each one of us. So what I regard as my freedom might well prove to be another's enslavement. In practice, a full-blown individualism ensures that strong individuals are the ones who flourish and enjoy their freedom, while weak individuals have increasingly fewer freedoms to appreciate.

Individualism then is fundamentally incompatible with a Christian world-view. For our understanding of human personhood is not that of the autonomous individual with inalienable rights to protect. It is rather that we are all creatures of a loving God, and as people we have responsibility for one another: just as we are stewards of the earth, we are also guardians of our fellow humans. Similarly, the notion of individualism flies against Christian norms of justice. My freedom does not exist in isolation from the needs of others; it is always to be tempered by, and understood, in that context. I cannot therefore exploit my own freedom and assert individual rights by trampling on another's weakness. The Old Testament principles of neighbourliness as well as usury are full of such cautions. Ultimately, then, individualism denies the meaning of who we are. It undermines the principles of right relationships and care for our neighbours which should be upheld above all else in a just society. In Christian terms, individualism is a contemporary idol which demands worship, but offers no salvation.

Economism. Lesslie Newbigin, amongst many others, has pointed to another legacy from the Enlightenment: the domination of religion and morality by economics. In that period, what came to be understood as satisfactory explanation changed in reference from some common sense of the ultimate and divine to a satisfaction with the partial and mechanistic. Concepts like stewardship are essentially Christian, in that they contain a sense of accountability to the creator, but the concept of 'rational economic man', which lies at the heart of modern economic life, depends on a fundamental autonomy in decision-making, with no sense of accountability whatsoever.

Today a large part of our social existence is dominated by the economic. One of the most destructive aspects of this is the reductionism it implies – when fundamentally non-economic categories are seen as uneconomic. Until very recently this was true of the environment, which was treated as a free resource. It did not have an economic price tag, and nothing else mattered. The fact that there were aesthetic, moral, social, cultural, ecological and religious reasons for respecting the environment was irrelevant.

Schumacher states this point passionately when he writes:

> In the current vocabulary of condemnation there are few words as final and conclusive as 'uneconomic'. If an activity has been branded as uneconomic, its right to existence is not merely

questioned but energetically denied. ... Call a thing immoral or ugly, soul-destroying or a degradation of man, a peril to the peace of the world or to the well-being of future generations; as long as you have not shown it to be 'uneconomic' you have not really questioned its right to exist, grow, and prosper.[1]

It is easy to see from our outline what implications this has had. We could look at contemporary thinking about the Welfare State. As well as its being anti-individualist, it is also 'uneconomic' and therefore must be dismembered. But it was never proposed for economic reasons. Its *raison d'être* is social, and humanitarian. It was developed by people who upheld a high view of personhood as rooted in the divine image and not as rational, autonomous, economic man.

No institution has been unaffected by this economism. All aspects of life have come under our scrutiny. It is 'uneconomic' to have more than 2.1 children, it is 'uneconomic' not to have two working parents, it is 'uneconomic' to allow universities and schools to educate their students along lines suggested by educators, it is 'uneconomic' to fund research that does not result in some sort of spin-off. It is 'uneconomic' to ensure that mental patients are fully resourced, 'uneconomic' to provide pensioners with adequate winter heating, 'uneconomic' to keep open hospital wards, 'uneconomic' to allow free access to museums and art galleries, 'uneconomic' to ensure historical treasures stay within the country, 'uneconomic' to employ active pensioners, 'uneconomic' to visit distant relatives, 'uneconomic' to maintain the care of churches and cathedrals. The quality of life, the meaning of community, the heritage of history, family life, education and medical care all shrink before the demand to be economic.

We could illustrate this graphically by referring to pornography. It is one of the biggest areas of growth in consumption over the last two decades so that the pornographic industry is now very big business. In a very real sense sexuality, intimacy and deep meaningful relationships have become economically exploited and economically defined. Individualism also comes in here of course, because pornography is the ultimate in individualist sexuality. It is also 'safe': no physical diseases can be caught, and no real relationships can get in the way of autonomous freedom. Sex is now a commodity which can be bought and sold on the market, with large revenues, and soft porn (much of which contains advertising for the much more destructive hard porn) is available in almost every newsagent's shop in the country. The difficulty of enforcing any ban on pornography, or restrictions on outlets, indicates the extent to which the threat to profits can prove very powerful. To run down such a lucrative trade would surely be uneconomic. Yet the underlying damage it does to actual relationships has yet to be told. The effects of being constantly faced with degrading and dehumanizing images of women, of being placed in a 'master-slave relationship' with some of the images offered makes deep inroads into the male psyche. It is not surprising that many men find that they cannot make deep, intimate relationships with women after a long-term addiction to porn, and that for many counsellors it can take years of therapy to undo some of the damage. For women too, their person-hood, their humanness, has been violated in the name of economism, and they have been reduced to something far less than the value with which God has created them.

In this and in many other examples the poverty of economism is very evident. Economic values have overridden all others, and the concept of 'autonomous economic man' has replaced the Christian idea of living responsibly as members of the kingdom of God. For God has given us a rich creation where things are meaningful for so many reasons. We are surrounded by realities which have no price tag, which are simply non-economic, not uneconomic, because God has not made them for economic reasons. In fact this incorporates the most funda-mental aspects of life. The givenness of love, friendship, worship, sunsets, musical sounds, the gentleness of a baby's face, all of these are part of the fullness of God's creation, and cannot be simply reduced to an economic dimension of it. In fact we live in a value-soaked universe, where norms of beauty, and truthful relationship and communal responsibility, go alongside our careful stewardship of the earth's resources. But to reduce all this to the one word 'uneconomic' is to spit in God's face and to erect mammon in God's place.

Relativism. In one sense, of course, relativism is unproblematic. It is simply an acknowledgment that we live in a dynamic, changing world; history and culture provide the backcloth against which we can more fully understand our own time and society. It can mean too that we must learn to be tolerant in the light of views other than our own, and that we must always be humble seekers after God, rather than those who believe that their own credal articulation exhausts and enshrines the whole of truth.

Yet contemporary relativism means more than this, because the concept of the autonomous individual also lies at the heart of this perspective. My autonomy extends to having permission to construct my own framework of meaning, and my own system of values. For there can be no truth outside myself. Where else would its origin be? Nor is there any coherent meaning which is external to my own perception of reality. Meaning can only be that which I impose upon a situation. Fundamentally, a relativist assumption says there is no truth. There are pragmatic ways of operating, values which derive from our autonomy, but no truth. At the very best, there are only well-meaning opinions.

It is important to see what a new departure this is from the Enlightenment heritage. There is no longer the tenacious faith, for example in the objectivity of science. For science has its own paradigms, its own meaning frameworks. The rising influence of the social sciences has reversed the former dependence of sociology and psychology on the 'objective methods' of physics and chemistry, so that the relativism of the social sciences has begun to affect other areas. The movement is a powerful one in the theory of ideas, and it also has many implications which extend beyond academic analysis into everyday life.

Within this framework there is blasphemy, of course – the blasphemy of dogmatism. Just as one of the most condemnatory words in contemporary culture is 'uneconomic', another is 'intolerant'. And intolerance is redefined not as being unable to see another's point of view, but believing fervently in something which you maintain is truth. What is interesting is that intolerance and relativism live side by side. Overhearing conversations in relaxed social gatherings, or listening to letters written to the media, it is never long before some very strongly held view is stated vehemently, and from the position of unassailable rightness. The very juxtaposition of such contradictory opinions, all vehemently held and expressed, reinforces the argument for relativism in the minds of those for whom there is no truth, only opinions.

There are considerable implications of this position in a multi-faith culture. Just as many different opinions reinforce the view that there can be no ultimately true position, so relativism assumes that many faiths reinforce the idea that there can be no true faith. Religious faith is a product of certain social, historical and economic factors, coupled with a non-acceptance of a modern scientific mind-set. Interestingly, it has been the Islamic faith which has contested this most strongly in the last decade. There is one true faith, they argue – Islam. The insistence on defining everything from a Muslim perspective has winded our British pragmatic relativism. The call for state-aided Muslim schools and Muslim blasphemy laws has taken us by surprise, for many Britons no longer possess the categories for understanding such certainty.

For the Christian, therefore, the problem becomes confounded. We have both to reckon with the relativism of the culture, and also the increasing non-relativism of those religious groups which have made their home here, and which are growing in membership and strength. We have therefore to maintain firmly our own commitment to Christ as the only Way, Truth and Life, but to do so in a way which is compatible with respecting and acknowledging those whose religious commitment is different. It means too that we need to be more urgent in our evangelism, and in the way we approach the task of proclaiming the gospel of truth in a relativist society. Yet there is more to work with than we might realize. For although relativism might be one of the most powerful of our contemporary idols many people do not (and indeed cannot) live fully within a relativist framework. Many live as though life does have some meaning other than that constructed by themselves, as though there are externally valid norms of justice and fairness, and as though love does exist and is to be sought after. Many people too spend their lives searching for deeper levels of significance which can both exist in their experience, and also be seen as somehow there in the nature of reality itself. In fact, this searching after God is still a feature of our society in the 1990s. As Christians this should not surprise us, because we are the creation of this God. The search is to do with the very root of our humanness.

Search for meaning. A deep search for meaning is therefore part of our contemporary British culture, just as in other forms it has been part of all secularized culture. The idols of our time have cut us off from the roots of our personhood, and given us false directions in which to travel. The searches which we witness today give more weight than ever to the suggestion that we are moving not only into a post-Enlightenment, but also into a post-secular, culture. I have already mentioned the growing interest in other faiths, in new cults and sects, and the steady revival of old forms of astrology and the occult. Equally significant is the dramatic take-off of New Age thinking, which draws on strange forms of medieval occultism as well as on earth, sun and moon worship, and other forms of primitive paganism. Shops selling New Age music, curios and symbols have begun to proliferate, especially in the West Country where some devotees have claimed that pagan forms of worship have their natural root. Some have seen a link with Eastern pantheism, but the movement is wider than that, incorporating a religious eclecticism which experiments with any and all forms of religious expression. Yet whilst it might be seen as a challenge to the scientism, economism and individualism of the age, it goes in a direction which is equally idolatrous, and in many ways more blatantly so.

The rise of New Age thinking has brought great alarm to many Christians. Yet in many ways it is nothing other than the contemporary mind searching after a deeper meaning and reality. It is another of the age-old attempts to find a focus of worship. If the Christian gospel is true, then what it says fundamentally about human personhood is that we are made for God, and that our hearts will be restless until they find their rest in that same God. This is one of the most contemporary, as well as one of the most ancient, expressions of restless hearts.

Conclusion

If my analysis of contemporary secularism is valid, then it would surely follow that the way we have tried to combat it has often been misdirected. We have so often missed the underlying world-view and have focused upon certain symptoms which we have challenged and not been heeded. The task is much bigger than that. In fact it is a mammoth one, both in terms of the way in which we present the gospel to our culture, and in the way we live our own lives as Christians within our churches, families and communities. Too often we have failed to understand the nature of 'idolatry', and have taken many of these aspects of our contemporary culture into our own thinking, living and worship. Very often the church itself has been absorbed within a framework of individualism, and economism, and narrowed its challenge to one about morals and 'declining standards'. The task before the church in the 1990s, I believe, is a fuller and more demanding one. It is to recover a Christian view of personhood, and follow through its implications in all areas of life. This might involve working out methods of evangelism which recognize the world-view and patterns of thinking which exist amongst those to whom we bring the gospel. It might mean developing a new apologetic. It might mean committing ourselves to Christian education programmes which begin at a deeper level of analysis than that which we have come to take for granted. It might even mean developing a social programme based on a biblical understanding of the meaning of community and koinonia.

By now you may be feeling that the task is overwhelming. On the other hand, the gospel is a radical one, and calls for a radical response. If we cannot give it a whole-hearted response, preferring to stay within the world-view of economism, individualism, scientism and relativism, then we cannot blame our contemporary culture when it rejects what little of the gospel we offer them. Yet on the other hand, we have the biblical assurance that the onus for success is not ours alone. Fundamentally, we are reaching out to people in their created humanness, and to be human means to be made in the image and likeness of God. So even in the midst of deep secularism people can and do respond, because they can recognize something of the very nature of reality in the gospel. They know something of who they are, and what that means for the rest of life, and can respond to truth, even when caught up in idolatry. The Holy Spirit is the one who speaks the truth, and who will ultimately bring the will of God to fruition. This indeed puts our work into clearer perspective. For what is required of us is much more limited: not success, but faithfulness.

The 'new science'
and the gospel

Ernest C. Lucas

Recently Lesslie Newbigin, an elder statesman amongst missiologists, has been pressing the need for a 'missionary encounter' with Western culture. Christians, he says, have given a good deal of thought about how best to present the gospel in non-Western cultures, but have failed to do the same with respect to modern Western culture. When faced with the question 'What would be involved in a genuinely missionary encounter between the gospel and our post-Enlightenment culture?', he begins by saying that there needs to be an 'encounter at the intellectual level with what forms the heart of our culture – modern science'.[1]

For some evangelicals the intellectual interface between science and the gospel is still the nineteenth-century issues of uniformitarian geology and Darwinism. However, many non-Christians have lost interest in these issues and are caught up with new, exciting ideas arising out of what is called the 'new science'. Some claim that these ideas challenge the accepted world-view of Western culture, with its

Judaeo-Christian base, and point towards Eastern religions. In this way the 'new science' is one of the factors feeding the rise of New Age thinking. It would be wise, in terms of a strategy for a missionary encounter with Western culture, for evangelicals to stop what has become largely schismatic in-fighting over nineteenth-century issues to address the late-twentieth-century issues. If we do not, the battle for the gospel in our culture could be lost by default.

What is the 'new science'? I shall take my agenda from two books: *God and the New Physics*[2] and *God and the New Biology*.[3] However, one item needs to be added because it has come to prominence since these books were written – chaos theory.[4] In a brief survey, I will highlight the ideas or concepts which some claim arise from, or are supported by, the 'new science' and are supposedly more in tune with Eastern religions than with Christianity. I can do no more than outline how they arise out of science. Those who find the science baffling can skip these brief explanations. What will influence the general public is the ideas and concepts said to be derived from the science and the simple *claim* that they have scientific backing. I hope that those who do have the appropriate scientific expertise will make the time and effort to critique this claim in detail, something which I cannot do here. Also, I do not have the space, nor the philosophical and theological expertise, to provide a detailed Christian response to these claims. What I hope to do is to bring the agenda to the attention of evangelicals, most of whom seem unaware of it, and to suggest some possible approaches which might prove fruitful for a biblical response.

The new physics

By the late nineteenth century, classical physics, that based on the foundations laid by Galileo Galilei and Isaac Newton, seemed to provide an almost totally satisfactory account of the material world. In 1900, the great physicist Lord Kelvin[5] said that there were only two 'clouds' on the horizon of physics – how to explain the radiation of heat and light by a 'black body' (the perfect type of radiator) and the Michelson-Morley experiment to measure the speed of light. These two 'clouds' soon burst and blew apart the edifice of classical physics. Out of them came, respectively, quantum theory and the theory of relativity, which form the heart of the 'new physics'. I will summarize the more important challenges which, some claim, the new physics raises for Christian thinking.

The theory of relativity

The Michelson-Morley experiment failed to find any difference in the apparent speed of light, whether it was measured in the direction of the Earth's motion or perpendicular to it. The oddity of this can be appreciated if you think of two cars approaching a crossroads. If they are travelling head-on, each at 30 miles per hour, to the driver of one car the other will appear to be travelling towards him or her at 60 miles per hour. If, however, as that driver crosses the junction at 30 miles per hour, the other car is approaching along the road to his or her right at the same speed, its apparent speed of approach will be 30 miles per hour. This is what classical physics predicted. Light did not meet these expectations.

Albert Einstein's answer to the problem was to propose that the speed of light is a constant which has the same value no matter from what 'frame of reference' it is measured. He also proposed the principle that nothing can travel faster than light. These principles lead to some surprising predictions concerning bodies travelling close to the speed of light,[6] for example: their mass should increase, time will slow down for them; they will become foreshortened in the direction of travel. Since in everyday life we do not travel at anything more than a minute fraction of the speed of light we are unaware of these phenomena. However, they have been proved true for sub-atomic particles moving at close to the speed of light.

Interesting as these predictions are, more important from our point of view are two other consequences of the theory. The first is the well-known equation:

$$e = mc^2$$

where e stands for 'energy', m for 'mass' and c for the speed of light. This states that matter and energy are equivalent and inter-convertible. It provided the key to unlock nuclear power.

The second consequence is the unification of space and time. According to the theory of relativity, time can no longer be regarded as an independent entity separate from the three spatial dimensions of length, depth and height. Instead, we must think in terms of unified, four-dimensional, space-time. This puts a new slant on an old debate. Classical physicists debated whether or not there was such a thing as absolute space – a 'structure' existing separately from the material 'contents' of the universe. The debate now continues about space-time. There are two main positions. *Substantivalists* believe that space-time does exist separately from the material objects which 'fill' it. *Relationalists* deny this and argue that space-time is simply a way of talking about the relationship between material objects. Moreover, some argue, the time sequence of events has no objective significance since, as we have seen, the rate at which time passes differs for bodies travelling at different velocities. This, they say, leads to a view of ultimate reality as a timeless, inter-related unity, which is the view of it held by some Eastern religions.

Quantum theory

Max Planck solved the black body radiation problem. He proposed that energy cannot be emitted or absorbed by a radiator in amounts of any quantity whatever, but only in 'packets' or 'quanta' of fixed amount. The amount depends on the frequency of the radiation carrying the energy and is expressed by the equation:

$$e = h\nu$$

in which ν stands for 'frequency' and h is an unchanging fundamental constant called 'Planck's constant'.

The idea that energy is 'quantized' has as strange and far-reaching consequences as the simple propositions behind relativity theory. One of the most famous is Werner Heisenberg's Uncertainty Principle. Heisenberg showed that quantization puts limits on how accurately we can measure certain things. Suppose that we want to determine both the position (x) and the momentum (p = mass × velocity) of a material particle. Heisenberg showed that the uncertainty in the position (Δx) is related to the uncertainty in the momentum (Δp) by the equation:

$$\Delta x \times \Delta p \geq h/2\pi$$

This means that the more precisely we know the position of the particle (the smaller Δx is) the greater our uncertainty about its momentum (the larger Δp becomes). Because of the size of Planck's constant (h) this problem only becomes noticeable at the small distances and masses that physicists meet at the atomic level. The best that they can do at this level is talk in terms of the probability that a particle is at position 'x', or has a momentum 'p'.

What is the cause of this uncertainty? Einstein and Planck believed that it is a result of our ignorance, that there are underlying factors as yet unknown to us which would remove our uncertainty, if we knew them. Heinsenberg believed that it is the result of a fundamental randomness inherent in the nature of reality. Einstein recognized the possible theological implications of this when he rejected Heisenberg's view, insisting that God 'does not play dice'. If Heinsenberg is right, what *does* the inherent randomness imply concerning the nature of

God the creator (is he capricious?) and his sovereignty over the creation (does the Uncertainty Principle limit his knowledge?)?

By the end of the nineteenth century, light had come to be thought of as a wave of energy. This seemed the best way to explain its properties. However, in 1905 Einstein showed that the recently discovered 'photoelectric effect' could only be explained if light was regarded as a stream of energetic massless particles ('photons') whose energy is quantized according to Planck's equation. But this particle picture of light cannot explain other phenomena (such as diffraction) which are explained by the wave picture of light! To add to this puzzle, it was found that electrons, which were initially regarded as particles with a definite mass, sometimes behaved as if they were waves of energy with a wavelength (λ) related to their momentum (p) by the formula:

$$\lambda = h/p$$

On this basis Erwin Schrödinger developed a form of quantum theory called 'wave mechanics' which treats all sub-atomic phenomena in terms of the mathematics of waves.

The odd behaviour of light and electrons led physicists to accept the Principle of Complementarity. This is the recognition that some phenomena can be understood adequately only in terms of mutually exclusive but complementary pictures. Because they are mutually exclusive, both pictures cannot be applied at one and the same time. What determines whether an electron behaves like a wave or a particle? One answer is that the experimental set-up we use to observe the electron determines this. In other words, *how* we look at it determines *what* we see. A similar question can be asked about the position of an electron, given that quantum theory tells us that we can only predict its position in terms of probability. If there are finite probabilities of it being at positions x_1, x_2, . . ., what determines the fact that we actually see it at position x_1? Again, some suggest that the very act of observing it 'fixes' it at that position. It is argued from this that since it is humans who decide what to observe and how to observe it, human consciousness plays a part in determining the way the world is. Some see in this a possible solution to the problem of free will and determinism; others see it as evidence of the inter-connectedness of all things, and in particular of the worlds of consciousness and matter.

One way of resolving the wave-particle duality mathematically is a form of quantum theory called 'quantum field theory'. This treats 'particles' not as entities in themselves, but as the result of interactions between energy fields. Energy fields, like waves, spread out in space. Where two fields meet, they interact in a way that may have either wave-like or particle-like characteristics. According to this approach ultimate reality is a set of interacting energy fields.

The final aspect of quantum theory with which we shall deal (and we are leaving out several which have some claim on our interest) is the Bell effect, named after one of the physicists who has studied it. Sometimes a sub-atomic event produces a pair of particles which fly off in different directions. Quantum theory predicts that, from then on, the characteristics of these two particles will be linked, however far apart they go. For example, sub-atomic particles have a characteristic called 'spin'. If, when the two particles are produced, one of them has a spin of 1 and the other has a spin of -1, throughout their lifetime their combined spin will always be zero. Now it is possible to change the spin of a particle. If the spin of one of the pair is changed from 1 to -1, quantum theory predicts that the spin of the other will instantaneously change from -1 to 1, even if it is millions of miles away. This is inexplicable by the normal law of causality. According to this, for one event to cause another, information must travel between them. But the theory of relativity says that this cannot happen faster than the speed of light (information has to be carried by something – a light beam, an electric current, *etc.*). So how is the Bell effect produced? No-one knows, but experiment suggests that it is a reality. Here, some argue, is the ultimate evidence of the oneness of all things. What happens to a particle in one part of the universe effects a particle in another, far-distant part without any physical cause-and-effect link.

Gary Zukav[7] sums up the conclusions of some physicists regarding quantum theory: 'The study of complementarity, the uncertainty principle, quantum field theory . . . produces insights into the nature of reality very similar to those produced by the study of eastern philosophies.'

Cosmology

At present the generally accepted scientific view of the origin of the universe is the 'Big Bang' theory. According to this, our universe began with an enormous explosion of energy about 15,000 million years ago. There is good observational evidence to support this theory.

Inevitably scientists ask. What caused the Big Bang? Until recently they had to admit that science could give no answer. However, some now claim that quantum theory can provide the answer – the universe is the chance product of a quantum vacuum. It arose spontaneously out of nothing! This last statement is rather misleading. A quantum vacuum is not 'nothing' in the commonly accepted sense. It is seething with activity, full of random comings-to-be and fadings-away. This is because the Uncertainty Principle will not allow us to say of a particular point in the vacuum at a particular moment that there is absolutely nothing there. *On average* there is nothing there, but there is always a finite possibility that something will come into existence there for a brief moment and then fade away.

The 'inflation' theory of the origin of the universe argues that a 'bubble' of space-time might have come into being in a quantum vacuum and then suddenly expanded to cosmic proportions. This theory is very speculative and has a number of unsolved problems associated with it. However, on the basis of it, some claim that there is no need for a creator God. At best he is redundant, worked out of a job by quantum physics.[8]

The new biology

Molecular biology

Molecular biology began in the late 1940s as a result of applying physics and chemistry to the study of the living cell. Its first great success, signalled in 1953 by the determination of the three-dimensional chemical structure of DNA, was the elucidation of the molecular basis of genetics and the unravelling of the genetic code. Since DNA governs the development and behaviour of the living cell, this success led some to the conclusion that living organisms are 'nothing but' collections of interacting atoms and molecules.

This view is an example of philosophical *reductionism*. It claims that humans are to be understood by reducing them to their component parts, living cells. These in turn are to be understood by reducing them to their component parts, atoms and molecules. This shows that humans are only physico-chemical machines.

Nowhere in this process of reduction has there been discovered any hint of a 'soul' or 'spirit'. Molecular biology seems to leave no room for talk of humans as 'made in the image of God' and having an 'eternal soul' which needs to be 'saved'.

Biological evolution

When Darwin published *On the Origin of Species* in 1859, he was not able to propose a convincing theory of the hereditary mechanism behind the rise of new species. In particular he could not explain how there could be both constancy and variation in inherited characteristics and why, when a new characteristic appeared, it should not disappear over a few generations due to 'dilution'.

The situation was changed by the rediscovery in 1900 of Mendel's work on genetics (originally published in 1866) and the growing understanding of the subject which this stimulated. This, coupled with other developments in biology, especially in the understanding of the living cell, led to the 'new synthesis' or 'neo-Darwinism' in the 1930s and 1940s. This is the basis of modern evolutionary theory. However, there is still debate over the mechanism of evolutionary change. Those who claim that this debate indicates a rejection of evolution by biologists are mistaken. What is being questioned is not *whether* evolution took place but *how* it works. It would not be surprising if eventually an acceptable theory is produced which combines some of the ideas currently under debate.

One concept plays an important part in all these ideas – 'randomness' or 'chance'. It is well-established that genes (the units of hereditary material) undergo random changes, called 'mutations'. Also, in sexual reproduction, the egg that will grow into an offspring receives the genes for particular characteristics from its parents in a random way. The importance of chance in modern evolutionary theory is indicated by the following well-known quote from Jacques Monod, a Nobel laureate in molecular biology:

> Chance alone is at the source of every innovation, of all creation in the biosphere. Pure chance, absolutely free but blind, is at the root of the stupendous edifice of evolution.[9]

Monod goes on to claim that this proves that there is no purposeful creator behind the existence of living beings.

Chemical evolution

As the physico-chemical basis of life became better understood, chemists and biologists began to theorize about how life might have arisen on the Earth by natural processes involving the random combination of suitable chemicals (note again the importance of this concept of randomness). They have had some, very limited, success in producing important biological molecules in laboratory simulations of the conditions which they conjecture (perhaps wrongly) existed on the early Earth.

It is sometimes objected that the idea of chemical evolution violates the Second Law of Thermodynamics. Put briefly, this Law states that, in a closed system close to equilibrium, all spontaneous processes result in an increase of disorder in the system. What chemical evolution proposes is spontaneous processes which result in an increase in

131

order – the production of complex molecules which order themselves into a living cell.

This objection ignores the limitations of the Second Law. Firstly, the Earth is not a closed system. It constantly receives energy from the Sun in the form of heat, light and other radiation. This alone, under certain circumstances, allows spontaneous processes leading to an increase in order to occur. Secondly, the last twenty years has seen the development of a new area of science, non-equilibrium thermodynamics. This has shown that if energy is fed into a system which is far from equilibrium, the result can be the production of order out of chaos.[10] This results from what are called 'dissipative processes'. Here, claim some, is the ultimate answer to the origin of life:

> In the modern world view dissipation has taken over one of the functions formerly performed by God: it makes matter transcend the clod-like nature it would manifest at equilibrium, and behave instead in dramatic and unforeseen ways, molding itself for example into thunderstorms, people and umbrellas.[11]

Ecology

Belief in the rise of new species by natural selection is one of the factors which led to the development of ecology as a distinct scientific discipline. Instead of studying isolated individual creatures or species, it studies how creatures interact with one another and with their environment.

Ecology has led to a stress on the oneness of nature, which parallels what we have seen arising out of quantum physics. Perhaps the best-known expression of this is James Lovelock's concept of 'Gaia'.[12] Gaia is the planet Earth seen as a 'holistic' self-regulating system, in which the activities of the living beings cannot be untangled from one another, or from the complex processes of geology, climatology and atmospheric physics. Whatever Lovelock intended, some have made this the basis for a religious, pantheistic world-view.

Chaos

The scientific meaning of 'chaos' can be illustrated by the simple equation:

$$x_{n+1} = ax_n (1 - x_n)$$

This equation is used to 'model' the behaviour of animal populations.

When this is so, 'x' is a measure of the population size, measured on a scale such that x varies from 0 to 1, and 'a' is a measure of reproductive effectiveness or fertility. The equation represents a 'feed-back' system. As the population grows (x increases) so do the restraints on the population ((1 − x), representing, for example, food resources, decreases and counter-balances x).

Anyone with a programmable calculator or a small computer can investigate the properties of this equation by putting in initial values of a and x_0, calculating the value of x, and repeating the cycle several times. The following table gives a sample set of results for $x_0 = 0.6$ and varying values of a:

a = 2.7	a = 3.1	a = 3.5	a = 4
0.648	0.744	0.840	0.960
0.616	0.590	0.470	0.154
0.639	0.750	0.872	0.520
0.623	0.582	0.391	0.998
0.634	0.754	0.833	0.00641
0.626	0.575	0.486	0.0255
0.632	0.758	0.874	0.0993
0.628	0.569	0.385	0.358
0.631	0.760	0.828	0.919
0.629	0.565	0.498	0.298
0.630	0.762	0.875	0.836
0.629	0.562	0.383	0.547
0.630	0.763	0.827	0.991
0.629	0.561	0.501	3.514
0.630	0.764	0.875	0.136
0.630	0.560	0.383	0.469
0.630	0.764	0.827	0.996
0.630	0.559	0.501	0.0154
0.630	0.764	0.875	0.608
0.630	0.559	0.383	0.228

When a < 3, x soon settles down to a single fixed value, having oscillated around it for a few cycles. When 3 < a < 3.45, x soon settles down to oscillating between two fixed values. When 3.45 < a < 3.6, x soon settles down to oscillating between four fixed values. When a > 4, the value of x varies all over the place and never settles down. This is what is meant by 'chaotic' behaviour.

Three points are worth noting about chaotic systems. First, they are not chaotic in the popular sense of behaving in a way that has no explanation. Their behaviour is fully determined by a mathematical 'law'. Secondly, in practice that 'law' could never be deduced by observation of the system. A scientist who obtained a set of observed results such as that in the right-hand column of the table above could not tell whether they represented a chaotic system or a truly random one. Even if that scientist had reason to believe that it was a chaotic system, it would not be possible to work back from the figures to the underlying equation. Thirdly, as anyone with a calculator or computer can check, a very small change in either a or x_0 produces a major change in the sequence of numbers produced after the first few cycles of calculation. This means that in practice anyone who sets up a chaotic system cannot predict its behaviour beyond the immediate future, because any minute error in setting up the initial conditions soon produces major departures from the predicted course. In other words, chaos introduces an element of practical unpredictability into the world of ordinary experience similar to that which quantum theory introduces into the world of atomic phenomena.

What are the theological implications of chaos? This question is only just beginning to be debated. We will look at a few provisional reflections later.

Some preliminary responses

In this final part of the essay, I cannot do more than outline some preliminary responses to the issues raised above.

God and nature

The challenge of the 'old' science was its mechanistic determinism. For many it seemed to shut God out of nature. The problem was compounded by a strategy adopted by many Christian apologists, the so-called 'God of the gaps' approach. This invoked God to explain what the scientists could not, and it used this appeal to God's action as evidence of his existence. The trouble was that the mechanistic explanations of science advanced to fill the gaps and God seemed to become increasingly unnecessary. It is against this background that the claims that quantum theory can explain the 'Big Bang', and that non-equilibrium thermodynamics explain the origin of life on Earth, seem to make God redundant, and more probably non-existent.

Both the Christian apologists and their opponents have committed a theological error. The God of the Bible is not only the creator who brought the universe into being out of nothing (Heb. 11:3), but also the sustainer who is constantly keeping it in being (Col. 1:17; Heb. 1:3). Because of this, when Christian theologians have spoken of God as the 'first cause' they have not meant this in a temporal sense – that he was the first in a chain of causes, *e.g.* 'setting off' the 'Big Bang'. They have meant that he is the cause of all existence. Everything that comes into being, and everything that continues in being, does so because he wills it.

God's existence is not evidenced by gaps in the workings of the universe. Arguably there should be no such gaps if he is a competent creator. It is evidenced by the very existence of the universe. This is not a conclusive argument. The unbeliever is always free to insist that the universe just *is* and needs no explanation. However, the Christian is also free to insist that the existence of quantum laws is so incredible that belief in a God who created and sustains these laws and the universe is quite reasonable. These laws allow for the existence of a quantum vacuum out of which a cosmos, which produces rational beings who understand these quantum laws, can be born.

The same kind of considerations apply to non-equilibrium thermodynamics and dissipative processes with regard to the origin of life. When faced with the theory of evolution Archbishop Frederick Temple is supposed to have said, 'We used to believe in a God who made things. Now we must believe in a God who made things make themselves.' Which kind of God is more awe-inspiring? Would we marvel more at the ingenuity of an inventor who made a robot, or the ingenuity of one who made a robot which could design and make other, novel, robots?

For those who take the biblical concept of God seriously, the laws of nature are not an autonomous system. They proceed from the mind of God and are kept in being by him. They can be seen as his 'normal' activity in the realm of nature. Their regularity does not shut him out of that realm, but is an expression of what the Bible calls his 'faithfulness'. God is free to act differently when to do so is in accord with his purposes, which are wider than simply maintaining the natural laws. This, however, leads to the subject of miracles, which we will not discuss here.

Failure to recognize the laws of nature as God at work limits his providential activity to either the realm of history (where he works by influencing people's hearts and minds) or to miracles in the realm of nature. The Bible does not restrict it in this way. The sun and the rain, the cycle of the seasons, the natural provision of food for the wild animals and birds, are all part of his providence.

Evangelical apologists seem to have been slower than others to recognize the unbiblical nature of the 'God of the gaps' argument and to reject it. I think this is because we have tended to emphasize the transcendence of God over his creation and to neglect the balancing biblical teaching about his immanence within it. This may have been due to a fear of pantheistic ideas creeping back into Christian theology. However we must not let that fear, perhaps in the form of a reaction to modern 'process theology', cause us to neglect an aspect of biblical teaching. Rather, we must find ways of expressing it which avoid the taint of pantheism.

God and chance

If, as the Bible claims (Ps. 19:1; Rom. 1:19–20), the universe reflects something of God's nature, what are we to make of the importance of random processes within it? The problem is twofold. First there is the claim that because random processes may have given rise to the cosmos and played a key rôle in the rise of life on Earth, there is no place for a purposive creator. Secondly, there is the question whether a universe full of random processes is compatible with the nature of God as revealed in the Bible.

The debate about God and chance is clouded by confused thinking. This has been exposed very well by Donald MacKay.[13] The confusion arises largely because of a difference between the popular use of the words 'chance' and 'random' (which includes the idea of lack of purpose) and the scientific use. Even scientists confuse the two uses! In science a 'chance' or 'random' event is one that has no *known* cause and is therefore *unpredictable*. It is a reference to our ignorance. To say more than that about it is to go beyond science proper into metaphysics. Given this meaning of chance, it is a logical blunder to speak of it (as Monod does in the quote given earlier) as a *cause* of anything. MacKay is right to call such a use of it mythological, making 'chance' into a 'god'. When scientists attribute an event to 'chance' they are saying that its cause is unknown to them, nothing more.

The absence of a known cause does not mean that there is no cause. To say that something is unpredictable by us is not to say that it is absolutely unpredictable. There is one (minority) interpretation of quantum theory which assumes that behind the quantum events there is a 'hidden variable' which, if known to us, would enable us to predict them. Chaotic processes are predictable in principle (they can be expressed in mathematical relationships), the problem they pose is a practical one of setting accurate boundary conditions.

I see no problem in believing that God is the 'cause' of random quantum events in the sense that he created and sustains the quantum laws. Moreover, what seem random events to us because of our limited knowledge may be quite purposive from his point of view. For the same reason chaotic processes need present no mysteries to an omniscient and omnipotent God.

But would the faithful, loving God of the Bible have any place for such random events in his creation? There are reasons for answering 'Yes', because random events can have a positive value. Consider some of the uses we make of them.

1. To ensure fairness, *e.g.* the toss of a coin in some sporting contexts.
2. To create interest. My young son is more interested in playing me at snakes and ladders (where the chance of winning depends on the fall of the dice) than at chess (where my experience and skill are greater than his).
3. To aid skill development by presenting new, unpredictable challenges.
4. Random search processes have proved to be an efficient way of exploring the potential of situations. This is used, for example, in computerized design processes.
5. To provide in-built resilience. Random mutations can be seen as a way in which God has made plants and animals resilient in the face of changes in their environment.

Here, I suggest, there is a credible basis for including random events within the providence of God.[14]

I think that a much more debatable suggestion is that the unpredictability of quantum events and chaotic processes makes them the possible locus of God's interaction with his creation in a way that preserves our freedom.[15] I am not sure that an omnipotent, omniscient God needs such a 'smoke-screen'. He could work in a hidden way just as well in a physically deterministic sequence of events of which he was the author.

Reductionism and human dignity

The natural sciences are reductionistic in *methodology*. Complex systems are studied by taking them apart and seeking to understand the bits and pieces and how they fit together. This methodology has proved very successful. This is why there is a great temptation to assume that the reductionist explanation of something is the *only* one. This, however, is not a 'scientific' deduction, but an assumption, an act of faith. There are grounds for believing that it is misguided.

The fact is that there are many scientific theories and concepts which are essential for understanding systems at a particular level, but which have no place at the lower level that results when the system is taken apart, and which cannot be explained by the theories that apply at the lower level. The genetic code is essential for understanding the working of a living cell, but it cannot be reduced to, or deduced from, the chemistry and physics of the nucleic acids which make up the DNA which carries the code. Numerous examples like this lead many scientists to argue that as systems increase in complexity, truly novel phenomena appear which cannot be explained in a reductionist way.[16] The whole *is* more than the sum of its parts.

In any case one must ask the question, Why should we assume the simplest level, in terms of physico-chemical organization, to be the most fundamental level of reality on the basis of which the other levels must be understood? Why should we not take consciousness as the most fundamental level? The answer may seem obvious – because conscious beings evolved (by chance!) out of the simple bits and pieces. But that assumes what is not proven – that there was no conscious being (God) overseeing the evolutionary process.

Christians cannot accept a reductionist view of human beings. We believe that the human person cannot be explained simply in terms of the physics and chemistry of matter. There is a human spirit, made in the image of its creator, which though expressed through the material body is not to be simply identified with it. The 'spirit' is not to be thought of as another 'bit' which could be discovered along with the other bits by a reductionist methodology. It is more like the meaning of this paragraph. The meaning is not to be identified with the letters which carry it. No amount of study of the individual letters, or even words, in isolation will reveal the existence of the meaning. It can be found only when the paragraph is taken as a whole. Of course the meaning will disappear if the letters are erased. However it will not cease to exist because it still exists in my mind. I can express it again, perhaps in different letters (Greek or Hebrew). For me this is a helpful analogy for thinking about the Christian doctrine of bodily resurrection.

Reductionist philosophies have great difficulty in preserving any concept of human dignity because their logical end is the conclusion that we are nothing but robots programmed by the impersonal laws of physics. For some the 'new physics', with its suggestion that the consciousness of the observer affects the matter which is observed (at least at the atomic level), seems a way out of the mechanistic strait-jacket. However, it is an illusory one. That consciousness is still determined solely by the laws of physics. If appeal is made to their probabilistic nature, it must be pointed out that this does not provide a basis for belief in free, rational behaviour. Rather it suggests random, irrational behaviour. For Christians, the basis for human dignity is the belief that each individual bears the image of God.

The 'new science' and mysticism

The aspect of the challenge of the 'new science' which evangelicals are least well-prepared to face is the claim that it validates the world-view of Eastern mysticism. Mysticism has not been a notable feature of evangelical experience, and evangelical theology has never got to grips with it.

In fact the claim that quantum physics validates Eastern mysticism rests on a shaky basis. Those who make this claim frequently do so on the basis of controversial and contested theories or interpretations of quantum phenomena. An example is the view that quantum theory leads to the conclusion that consciousness determines the way the world is. Many physicists and philosophers of science contest this.[17] So the claim rests on a selective and debatable understanding of modern physics. Much the same can be said of its use of Eastern mysticism. According to those who know about the Eastern traditions, the writers who make this claim do so on the basis of a very truncated and unreal picture of them.[18] In addition it must be said that the aspects of mystical experience to which these writers refer are not uniquely Eastern but can also be found in the Judeo-Christian mystical tradition.

The claim is at heart a reductionist one. It is ironical that those who make it do not recognize this, but usually assert that they are presenting an antidote to the mechanistic, reductionist mind-set of Newtonian physics. However, they are assuming that ultimate reality is to be found by reducing everything to the level of sub-atomic particles. At this level, they claim, we see that everything is bound up in an inter-related oneness. Therefore, they conclude, the separateness and individuality which we see at the macro-level of everyday experience is an illusion. As we have seen, this reductionist approach needs justification and should not be allowed to go unchallenged.

Having said all this by way of criticism, there are, I think, two questions which we must ponder and pursue. The first is: Assuming that there is an inter-related oneness of all things at the sub-atomic level, what do we have to say about it as Christians? Personally, I do not find it in any way surprising. If the universe is the creation of the one and only creator and is constantly kept in being by him, I would expect there to be a fundamental coherence and unity about it. Moreover, the

Christian concept of God is a trinitarian one, that God is in himself a harmonious inter-relationship of persons. Is it surprising if his creation reflects something of this as it reflects his glory? In God himself, the harmonious inter-relatedness does not lead to loss of individual identity. This must lead Christians to reject the idea that the individuality we experience at the macro-level is illusory. I hope that others will take up and develop these trains of thought into something more substantial.

The second question is: What are we to make of the mystical experience of oneness? This is where the absence of any deep study or understanding of mysticism leaves us evangelicals at a loss. I can only make some tentative suggestions. It may be a genuine experience of God, who is one. I question whether this is so when the experience is said to lead to a loss of personal identity. The biblical picture of our relationship with God is that of human lovers, husband and wife. In this relationship there is a unity which comes from them giving themselves to each other. But there is also an individuality which results from each accepting the other and affirming the other's worth. Another possibility is that the mystic is experiencing the unity of God's creation, of which humans are a part. If so, this can rightly lead to a sense of awe and wonder which stimulates worship of God. However, to seek the experience of oneness *for itself* is to take the road to idolatry, to put the creation before the creator. Finally, the experience may be illusory, either self-induced or a demonic deception. How are we to test these possibilities? I must leave others to answer that. Since this is intended to be no more than an exploratory and provocative essay, it seems right to end with an unanswered question.

The gospel and Hinduism

Saphir P. Athyal

From one viewpoint, Christianity is just one of the major religions of the world. But to Christians, confronting religious pluralism with evangelistic outreach has always been a key task from the very inception of the church, because of their deep conviction that there is salvation only through Jesus Christ, the unique self-revelation of God. Although the Christian movement began in the midst of Jewish Palestine, it soon spread into the Graeco-Roman world, and there it confronted complex religious systems not unlike the religious pluralism of today. The church's earliest encounter was with Judaism. In the first century, rabbinic Judaism was engaged in extensive missionary activities, and many Gentiles were attracted to the Jewish fold. Others became 'God-fearers' without embracing everything in Judaism. But the Christians, because of the very missionary nature of their faith, went to the nations and shared a gospel that made total demands of all who accepted it. Inevitably this produced much conflict. Meeting the devotees of other religions on their respective soils became a theological challenge in ways not previously faced by God's chosen people.

The issue of religious encounter has become particularly urgent today because of significant developments of recent decades.[1] Two world wars, much international interaction, advanced technology in communication, the migration of peoples – all these mean that on the global level all peoples have become neighbours to one another. Religious pluralism has long been a phenomenon in Asia and Africa where Christians have always lived. As far as the West is concerned, however, it was only missionaries who went to far-off lands who faced the issue. But now, with the aggressive missionary penetration of the West by other religions, and the extensive scientific study of them in Western institutions, along with people of other faiths settling in increasing numbers in the West, even Western people are finding themselves in an unprecedented way in religiously pluralistic situations. The church, which since the fourth century through the Emperor Constantine made Christianity the official religion of the Roman Empire, has had prestige and power in the West until the twentieth century. But Christendom no longer exists. The rise of ideologies such as Communism, secularism and atheism, along with the appeal of Eastern religions in the West, especially through the New Age movement, has stripped Christianity of the high position it once held in many Western nations. Also, a cursory overview of some 500 years of Roman Catholic and 250 years of Protestant missionary work in Asia reveals little evidence of significant church expansion. Today hardly 5% of Asia is Christian, and this despite all the extensive Christian service rendered to Asian peoples and their societies.

What this means is that the global church today must reaffirm the rôle it had 2,000 years ago when it first emerged in the Near East – a servant and not the master, whose triumph is the despised cross lifted up, and whose method of conquest is selfless love, 'becoming all things to all men' (see 1 Cor. 9:22), that it might win some to faith in Jesus Christ. It is in this changing context that we have to view the world and its peoples.

Specifically, the Hindu world consists of some 650 million people: approximately 13% of the world's population. The essence of the Christian gospel and the major tenets of Hinduism may be studied from a variety of perspectives: the complex nature of Hinduism; the Christian understanding of God's dealings with Hindus; the challenge of Hindu Renaissance to Christianity; the Hindu-Christian mutual influences; the present state of Hindu-Christian dialogue; the Bhakti movement and its points of contact with Christianity; the distinctive doctrinal differences between the two religions; the eternal destiny of those Hindus who never rejected Christ because they had never heard of him; and the present climate of evangelization in India. Whereas only a few of these concerns can be addressed in this essay, major attention will be given to Hindu-Christian dialogue. Even this discussion is bound to be brief and quite inadequate.

Our approach to other faiths

Generally, Western Christians have had a negative attitude to other religious systems. They have all too easily overlooked many aspects of the Christian religion; its troubled history, and its flawed practice, have frequently been contrary to the standard of Jesus Christ and its biblical rootage. At best, their interest has been largely academic, approaching other systems of faith from only an anthropological or a historical perspective. Even the comparative religious approach has often been prejudicial. The temptation has been to compare the best in Christianity – its biblical and ethical distinctions – with the worst expressions of the popular practices of other religions. This is quite unfair and altogether improper.

Actually, comparing religions with one another is a futile exercise. But if it is found to be warranted, it should be strictly confined to corresponding levels of reality such as the level of popular practices, the level of historical development, the level of inner experience, or the level of doctrines and theological concepts. At the doctrinal level, we will find in Hinduism profound thoughts that are assertions of truths far removed from, and even diametrically opposed to, those of Christianity. Hence we would stress that it is naïve for one to compare the sublime elements of the Christian religion with the lowest forms of Hinduism. It must be kept in mind that what Christians commend to non-Christians is not a Christian religious system but the person of Jesus Christ.

What is the nature of God's work among the people of other religions? While Christians might readily concede that God has his own ways of dealing with individuals who belong to other faiths, some contend that this is quite impossible. To them, other religious systems are totally misleading and deceptive, if not outrightly devilish and demonic. In Judaism and Islam one finds a valid and meaningful, though partial, self-revelation of God, and we have not sorted out where in the whole picture these religions belong.

We believe that history is the scene of God's actions and that the Christ event, his death and resurrection, is the central focus in the salvation history that transforms, guides and judges till the end of time, when Christ will consummate his redemptive purpose. If major world events, the gospel and God's kingdom reaching out to all nations, and human renewal programmes that bring about freedom, liberty and social justice, are all components of this history of which Christ is the Lord, where do the religions and their history fit into this overall history?

> Evangelicals have tended to be ahistorical, because they think in terms of belief systems. They have not really taken the historicity of Christian revelation seriously. So when they think of other religions, they also tend not to take their historicity seriously. But if the event of Christ were decisive for all history, then the world of religions as part of history is affected by it. Our agenda is to discern how.[2]

It should be further noted, however, that just as in secular history there have been the good and the demonic, love and hatred, victories and failures, so also in all religious systems there exists truth and falsehood, light and darkness, positive guidance and much deception. As in history many forces opposing the cause of Christ's kingdom have worked effectively, so also there are many aspects in all religions which oppose the truth as it is in Christ.

The Bible makes abundantly clear that those outside the covenants of both the Old Testament and the New Testament have some general knowledge of God, and that God reveals himself to them and deals with them. Often this is described in terms of his general revelation. A detailed examination of the relevant biblical passages is not within the scope of this essay, but a few should be noted briefly.

All humankind, and not just the chosen people, are created in the image of God (Gn. 1:26), and whatever aspects of this image were not lost by the sin of Adam must remain in all people (Gn. 9:6; Jas. 3:9). God's covenant with Noah was with all humankind and the whole creation (Gn. 9:9–10). Abraham included peoples other than the descendants of Jacob when God made a covenant with him (Gn. 17:1–9). Melchizedek, the 'priest of God Most High' (Heb. 7:1), and Job, who was 'blameless and upright' (Jb. 1:1), stood in close relationship to God though they were outside the covenant. Balaam was a Moabite to whom and through whom God spoke (Nu. 22 – 24). Cyrus is spoken of as 'my shepherd', *i.e.* as a servant of God (Is. 44:28 – 45:1), and Assyria, a rod in Yahweh's hands (Is. 7:17; 10:5). Amos speaks of how, while God brought Israel from Egypt, he also guided other nations (Am. 9:7).God not only spoke to the people of Nineveh but also heard their prayer and cared for them (Jon. 4:11). The wise men of the East at the time of Jesus' birth were guided by

God, both by the star and also in their dream (Mt. 2:1–12).

Peter, in the story of Cornelius, admits that God does not show partiality but 'accepts men from every nation who fear him and do what is right' (Acts 10:34–35, see also 10:4), but goes on to proclaim 'a message through which you and all your household will be saved' (Acts 11:14). God's eternal power and divine nature are made plain to all peoples (Rom. 1:19–20) to such an extent that they are held accountable for a proper response. What is required of the law is written on their hearts (Rom. 2:15). At Lystra, Paul would say that as far as all nations are concerned, God 'has not left himself without testimony' (Acts 14:17).

These and many other passages are well-trodden areas. They do not imply that salvation is to be found in every religious tradition, but that the people of other faiths are not cut off from God and his dealings. However, the main thrust of the Bible is the particularism of Yahweh and the uniqueness of Christ. There is only one gospel (Gal. 1:6–9), one Mediator between God and all people (1 Tim. 2:5–6), and only one name through which we are saved (Acts 4:12).

The question now surfaces, How are we to do justice to these two apparently divergent strands in the Bible, with respect to those outside the covenants and the knowledge of the gospel? One reflects openness and universality in its scope while the other is exclusive and particular.

There can hardly be any question that all peoples to some degree or other are the recipients of God's general revelation and general grace. Furthermore, clear choices are made whenever God confronts a person. Just as the gospel becomes good news only to those who respond positively to it and bad news to those who reject it, so also opposite responses must be possible with regard to God's general revelation. Paul in Romans 1 and 2 would emphasize the natural tendency of people to suppress the truth and thereby merit the condemnation of God. But if this is actually the only intended response to general revelation, if rejection of God is invariably the only response possible, then what is God doing, and in what sense is humankind 'without excuse' (Rom. 1:20)? So the basic question remains: Does God's general revelation have any necessary link with the overall purpose of God for all humankind? While the devil can distort much of God's light and truth and deceive people, is all of general revelation to be rendered so void that it has no continuity whatsoever to God's unique salvific revelation in Christ?

Paul's words at Athens to a pagan audience give us a clue in our search for an answer. 'God did this so that men would seek him and perhaps reach out for him and find him, though he is not far from each one of us' (Acts 17:27). To be faithful to our understanding and experience of the finality of Christ and his unique salvation, we do not have to reject outright all that we find in Hinduism or other religions. Whatever distortions and imperfections they may have, we must contend that God remains free to use any means he chooses to draw people to himself.

Towards understanding Hinduism

India has over 650 million Hindus. They also form significant segments of the population of Singapore, Sri Lanka and Trinidad. In addition more than twelve million Hindus are scattered throughout the countries of the West and are making an impact upon their separate peoples. Moreover, their numbers are increasing. But most importantly, Hindu thought, teachings and world-view are permeating many societies throughout the world. In the 60s and 70s, many Hindu gurus and religious leaders gained wide acceptance and considerable followings in the West. Many people went to India, having grown tired of the materialism in the West and sought what they regarded as the spirituality and peace of the East. Transcendental meditation, yoga, Hare Krishna and a host of other forms of Hindu faith are currently widely known throughout the world.

In recent years, however, the penetration of basic Hindu tenets into the mainstream of thought of Western society has been more effectively achieved through the New Age movement. Most of its teachings are based on the core concepts of Hinduism, and of Buddhism – which originally arose out of Hinduism as a protest to it. Hence there is nothing new about the New Age movement. Indeed, Asia has known the same teachings for many centuries. A recent Gallup poll shows that 23% of North Americans believe in the reincarnation of souls. The use of crystals, channelling, mental telepathy and astrology, commonly practised in the West, likewise today characterize this development. In such popular concepts as holistic health, transpersonal psychology, quantum physics, transformational politics, and even in many areas of public life in the West, one finds the far-reaching influence of Hinduism.

While the popularity of Hindu cults and sect groups in clearly distinguishable forms began to decline in the West in the late 70s, the steady expansion of Hinduism and its teachings in more subtle forms through the New Age movement gives much cause for concern. Hence, the issue before us clearly is a global one, and not just related to the Christian witness to Hindus in India.

A basic problem one encounters in seeking to understand Hinduism is that it is not a single coherent religious system but a complex family of varying religious traditions, practices and reflections on transcendent deities. On the one hand, Hinduism contains sublime forms of philosophical and devotional expressions of religious truth, but on the other hand, it has within it many degenerating religious practices, much overt spiritism and gross superstition. Hinduism today provides a laboratory, if one is needed, to study all stages in the long history of the evolution of religion from some of their more primitive forms to those which are regarded as ethically and philosophically most advanced. Hinduism should not be regarded as one religion but rather represents a jumble of interrelated religious systems.

Hinduism does not have any one founder; neither does it have any precise creed to which all its adherents subscribe. While some of its scriptures, like certain Vedas and the Bhagavad Gita, are more popular than others, Hinduism does not claim to have any one normative scripture that is binding upon all Hindu devotees.

Hinduism is interlocked with a unique way of life and a distinct type of culture. Many of those who belong to it were earlier absorbed into the overarching system as they become part of India's general culture. It is only in this sense that millions of tribals in India are considered Hindus. India's Census Commission of 1910 found it necessary to define 'a Hindu', and they set his marks as: being served by the Brahmins as priests whose authority is accepted, worshipping Hindu gods, having access to Hindu temple worship, recognizing the authority of the Vedas, maintaining caste distinctions, cremating the dead and not eating beef.[3]

The basic elements of the Hindu system often noted are membership in a caste, belief in the law of retribution through the concept of 'karma' and transmigration of souls, the monistic idea of the universe, and a sense of the reality of the unseen.[4]

It is widely recognized that the word 'Hindu' originated from the incorrect Persian pronunciation of 'Sindhu', which means 'river' – a reference to the Indus River and to the people who lived along its banks. As noted by leaders such as Jawaharlal Nehru, Mohandas Gandhi and Sarvepalli Radhakrishnan, the word 'Hindu' does not occur in any of its scriptures or ancient literature. Actually, its use referring to a religion belongs to a late period introduced by foreigners.[5]

The basic thesis of Hinduism is that all religions are valid paths to the ultimate Reality. As a result Hinduism has had no difficulty in absorbing into itself widely varying religious traditions, including some which initially opposed it. Its only difficulty is with those religions whose claims are exclusive and unique. Indeed, Hinduism's inclusive eclectic character is its fundamental characteristic. As a result, down through the centuries it grew and changed without developing any clear canon or rule. As with most other religions, it contains the distinctive aspects of folk animism, popular mysticism and a militant brand of fundamentalism, all intermingled within its philosophical structure. The religious pluralism within Hinduism itself defies any clear understanding of it. This becomes quite evident in dialogic discussions about the gospel and Hinduism.

The Hindus consider their religion as *sanatana dharma*, the eternal religion that is adequate for people at all levels and that embraces all the essentials of all religions. To them 'Christianity and Hinduism are not alternatives which call for a choice between the one and the other'.[6] In this sense they have serious objections to the concept of conversion and change of religion, which stands as a great hurdle to the gospel witness.

Hindu–Christian dialogue

The most popular concept today in inter-religious encounter the world over is dialogue. In this is meant an attitude of openness to religious pluralism coupled with a non-judgmental desire to understand and appreciate 'the other'. But by no means is there any general agreement as to the nature, content and specific purpose of dialogue.

There are widely varying approaches to Hindu–Christian dialogue and, for that matter, to any inter-religious dialogue. At one extreme are those who understand it to mean the common exploration of ultimate truth. To them this truth is manifold and inexhaustible, since the ultimate Reality is beyond human comprehension. The ancient Indian story of a king placing four blind men near different parts of an elephant and asking them to describe the animal illustrates this approach. The one who felt its tail said the elephant was like a rope, the one alongside a leg thought it was like a pillar, the third one at its side was sure it was like a wall and the last one at the trunk insisted that it was like a fat snake. Hence, the basic axiom of religious pluralism is that since God reveals himself in a multitude of forms the human response will be expressed in different religions. None of them represents completeness. Furthermore, they need to be seen together to get a fuller understanding of the ultimate Reality.

At the other extreme is the attitude that uses the context of dialogue for apologetics, or even polemics, for defending one's faith by argument or attacking the religion of the other. But neither of these can be termed as dialogue. In between these two extremes lie other understandings as to the nature of the dialogue. Dialogue may be aimed at highlighting the best values in the religions involved. This assumes that the partners have genuine respect for each other's religion even when each may be convinced of the unique validity of his or her own faith. It is argued that such discussion may clarify at the same time one's own beliefs and practices. It may bring enrichment to all who participate.

Another type of dialogue is one that has social upbuilding or the concerns of the community as its focus. Not all people are able to sense that social needs are related to their religious convictions. But people of all faiths, especially in a country like India, share a common awareness of their basic social and economic needs. All partners in such inter-religious dialogue should explore in their respective religions those elements that will provide them with specific counsel to bring about justice in society and personal dignity and freedom for all people.

I took the initiative some years ago during the 'Year of the Handicapped' to call together leaders in a small city in India to discuss our common responsibilities in terms of our service to the handicapped in our city. The group included several top government officers, influential people of the community and religious leaders. Most of them were Hindus with a few Muslims and Christians. At times in our discussions our varying religious convictions showed through, though all participants made a conscious effort to avoid expressing anything that even approximated their religious beliefs.

Still another kind of dialogue takes place when the central concern is one's personal spiritual quest, and the satisfaction of inner cravings through the interpersonal sharing of the partners involved. Beyond all the complex religious practices and traditions, confusing notions and doctrinal controversies, most Hindus and Christians have a deep desire to know God and live lives pleasing to him. Mutual sharing at an in-depth personal level in one's varied spiritual expectations, inner feelings about God, failures in the religious quest, and the religious discoveries of the partners, can prove to be a most fruitful type of dialogue. But this presupposes a high level of genuine friendship and the mutual respect of those involved. I have found this kind of dialogue to be very meaningful.

Yet another approach to dialogue is to consider it as a stage in pre-evangelism. True values and salient features of the religion of one's partner are recognized with the purpose of building bridges. This is done with integrity and not as an evangelistic device. And yet, one's genuine desire is to win over one's partner. Hindus in the West make wide use of Christian notions and Bible quotations in their discussions with people of Christian background. So also do Christians. To the Christian, faith is not the sum total of all good and great values, but knowing, loving and serving a person, Jesus Christ the Lord. With no sense of triumphalism or spiritual superiority, but in gratitude to God for his grace, and in humility and love, the Christian earnestly hopes that the partner in dialogue will meet Christ in a personal way. This evangelistic desire should not be regarded as a hidden agenda or a deceptively concealed motive for engaging in dialogue. After all, no-one shares with another from the depths of his or her heart without the natural desire to impart and see received that which can only be regarded as of supreme importance in this life and the next.

The Indian context of dialogue

In India, where people of different faiths live together as neighbours, especially in urban areas, the mutual interaction and sharing of experiences and ideas is inevitable. They often work together on common projects, take part in common functions, exchange greetings, gifts and sweets during religious festival seasons, and share many experiences of life together. This means that dialogue, in the broad sense of sharing significant life experiences and engagement in 'neighbourliness', takes place all the time. While most often such encounters happen by chance, true dialogue only eventuates when deliberate efforts are made to share ideas, aspirations and inner struggles. Mutual sharing of life makes more demands on a person than just living together with its inevitable unstructured interactions.

Dialogue at the level of popular traditions, beliefs and religious practices is very difficult to achieve. When this takes place the differences between Hinduism and Christianity are seen to be deep and starkly clear. In the ensuing tension friends often are reluctant to press the subject very far.

Discussions at the level of disclosing one's deep inner cravings for God and frank personal sharing between Hindus and Christians occur still less frequently. While such an encounter can prove to be a very meaningful experience for both, it takes a great deal of mutual respect, love and confidence before people are willing to share in any degree of depth.

Most of the dialogue in India takes place in formal gatherings and on a philosophical or conceptual level. One is not quite sure as to what this type of encounter exactly produces, though all seem willing to admit that it sharpens one's academic understanding of the doctrines of both religions.

It is normally Christians who take the initiative in Hindu-Christian dialogue and not Hindus. One would have expected that Hindus would take an active interest in dialogue because of their tolerance of religious relativism and their openness to all religions as different paths to the one God. Moreover, Hinduism is currently going through a crisis, as are all other religions, because of secularism and modernity. India's growing middle class, along with many educated Hindus, give lip service to their religions because of the communities in which they live, yet they do not appear to take their traditional beliefs seriously. Moreover, Hinduism has no political clout or power, unlike Islam in Muslim countries. It would never stand against free interaction with people of other faiths. Atheism and secularism pose as the common enemy of all religions, and some scholars have even proposed that world religions should co-operate in order to fight it.

In some ways one can understand the lack of enthusiasm on the part of Hindus entering into dialogue with Christians. They constitute a predominant majority of over 80% of the population in India and do not feel the same need for recognition and acceptance that the people of minority religions do. Also, their basic notion is that all religions are essentially the same, and that the differences in their practices and historical expressions are not significant. While this results in their tolerance of all religions, it also means that they do not concern themselves with relating to other religions. Moreover, they are often suspicious of the motives of Christians in dialogue, feeling that it is a covert way of trying to convert them to Christianity.

There are a number of ashrams and centres for dialogue, as well as institutes for the study of religions, in India. Several leading denominations have commissions on Hindu-Christian relationships. One is overwhelmed with the reports of their discussions, consultations and writings on the subject of dialogue. But actual dialogue on serious religious themes is minimal. Those who engage in it are mostly from the intellectual level of society. The great majority are outsiders or Westerners and even some who are outside of the mainstream of the Indian Christian community.[7] Roman Catholics show more disciplined interest in this than do others.

When dialogue sessions are formally arranged, very few Hindus take part. In one such in which I participated in Bombay there were six Protestant and Orthodox Christians, six Roman Catholics and, in the place of six from other faiths we arranged for, only one Hindu, who came in for only part of the time. Usually those who come do so as an expression of charity to their Christian friends. Educated high-caste Hindus come for their own intellectual stimulation. Many of them more readily come to give a straightforward discourse on Hinduism than to engage in dialogue.

A matter of grave current concern is the rapid rise of Hindu fundamentalism, especially its more militant forms. This is no new development. For example, it was one such group that found Mahatma Gandhi's openness to the Muslim a potential threat to Hinduism and hence assassinated him. Political forces are prone to exploit the religious sentiments of people, stirring up tensions and communal fights to achieve their own goals. In the 1989 political elections in India, several fundamental Hindu parties won significantly, and thereby became an influential segment of the coalition government that rules the nation. They control a few state legislatures also. They take aggressive steps to discredit the Christians and oppose their activities. Earnest efforts are made to reconvert into Hinduism those who have accepted Jesus Christ. In the long run the new pressures they bring upon the church in India will invariably benefit it in terms of its self-examination and purification. Whether or not this will strengthen the faith and witness of the church is yet to be seen.

Many evangelicals have not entered into serious dialogue with Hindus because they are not convinced that the exercise is worth the demands it makes of them. The ability to discern 'core Hinduism' beyond its complex religious practices at the popular level, and to understand these fundamental concepts without any prejudice, requires patient study with an open mind. Just as Hindus have prejudicial opinions about Christians, so also the typical evangelical is totally negative when it comes to appreciating Hinduism as a philosophical system largely because of everything else that is associated with it. The predominant image of Hinduism is its cluster of idol worship, superstitions, the fear of spirits and demons, the evils of the caste system and endless meaningless rituals. Understandably the evangelical finds it difficult to appreciate and respect the basic fundamentals of the religion that shapes the Hindu's world-view and value system. The temptation is to dismiss the whole system as unworthy of serious consideration.

Also there is a reluctance to concede that there may be points of contact between Christians and Hindus relating to religious convictions. It is much easier to regard such an approach as syncretism. Besides, such a concession may threaten to devalue the evangelical's commitment to the uniqueness of Christ. Evangelical Christians would have no problem in relating to Hindus on matters of community life and social issues, and would be willing to participate with them in neighbourhood functions and events. But any toleration of the thesis that the one true God is near to Hindus, that they have some knowledge of God, and that God has his own way of dealing with them (Acts 16:27–28; Rom. 1:19–20) – all this is too incredible to grant. Evangelicals feel that to concede that God is working with people of other faiths, and therefore finds common ground with them, is too threatening to their own faith.

This negative reaction to the notion of dialogue is to a large degree conditioned by the fact that it is promoted primarily by more liberally oriented Christians. Evangelicals are instinctively suspicious of those who have abandoned the great fundamental of the Christian faith – the uniqueness and finality of Christ – and who downplay the imperative that the gospel be evangelistically proclaimed. Their reaction is similar to the earlier struggle when evangelicals avoided involvement in social issues because of their concern that the biblical gospel was thereby reduced to a mere 'social gospel'.

Yet another real difficulty is the widespread liberal notion that dialogue should be divorced from evangelistic witness. Evangelicals may be willing in a spirit of humility, friendship and respect for Hindus to engage in the sort of dialogue that will further mutual understanding. But they must be free to express their deep desire that their Hindu partners might come to acknowledge the lordship of Christ.

The purpose of dialogue

There is much of value and usefulness to inter-religious dialogue, and its positive benefits should be noted. We may note a few of them.

Dialogue in the broad sense of the word means bringing people of different faith commitments in a particular community to share their ideas, experiences and aspirations, and in a way to share their lives in order to develop community cohesion and mutual helpfulness. Dialogue at this level can promote freedom of expression, social ministries, the dignity of persons, the status of women, educational goals, social morality and a host of such beneficial concerns.

Dialogue also helps to clear up the misunderstandings and prejudices we all have of one another's religion and in so doing build mutual trust and social harmony. The greatest obstacle to genuine dialogue is not so much the different religious traditions and spiritual goals, as the ignorance which most people have of others, and the contribution this makes to mutual prejudice and bias. Christians do not realize the serious misunderstandings Hindus have about Christianity, its history, basic beliefs, religious practices and the motives behind the Christian's service and witness.

Again, in a situation where people of a minority religion are able to initiate dialogue, they derive psychological value in that it provides them with acceptance and hearing in the society. In India Christians are a distinct minority: 4% of the population at best. Inevitably the church projects the image that it is largely made up of low-caste people and tribals. In addition to this, a stigma is wrongly attached to Christianity that it is the religion of the colonialists and, as such, should no longer have a respectable place in the country. If the concern behind the dialogue is to promote the respectability and status of Christians in Indian society, then the tendency will be to emphasize Christianity's common grounds with Hinduism rather than its distinctiveness.

Some contend that an important value in dialogue is that it demands genuine respect for people as people. The Hindu participant is not primarily a target or object of evangelism. Dialogue makes Christians sensitive to the convictions and forces that shaped the Hindu worldview and Hindus personally. It is altogether right that Christians attempt sincerely and truly to understand and identify with them. Once genuine respect is established, meaningful listening will follow. Proclaiming the gospel to people on a 'take it or leave it' basis is certainly not becoming 'all things to all men' that by all means one might 'save some' (1 Cor. 9:19–22). Sharing the gospel is not blaring it.

Moreover, dialogue serves to expose its participants to one another, making them transparent to one another, provided they engage in it with integrity and humility. People need to be open to questioning and to criticism. How else can they be authentic in their witness?

Even though one accepts the above and many other values of dialogue, the basic question remains as to the central goal of Hindu-Christian dialogue. In dialogue, once mutual misunderstandings have been removed, and the values and riches in both faiths have been recognized, all become conscious of the shortcomings of their respective religions, and seek to identify and work together on pressing social issues. This is altogether commendable. But if on matters pertaining to personal faith they agree to disagree as good friends who esteem each other, then where do they go from there?

In certain Christian circles, the ultimate goal to be achieved through dialogue is to create a community of peace, justice and unity. The argument is that thereby Hindus and Christians living in such community will increasingly recognize their mutual interdependence and responsibility to each other. Their concern will be to strengthen all human links and common values, and not occupy themselves with the religious traditions and practices that divide them.

But is it not very idealistic to expect to create this kind of a community? Is this not a quasi-reproduction of something akin to a redeemed and redeeming community within the larger community? Does this not approximate what the Christian church is expected to be within the larger human community?

Also, what is the spiritual dimension of such a community? Wesley Ariarajah, the Director of the Sub-unit on Dialogue of the World Council of Churches, comments:

> What does the future hold for Hindu-Christian dialogue? Some wish to see the Christian and the Hindu as deeply and firmly rooted in their respective traditions, but in truly mutual relationship and partnership. Others wish to see this relationship essentially as a transforming friendship where the two traditions would interpenetrate and transform each other. Still others may wish to see only relative value in the historical expressions of religious life and see the emergence of an authentic religious life for contemporary society that has the imprint and input of the spiritual resources of the different traditions.[8]

In this kind of approach the central concern of the Christian witness is to further the common struggle for social justice, human rights and community peace. The most significant area of Hindu-Christian relationship lies 'not so much at the level of the recognition of doctrinal excellence, of belief systems or even of the depth of piety, but at the point of the recognition of the liberating potential of religions', and the special contribution that Christianity can give is the distinct message it has in this area.[9]

Dialogue in which the main objective is social justice, or identifying the common denominators between religions to promote social unity, or the joint search for truth, can hardly be reconciled with the heart of the Christian faith.

Our interest in dialogue is not to get converts to add to the numerical strength of the Christian community. Nor is it to prove the superiority of Christianity over Hinduism. We know only too well the past history and present problems of the church to engage in such a futile exercise. But dialogue provides an opportunity when God, who already deals with our partner in various ways, may use our witness to lead him or her to the truth. A person to whom the lordship of Christ has become the central force in transforming and energizing him or her cannot engage in dialogue without the inner hope and prayer that the Hindu partner in dialogue might also come to know the Lord. This is not because of his or her religious allegiance, but because of the redemptive concern of Jesus Christ for all people. Christians have the same spiritual concern for nominal church members.

Because Christians are commanded to love their neighbours as themselves, they need to identify and genuinely respect and understand the people to whom they bear witness. Therefore, dialogue with integrity and love is their duty. But they should not think that dialogue makes the gospel more readily and gladly acceptable. The offence of the gospel will always remain because of the demands it makes. But if Christians more effectively engage in dialogue with people of other faiths, as well as with their fellow Christians, then there is the possibility that the gospel will increasingly call people to faith in Jesus Christ.

Agreed in principle?

The pursuit of the Christian mind in politics

Martyn Eden

I f this writer appreciates John Stott for one thing more than any other, it is for his example of, and commitment to, relating the Bible to modern life. It is one thing to claim orthodoxy in holding a high view of Scripture, but it is another thing entirely to grapple with the complexities of contemporary issues in order to develop a consistently biblical understanding and practice in relation to them. To this end, John Stott has made great use of the idea of the Christian mind. He defines this as, 'a mind which has firmly grasped the basic presuppositions of Scripture and is thoroughly informed with biblical truth'.[1] There are dangers with this idea, either of intellectual élitism or of dilettantism. Harnessed as it is by John Stott in his *Issues Facing Christians Today*, however, it offers a way of avoiding the twin horrors of glib superficiality and of reading one's own presuppositions into Scripture.

Nowhere are these horrors more prevalent, and the need for a Christian mind more evident, than in the political arena. After more than half a century of steering clear of politics, British evangelicals have been reclaiming the heritage of William Wilberforce and the 7th Earl of Shaftesbury, Anthony Ashley Cooper, and are once again becoming politically active. Parliamentary debates on Sunday trading, abortion and embryo experimentation have spurred a significant number of evangelicals to lobby their MPs and to campaign in support of measures to give legislative expression to Christian values. In relation to this narrow band of issues there has been a reasonably clear articulation of the biblical perspectives, and a fair measure of unity amongst evangelicals. Sadly, the same could not be said in relation to the vast majority of issues on the mainstream political agenda. On these, evangelicals are either silent, or seem to reflect the essentially secular thinking of the major political parties. In other words, there is only very limited evidence of a Christian mind in British politics. In the light of Harry Blamires' statement of 1963 that 'There is no longer a Christian mind',[2] perhaps this ought not to surprise one, but it is still an unacceptable state of affairs.

Faith and politics have never been comfortable with one another unless believers were willing to compromise their faith. A person's faith determines his or her first loyalty and commitment. Since for a Christian this belongs to Christ, it cannot be given to a political leader. Thus, the early Christians were persecuted for refusing to worship the emperor. Then again, it is an embarrassing fact that religion has been one of the principal causes of war, all the way from the Crusades to modern conflicts in Northern Ireland, Sudan or the Lebanon. Moreover, since the eighteenth century, the heirs of the Enlightenment have striven to keep religion out of politics. When, on the publication of the 'Faith in the City' report, for example, the church was told to look after souls and leave politics to the politicians, this was no more than the outcome of a long secularization process which has made politics autonomous and marginalized faith to the purely personal sphere.

If Jesus is Lord, however, as we profess, there can be no autonomous spheres of life, excluded from his lordship. It is sad yet understandable when non-believers are not interested in a Christian perspective on political issues, but the absence of a distinctively Christian mind amongst Christians in politics is a cause for grave concern. This is made the more so by the reawakening of interest in politics amongst evangelicals. Are their political contributions to be rooted in biblical values and presuppositions, or will they merely assimilate secular thinking and 'sanctify' it with proof texts? There is some evidence to suggest that the latter is happening.

What principle?

The most obvious example is the way in which most British Christians have accepted the left/right divide in politics and identified with one side or the other. It used to be said that the Church of England was the Conservative Party at prayer, and Nonconformists were more likely to be linked with the Liberal or Labour Parties. In the early 1980s one had the impression that quite a lot of evangelicals backed the SDP, but that is so no more. However, regardless of which party they supported, either as members or simply as voters, there are few grounds for believing that their support was prayerfully thought through from biblical principles. First, none of the parties appealed for support on a religious basis. Secondly, students of voting behaviour have found little evidence of religious affiliation being a significant factor in determining how modern British electors cast their votes. The exceptions have tended to be associated with historical factors.

> Thus, Irish voters (of whom there are over a million) are nearly all Catholics and mostly Labour, but the basic reason for this is that the Irish dislike the Conservative Party for historical reasons. Welsh rural voters are mostly Methodists and mostly anti-Conservative (being Liberal, Labour or Plaid Cymru), but this is also for historical reasons.[3]

The two factors which do seem to have strongly influenced voting behaviour in the recent past are social class and parental example. However, even social class has diminished in significance in the last two decades as affluence has increased, and as trade union membership has spread amongst the middle classes. There is now some evidence to suggest that 'electors are individually motivated, spending time to gain information about what the parties have to offer and "buying" whichever package appears to them to be most advantageous'.[4] Whilst recognizing that very small numbers of people can get lost in opinion polls, it is disconcerting to find no evidence that the voting behaviour of the 13% who describe themselves as very religious is distinctively different from the rest of the population.[5]

Moreover, when one examines the speeches and writings of politicians who attempt to find biblical roots for what they have to say, two things are immediately obvious. The first is the dearth of them, and the second is the way in which the Bible is hijacked for political ends. An example of this is to be found in Mrs Thatcher's address to the

General Assembly of the Church of Scotland, sometimes called the 'Sermon on the Mound'. The relevant paragraph of the address is as follows:

> We are told we must work and use our talents to create wealth. 'If a man will not work, he shall not eat,' wrote St Paul to the Thessalonians. Indeed, abundance rather than poverty has a legitimacy which derives from the very nature of the creation.[6]

In using 2 Thessalonians 3:10 in this way, Mrs Thatcher suggests that St Paul was urging the Thessalonians to create wealth. A careful study of verse 10 in context shows that this was not so. A prominent theme of both letters to the Thessalonians was the 'end times' and the return of the Lord. In the second letter, St Paul deals specifically with the 'lawless one' who will attempt to lead Christians astray before the Lord returns. Paul also warns against idleness in both letters. Leon Morris exegetes verse 11, giving the context of Paul's comment, as follows:

> The idea that the second advent was near seems to have convinced them that it was useless to work for their living; and, not content with being idle themselves, they were busying themselves in the attempt to make others idle also, probably urging them to give themselves over to nothing but preparing for the great event. Such conduct is castigated.[7]

Interestingly, a second example involves Eric Heffer using the same text in an equally inappropriate manner, for quite different political ends. In his contribution to *Faith in Politics*, he writes:

> Everyone has a right to a job. 'He that does not work, neither shall he eat', is not just a socialist idea; it is also a Christian one. Obviously, those who, because of misfortune – through illness, disability or enforced unemployment – cannot work, should be helped by society as a whole by right and not by charity.[8]

The same verse is being used in support of very different political goals, neither of which has anything to do with the meaning of the original text.

John Selwyn Gummer supplies the third example when he interprets Luke 21:4 (or Mk. 12:44) in support of private charity as opposed to tax-funded public welfare.

When Christians campaign for higher taxation to fund greater government spending on social security, there are some real economic consequences which we shall come to later. Yet there is also a very real religious concern. The widow *gave* her two mites, she was not assessed two mites for tax purposes. There is a freedom in Christian giving which makes it sit uneasily with compulsory taxation.[9]

The stress on 'gave' is Gummer's. There are two observations regarding this. First, the best translation of the word in the Greek text (*ballei*) is 'to throw', 'to cast' or 'to put', rather than 'to give'. So Gummer is unwise to pivot his argument on this particular word. Secondly, and more significant, is the fact that the usual understanding of Jesus' teaching here has nothing to do with the balance between private charity and state welfare. Most commentaries explain this passage in terms of the contrast between the showy but shallow religion of the scribes and the genuine but discreet devotion of the poor widow.[10] Only Jesus, with his unique insight, knows that she had given her all, meagre though it was, whereas everyone knew that the scribes had given a lot more, albeit a much smaller proportion of their resources.

Another principle

No-one who holds a high view of Scripture as the uniquely inspired Word of God can be happy with such eisegesis, regardless of the end which it serves. It is, however, only a symptom of a much deeper problem which Clark Pinnock has dubbed 'ideological entrapment'. Pinnock argues that radical Christians have been seduced by the utopian myth of socialism and have 'connected the cause of God's kingdom quite deliberately and intimately with the cause of Marxism or socialism in some milder form'.[11] He is not alone in making this accusation. Lloyd Billingsley, in his acerbic book *The Generation That Knew Not Joseph*, has likened contemporary Christian radicals to those who, like Hewlett Johnson, the former 'Red Dean of Canterbury', idolized Stalin and saw his regime as 'ushering in the very kingdom of Christ on earth'.[12] He complains bitterly that, 'to be politically aware or socially active is automatically assumed to mean an inclination to the left. Evangelicals are great faddists, and this is one more fad, as other signs show'.[13] Billingsley cites many examples of alleged left-wing bias and concludes:

Instead of following the biblical injunction for just weights and a just balance, the socialist evangelicals have two moral measuring systems: a lenient one for socialists and a strict one for everybody else, particularly the United States.[14]

Similar sentiments have been expressed in Britain, in the 1978 Reith Lectures by Dr Edward Norman,[15] and more recently by Rachel Tingle. In *Another Gospel?*, Ms Tingle complains about the growing influence of the political left in the General Synod of the Church of England and amongst its bishops. She is disturbed by the way in which 'the biblical concepts of "justice", "peace" and "liberation" have been used to gain uncritical support for political programmes which will create neither peace, justice, nor liberation'.[16] She is particularly antagonistic to the radicals' enthusiasm for 'kingdom theology', which she dismisses as heresy.[17]

The gist of these protests from the right is that the church in Britain (and America), including its evangelical wing, is becoming politicalized and hijacked by the political left. The main objections to this are, first, that socialism does not work. It has betrayed the poor because it has failed where the opportunity existed to create the wealth that would have brought them genuine liberation.[18] Secondly, it has inspired and sustained oppressive regimes which have killed and tortured millions.[19] Thirdly, it is distracting the church from its proper calling to preach the gospel, care for souls and stand up for biblical moral standards.[20] There is undoubtedly some truth in these objections, but also some grounds for argument. Notwithstanding the evil records of socialist regimes in Eastern Europe and China for oppression, the left does not have a monopoly on this. There is also a clear biblical case for including social action as an element of the church's mission. But the principal difficulty which this writer has with these protests is the alternatives which are offered in place of socialism.

One alternative, represented by Edward Norman, is for the church to stay out of politics altogether and concern itself with 'the ethereal qualities of immortality'.[21] The other writers quoted seem to oppose the leftward drift largely because they espouse another set of political values – those generally associated with the right. Clark Pinnock is the most explicit. Although he disavows wanting 'to tie Christianity to the capitalist ideology in the way the left-wing churchmen tie it to socialism',[22] he does not hide his admiration for capitalism:

Market economies on the other hand have been remarkable and even spectacularly successful in raising the standard of living of whole populations. No system has ever been so effective in wealth creation and productive power. It is not an exaggeration to say that capitalism is unique in its capacity to generate wealth, and not outlandish to claim that it represents one of the best blessings ever to have been bestowed upon humanity.[23]

That is a hugely sweeping claim and it provokes this writer to question whether those who think like this have not also succumbed to some sort of ideological entrapment. Does not this claim ignore the serious moral flaw at the heart of capitalism? This lies in the assumption that the unconstrained pursuit of self-interest is an acceptable motive. Yet in the Bible, no accusation is more damning than that which says 'everyone did as he [or she] saw fit' (*e.g.* Jdg. 17:6; 21:25). Thus the capitalism which Professor Pinnock sees as one of the greatest blessings bestowed on humanity finds no objection to a free market in drugs, pornography and prostitution, provided that they are profitable. So long as individuals are free to choose whether they will supply and demand these goods and services, capitalism remains neutral about them. Indeed, that is the reason why capitalism needs the moral framework which Christianity used to supply. For its own survival, capitalism requires certain standards of honesty and truthfulness, which it cannot generate within itself.[24]

Of course, it may be true that because of the fallen nature of humankind, we do operate on the basis of self-interest, but this is certainly not the biblical ideal. First, this ideal recognizes that we are accountable to God for what we do with his creation. Secondly, it teaches us to love our neighbour as ourselves, and we recall that Jesus' summary of the Law was set against a background of Old Testament values which included a proper concern for the weak and vulnerable. On top of these, Jesus added the values of his kingdom: 'seek first his kingdom' (Mt. 6:33); 'You cannot serve both God and Money' (Mt. 6:24; Lk. 16:13); 'where your treasure is, there your heart will be also' (Mt. 6:21; Lk. 12:34), *etc.* Yet, capitalism seems to assume that everyone is entitled to, and desires, more and more goods and services. This is surely alien to the biblical Christian perspective, though it reflects very well the consequences of the fall. To be fair, there are plenty of capitalists who moderate their behaviour to be good employers and altruistic citizens, but their motivation for doing this has nothing to do with theoretical capitalism. So why do so many Christians espouse capitalism as if it were naturally congruent with the values of the Christian gospel?

This question is not asked to provoke another round in the left-right battle for it is not this writer's purpose to support either side. Rather, it is a prelude to urging Christians to abandon the battle altogether, in favour of seeking a more holistic Christian mind in politics. The conflict has gone on too long, dividing Christians and damaging the credibility of the gospel. Moreover, it is a pointless struggle, because neither ideology can stand up to a thoroughgoing biblical critique.

Conflicting principles

There is no shortage of critiques of socialism and capitalism, but very few writers have undertaken a simultaneous analysis of both in relation to the teaching of the Bible. It is beyond the scope of this essay to do this systematically and comprehensively, but it might be instructive to examine the presuppositions of each with regard to human nature, and contrast these with the biblical doctrine of 'humanness'. Assumptions about human nature lie at the heart of all social theories, and any economic or political ideology which assumes too much or too little will be inherently flawed. Indeed, Clark Pinnock recognizes this when he claims that 'the market approach works well because it is realistic about human nature whereas socialism presupposes saints'.[25]

There is, in fact, no single view of human nature either on the left or the right. Marxist structuralists, such as Althusser, reject the very idea of a general human nature because it is incompatible with the implications of historical materialism: 'The only general characteristics which human beings have according to the requirements of historical materialism, are those which are determined by a definite mode of production and must have a class character.'[26]

On the other hand, Marxist humanists recognize that without a constant factor in humanness, the whole idea of an ongoing historical process, which is central to Marxism, would be untenable. The view of human nature held by this school, which harks back to much in Marx's own writing, has three principal elements. First, it is naturalistic in that human beings are seen as the product of biological evolution rather than supernatural creation.[27] Secondly, it sees human beings as social beings because they must eat to live, producing to eat, and production is a corporate activity.[28] Thirdly, it is optimistic about human potential.[29] People are potentially good and capable of perfection in this life, given the right social and economic conditions. Actually, people are generally far from perfect because of the alienation they experience in the capitalist system, which breeds false ideological consciousness. The whole thrust of the socialist movement is to liberate people to fulfil their potential by eliminating all those forces which cause their alienation: the private ownership of the means of production, a division of labour, competition and the exploitation of labour. Perfection involves being a good comrade and citizen, working for the good of society and others and not just in the pursuit of self-interest. There are, of course, many on the political left who would not accept all of this, but it is generally true that they take an optimistic view of human nature: if only we can get the social structure and education right, we can expect people to behave in a socially noble manner.

There is also no simple consensus about human nature on the political right, because it has drawn on a number of quite different strands of thought. One of these is the individualism and work ethic of the Protestant Reformation, which holds that people can influence their own economic condition by working hard and being frugal. Another strand is the Malthusian assumption that people are 'really inert, sluggish, averse from labour, unless compelled by necessity', hence the importance of the profit motive. Bentham's pleasure/pain principle also has its place: people seek to maximize their pleasure and minimize their experience of pain. The free-market liberal emphasizes personal responsibility, and wants a minimalist state so that individuals can pursue their self-interest: but traditional British Conservatives follow Benjamin Disraeli in taking a more paternalistic approach in accepting a duty to help those who cannot help themselves. Nevertheless, they are more or less agreed in taking a much more pessimistic view of human nature than those on the political left – hence Pinnock's jibe, quoted above.

A Christian critique will surely want to find fault with both sets of views. The biblical view is of humans created by God in his own image and of his love for us to the point of his self-giving on the cross in the person of Jesus. This reflects both the intrinsic value and significance of each individual and the inherent dignity of humankind even in our fallen, sinful state. The Bible reflects a realism about human beings which stands between the naïve optimism of the left and the dark pessimism of the right. It does not see humans as perfectible in this life but it promises perfection through Christ's sacrifice, when he returns, and the sanctifying work of the Spirit in the meantime. John Stott has himself summed up the biblical critique in this way:

> Thus, to indulge in a blunt oversimplification, both main political ideologies in western societies appeal to Christians for different reasons. Capitalism appeals because it encourages individual human initiative and enterprise, but also repels because it seems not to care that the weak succumb to the fierce competition it engenders. Socialism appeals, on the other hand, because it has great compassion for the poor and the

weak, but also repels because it seems not to care that individual initiative and enterprise are smothered by the big government which it engenders. Each attracts because it emphasizes a truth about man, either the need to give free play to his creative abilities or the need to protect him from injustice. Each repels because it fails to take with equal seriousness the complementary truth.[30]

Therein lies the thrust of this essay. Both socialism and capitalism are inadequate because they each overemphasize a particular value – or cluster of values – to the neglect of other values. In two helpful articles in *Third Way*, Peter Broadbent has shown how the main streams of British political thought attach different importance to each of four key values: justice, equality, freedom and interdependence.[31] Traditional liberalism is rooted in 'atomistic individualism'. As a result, equality becomes equality of opportunity, and justice means everyone being rewarded in relation to the use they make of their talents. Freedom of choice is the primary value but it is a freedom under the law so that one person's enjoyment of freedom does not curtail another's.

Mrs Thatcher's brand of politics has been much influenced by traditional liberalism but modified it significantly. Freedom is still the key value, but justice and interdependence are played down, and equality of opportunity becomes comparative equality. The driving force behind these changes of emphasis is the place of the market in New Right thinking. The market is seen as a neutral mechanism which satisfies consumers' wants and is incapable of injustice. Nothing must be allowed to interfere with its operation because that is how problems are caused.

As was evident from the frequent 'spats' between Margaret Thatcher and Ted Heath, classical British Conservatism stands for a different value mix. It is strongly wedded to tradition and 'the wisdom of the ages' and has a romantic belief in enlightened paternalism, tempered in practice by a pragmatic pursuit of consensus. Given these emphases, Conservatives have little time for egalitarianism *per se* but there is a respect for the value of the individual, so that justice and fairness are seen as important. The key value is still freedom of choice.

For Socialists, the priority is always equality and other values tend to be defined in relation to this goal. 'Justice becomes the means to the egalitarian end ... and freedom is defined in terms of fulfilment, with the individual achieving that fulfilment only in a context of renewed social relationships, where justice and co-operation ensure the goal of equality.'[32]

Biblical principles?

In the light of his analysis it is easy to understand the divisions which characterize British politics, but it is none the less important to show how Christians who are called to be politically active can avoid being sucked into the left / right divide. The motive for attempting this is not a fear of controversy *per se*, but a wish to operate within a distinctively Christian framework rather than one defined by secular ideologies. Nor is it imagined that there is to be found in Scripture a complete philosophical system which when applied in politics will answer every problem and see off all existing ideologies. But, if Jesus is to be Lord of our politics as of every other sphere, then there have to be some distinctively Christian perspectives which we can bring to the political arena. The search for these is the business of the Christian mind in politics.

This search raises two sets of questions about how the Bible can be related to day-to-day politics without committing any of the *faux pas* already identified. The first set of questions is about how one hears the whole Word of God on a particular issue in contemporary society. Once we believe that we have done so, we then face questions about how we feed that Word into the political process in such a way that its relevance is recognized even by those of other faiths or none. Unfortunately, the former questions belong in the territory of the Bible scholar whilst the latter are usually tackled by ethicists or sociologists. Communication between them, and with the rest of the church, has not always been calculated to help the Christian politician. The Christian mind in politics needs both to be willing to straddle the disciplines, and to be capable of earthing them in the real world. Add to these demands the complexity of modern life and political issues and one reaches the unavoidable conclusion that the Christian mind belongs to a community of believers and not to single individuals.

If this community eschews proof-texting, how does it discover the whole Word of God about a particular issue? The most popular approach is to harness the fourfold scheme of biblical history: the creation, the fall, the redemption and the consummation or end times. Good examples of the application of this scheme are to be found in John Stott's *Issues Facing Christians Today* and Richard Mouw's *Politics and the Biblical Drama.*[33] An alternative model is to use the major doctrines of the Christian faith as 'theological entry points' – points of doctrinal or theological emphasis which have relevance to politics. This is the approach of Philip Wogaman in his stimulating *Christian Perspectives in Politics.*[34] Whichever approach is used, the aim is to identify the sort of

Christian principles about which William Temple used to speak and write.[35] They stand somewhere between the text of Scripture and detailed political policies. They are sometimes called 'middle axioms'.[36] An example would be:

Biblical statement	Middle axioms	Concrete situations
God created us in his own image.	Humans are equal in the sight of God.	Public policies in favour of equality/against inequality.
	Humans need to work and be creative to be fulfilled.	Policies to maintain full employment, etc.
	Humans are social beings.	Institutions which give expression to this.

These approaches offer more hope of hearing God's Word than the echoes of our own prejudices which come out of the alternatives criticized above, but it would be dishonest to ignore the difficulties which even these involve. It has to be acknowledged, for example, that it is still possible to come up with conflicting insights from Scripture. Take the issue of nuclear defence. Some defend the retention of the nuclear deterrent to constrain an evil government on the basis of God's righteousness and justice, whilst others argue for abolition on the grounds of God's love. This is a gross over-simplification of the various positions, but there is no denying the fundamental disagreement between them despite the fact that each is sincerely argued from a legitimate biblical basis. This situation actually arose in a seminar on the nuclear issue organized by the London Institute for Contemporary Christianity and the Shaftesbury Project.[37] The way in which the principal protagonists responded was instructive. They continued their debate, off and on, for five years and complemented it with shared prayer and fellowship. Even then they did not see eye to eye on the issue, but some significant gains were made. Their mutual understanding and respect stood in stark contrast to the way many politicians behave towards one another. On the issue itself, they certainly focused more on what united them – the importance of peace-making – than they had at the outset. Those impatient for a cut-and-dried policy prescription would have been frustrated by this process, but they have to accept that where the Bible is not explicit, and that includes many contemporary issues, such a process is inevitable. It is also more Christlike than the unedifying spectacle of Christians attacking each other across the left/right divide.

Disagreement and debate are of the essence of healthy, democratic politics. This writer does not want Christians to opt out of this but to shift our debate to a lower rung on the ladder of abstraction, which links the Bible to day-to-day politics. If we could only agree on the principles we find in Scripture, it would not matter if we disagreed about the practical policies to be used to achieve them, provided we handled these disagreements in a Christlike manner. Indeed, it is arguable that the more widely-spread Christians are across the party spectrum, the more far-reaching would be our leavening influence. But when we are divided at the level of first principles, we tend to lose whatever leavening influence we might have had and we bring the Bible into disrepute.

There is, however, another potential risk attached to the articulation and pursuit of biblical principles in the political sphere and it is important that it is recognized. It is that in pursuing these principles one might secularize the Bible. The risk lies in thinking that the implementation of the principle is prima facie evidence of the Bible being applied when, in reality, it might be the outcome of non-believers employing totally secular methods. Thus, hypothetically, if plans to remove restrictions on Sunday trading were defeated largely through the efforts of secular trade unions protecting the interests of shop workers, it would not necessarily be a Christian act at all. In other words, there is an important distinction between the Bible and principles derived from it. This should not deter us from seeking and attempting to apply these principles, but it does suggest the need for the Christian mind to attend to means and motives as well as to ends.

Principles and practice

The second set of questions, concerning how we feed our biblical insights into the political process, is just as problematic. Not only does the intention run counter to the secularizing drift of the last two hundred years, but in a pluralist society, such as modern Britain is, it could provoke some very negative responses unless it is wisely done. So the way in which the Christian mind is expressed will count for a lot. Those called to do this will most certainly need the guidance and empowering of the Holy Spirit to produce the fruit which Paul lists in Galatians 5:22–25, in a milieu more familiar with the fruit of the old nature. Those who question whether it is possible for the meek and humble to survive, let alone succeed, in the political arena, would do well to reread the Beatitudes which immediately precede Jesus' teaching about being salt and light in the world (Mt. 5:1–16). We might also question the world's notions of success and failure. Christians like Wilberforce and Shaftesbury never won high office but they unquestionably had political impact. Admittedly, British politics has changed much since then, but the Green movement has had a parallel sort of influence in our own time. If Christians can persuade the major parties to adopt our principles, it matters not that we do not win office or the other symbols of worldly success.

Given the complexity of many contemporary political issues, there is also a need for humility even in claiming that our insight is of the mind of Christ. It is possible to approach a given issue from a number of different biblical or doctrinal starting-points and come to a variety of conclusions. How, for example, does one take account of the consequences of both the fall and the cross in framing a biblical perspective on prison reform? Philip Wogaman understands this when he suggests that, when we apply doctrine in order to know how to act in a specific situation, we should begin by treating doctrine as presumptive rather than definitive. There may be other ways of applying the doctrine than the one which first occurred to us. There may also be other doctrines relevant to our situation which, when recognized, will cause us to modify how we act. Our initial application of doctrine and Scripture should, therefore, be provisional until there has been an opportunity to test it against the insights of others. Thus Wogaman proposes that 'the most direct line of application of a given theological doctrine is presumed to be the right one to pursue unless and until it is shown, in fact, to lead to deviation from real Christian faithfulness'.[38] This is quite different from the tentativeness of a relativist, and seems to be a healthy way to cope with the complexity of life in the modern world.

Wogaman's proposal also reminds us that the goal of the Christian mind is a consistent and active faithfulness to Christ, and not just a matter of identifying an appropriate biblical idea as the basis for our thinking about a specific issue. Take, for example, the issue of public education in a pluralist society. Biblically-rooted Christians are convinced of the uniqueness of Jesus as Son of God and saviour, and will want to hold fast to this notwithstanding the large numbers from other faiths in the schools. But the Christian mind will also seek to be faithful to Christ in loving neighbours of other faiths, and reflecting divine justice and righteousness in relation to them. What constitutes faithfulness to Christ in this area may not be clear until this mix of biblical ideas has been thought, prayed, talked and lived out in practical terms.

More challenging still is the way in which human sin can make the application of a biblical principle impossible. The harsh reality of this was brought home to British Christians in 1990 when Parliament further liberalized the law on abortion, despite their campaigning and prayer to the contrary. There will be no avoiding the fact of sin until Christ returns, but that should not deter the development and expression of Christian thinking, for history also teaches that it is possible to tackle particular manifestations of evil – such as the trade in slaves, for example.

So, the Christian mind will be realistic about sin and eschew utopianism. It will also remember Lord Acton's caution about the corrupting effects of being close to the seat of power. There are too many political parties around the world labelled 'Christian' which seem to have forgotten their roots, for this warning to be ignored. The Christian mind will also be honest about the hurdles to be overcome in defining and agreeing biblical principles. It will anticipate resistance both from secular politicians, and from Christians already entrenched along the left/right divide. But it will persevere in showing how both socialism and capitalism are products of Enlightenment humanism,[39] equally rooted in distorted views of human nature, and alike in their neglect of important biblical values.

When opposed and ridiculed, those trying to express a Christian mind will point to the consequences of this neglect in terms of contemporary social decay. We will cite the current divorce rates, the number of one-parent families, the growing incidence of illegitimacy and rape, the number of abortions, the evidence of alcohol and drug abuse, and the neglect of old people, and we will call for the recovery of biblical values regarding the family and sexual morality.[40] We will also draw attention to the way people with a physical disability or a mental handicap are marginalized and ask what happened to real caring in the local community. The record prison population, and crime statistics, will provoke questions about the need to recover a biblical sense of right and wrong, and to restore it to the moral curriculum of our schools.

Warming to our task, the Christian mind spokespeople will go on to challenge the apparently idolatrous attitudes towards the market held by those on the political right. With such Christian economists as Alan Storkey,[41] we will reject capitalist determinism and begin to face up to the implications of our collective responsibility before God for the poor stewardship of the resources, gifts and opportunities which he has given us. At the same time, we will also resist the centralist instincts of the left, and sometimes of the right, too, and work for a diffusion of both power and responsibility to local communities, consistent with the biblical understanding of human nature.

171

It is beyond the scope of this essay to go on speculating about what the Christian mind in politics might seek to do and perhaps that is as well, for speculation is an easy substitute for action. The immediate challenge to Christians in Britain, especially to those who are politically active, is to give up conforming to the secular agenda epitomized by the traditional left/right divide, and replace it with consistently Christian responses to the needs of our nation and local communities. We shall probably disagree about detailed policies because we are different in so many ways, but we should surely seek agreement at the level of principle, if we take our principles from Scripture and endeavour to develop a Christian mind in politics.

Part Three
Living the gospel

Introduction to Part Three

Christians are not intended to be like tadpoles, practically all head and very little else. This advice, which John Stott has regularly given to students at the Institute for Contemporary Christianity, never fails to raise a smile, but it is a serious point that he is making. God wants us to love him with all of our heart, soul, mind and body – the whole person responding to him in a balanced manner. The Good News is about forgiveness, restoration and transformation to wholeness, so that believers become more like Jesus. These changes, which are a reflection of the new life in Christ, tell others that we are his disciples and commend the gospel to unbelievers. They are what qualify us to be salt and light in society. They certainly involve the mind, as Paul indicates in Romans 12:2, but they also touch every other part of us. Only thus can we really live the gospel.

Too many of us have made the mistake of falling into one of three traps. Our response to God may be largely cerebral, in terms of a sound grasp of Scripture and doctrine; or emotional, in terms of exuberant worship; or practical, in terms of caring social action. But few of us integrate all three in a spiritually mature balance. The purely cerebral response can be dry and even intellectually arrogant, rarely attracting others to Christ. The predominantly emotional response is warm and friendly, but it is not always capable of handling the intellectual challenges to the faith, which are many in a modern pluralistic society. The practical response may be strong on actually showing neighbour-love, but unless it is rooted in clear biblical convictions it runs the risk of drifting into a social gospel, indistinguishable from secular humanism. The mature Christian will have gone further than the rest of us in weaving the three strands into a single seamless garment which is worn with unselfconscious love and humility. Such a person is living the gospel.

How we go on from understanding the modern world, to being a people who live the gospel within it, is the general theme of Part Three. The individual chapters address the subjects of spirituality, authority in preaching, evangelism in the local church, and finding ministry effectiveness in the modern world, but they each reflect this general theme. To really live the gospel, we need a live spirituality. Spiritual life and growth are nurtured by the sort of preaching commended by James Packer. The content of faith has to be earthed in the context where God has put us. The model of local church evangelism analysed by Michael Green has at its heart a group of Christians whose lives reflect the gospel they reach out to share. Michael Cassidy also confirms this to be the key to effective ministry.

It is a happy coincidence, but not one without significance, that three of the contributors to this Part, James Houston, James Packer and Michael Green, are all members of the teaching staff of Regent College, Vancouver. As Dr Houston, its founding Principal, recounts in his opening paragraph, Regent College had a considerable amount to do with John Stott's initiative in setting up the London Institute for Contemporary Christianity, so it is appropriate that the link should be reflected in this volume.

The vision which inspired the founding of both centres went well beyond the conventional goals of academic institutions. Their distinctive aim was to equip lay people to penetrate the secular world with the gospel in ways that are not open to most pastors and clerics. Like the much advertised beverage, they can reach the parts that others cannot! However, to be effective in this rôle calls for both a personal integration of life under the lordship of Christ, and a commitment to proclaim the gospel. These are the themes of this section of the book.

James Houston is one of the few contemporary evangelicals who have really understood the importance of spirituality and the consequence of its neglect. How is it that 'born again' Christians are able to live quite comfortably in a secular society which, whilst it may tolerate religious faith in the private sphere, firmly denies it any place in the public domain? Houston finds the answer in a brand of piety which is little more than a set of do's and don'ts, and falls far short of being a living expression of the gospel. Too many of us have been influenced by a rationalism which tends to alienate mind from spirit, and leave us fragmented and lacking community. Dr Houston's antidote is the recovery of a full-orbed biblical and trinitarian spirituality which integrates knowing, feeling and doing. At its heart are prayer, self-giving and relationships, and it is a spirituality for all and not just for a priestly élite.

Underlying James Packer's essay on 'Authority in preaching' is a distinction between preaching and what he calls sermonizing or pulpiteering. All becomes clear when he defines preaching as 'the event of God bringing to an audience a Bible-based, Christ-related, life-impacting message of instruction and direction from himself through the words of a spokesperson'. He laments the decline in the frequency of such events, and suggests that low expectations are self-fulfilling. After analysing what it means for preaching to be marked by authority,

Dr Packer identifies some common hindrances to this, and four conditions that must be met if a preacher is to speak with genuine authority. The chapter is guaranteed to drive anyone aspiring to do so to their knees.

Such is the breadth of Michael Nazir-Ali's canvas that his essay could have been included in any section of the book. His discussion of the content of the faith is relevant to Part One, whilst that of the contexts in which divine revelation is given and received fits Part Two. At the same time, the chapter is a very personal reflection, and addresses the way in which Christians respond to the gospel, which makes it appropriate for Part Three, where it now appears.

The starting-point for Bishop Michael's essay is the paradox that God's Word – a word for all people in every age – can only be properly understood in relation to the contexts in which it was first given, and in which it is now received and lived. If we are willing to listen discerningly to the biblical insights of other contexts we can learn a lot. Bishop Michael goes on to illustrate this in relation to the doctrines of the Trinity, salvation, the incarnation and the atonement. The implication is a powerful one: no matter how substantial and orthodox the content of our faith is, it is worthless if it is not lived out in the context in which God has put us.

John Stott's links with All Souls Church, Langham Place, are well known. First as a curate, then as the rector, and since 1975 as Rector Emeritus, he has been involved in most of what has made that church so celebrated and effective in its ministry. Michael Green, himself well-known as an evangelist, and currently Professor of Evangelism at Regent College, is convinced that the local church is the primary agency in evangelism. He examines the life and activities of All Souls to discover what other local churches might learn from it in reaching out with the gospel to those who have a secular mind-set. The ten tactics he describes are neither the only ways nor foolproof techniques, but if they have not been tried already, most are worth considering in other situations. All Souls is certainly privileged in its peculiar combination of local opportunities and resources, but the key characteristics which have made it so effective are to be found wherever Christians are wanting to live the gospel.

Michael Cassidy's essay on 'The search for ministry effectiveness in the modern world' is an ideal chapter with which to end the book, because he confirms so much that has gone before. He identifies as the pre-requisites for ministry effectiveness a clear conversion, a good theological training and a well-disciplined personal life. He then proceeds to examine two spheres of ministry in which these can be applied, namely evangelism, and socio-political concern and compassionate care. In so doing, he speaks for all the contributors when he pays warm tribute to John Stott, not only for his public ministry but also for his private example. Those who have experienced only the former, know nothing of the time spent in prayer and study, and of the personal disciplines that are signs of one who lives the gospel which he proclaims.

MARTYN EDEN
DAVID F. WELLS

Spiritual life today

An appropriate spirituality for a post-modern world

James M. Houston

M y friendship with John Stott developed more closely when the London Institute for Contemporary Christianity – now part of Christian Impact – was first established in 1982. A major contribution to the original vision for the Institute came from a Christian business man, Ernst Van Eeghen, and his wife Erica, who, having visited Regent College in Vancouver, desired to help establish a similar venture in Europe. They were advised to locate it in London, where John Stott would be the ideal leader for such a Christian undertaking. Christian inter-disciplinary studies have been its emphasis ever since. Dr Stott's book on this theme was the product of these early years of the Institute.[1] The injunction of Matthew 25:31–46 has been long central to his vision of concern for the needy in the Third World, which was expressed in the Lausanne Covenant, of which he was the prime mover. Therefore this essay on spirituality bears in mind this balanced emphasis of both social and personal spirituality that John Stott embodies in his own ministry.

What is spirituality?

'Spirituality' is a word that has come into vogue today, partly in protest against a merely formal faith, and partly in the desire to renew the vitality of what is felt to be often lacking in religious practice. Spirituality refers to those attitudes, beliefs and practices that animate people's lives, to make them more sensitive to divine realities. In its original usage, *spiritualitas* was coined by the early Latin Fathers in North Africa, to designate all the activities of the Christian life as moved and inspired by the Holy Spirit, in contrast to the natural life of man. It was what the apostle calls *kata pneuma*, 'life according to the Spirit' (see Rom. 8:5).

'Spirituality' is also a word that is perhaps most characteristic of times of great social change and cultural upheaval. The word was first used in the fifth century, when the fall of Rome ushered in the earliest major upheaval after the bitter persecution of the church. It was then that the great spiritual renewal was identified with the Desert Fathers and their asceticism, which led to the rise of monasticism. This was motivated by the challenge of Matthew 19:16–22, to follow Jesus as his disciples. It was interpreted that to be a 'religious' was the 'more perfect way'.

In contrast, the second great social revolution was the Reformation, marked now by a rejection of monasticism. Luther's treatise *De Votis Monasticis*, in 1521, signals a new interpretation placed upon Christian spirituality, now in terms of the vocation of *all* Christians to express their faith in the market-place of life. This Protestant challenge was primarily felt by the Catholic Bishop of Geneva, Francis de Sales (1567–1622), who recognized that the growth of the church must be not by the clash of arms, nor by polemics, but by the deepening of the spirit of devotion among the laity.[2] Lay focus was now characteristic of some forms of French seventeenth-century piety, although 'La Spiritualité' came to be a pejorative term, to condemn the intensity of fervour of such laity as Madame Guyon.[3] So it was only later that Catholic 'spirituality' became an acceptable expression. However, in the Protestant world it has always been more acceptable to speak of a 'godly walk', or of 'practical divinity' among the Puritans, of 'holiness' in the Methodist tradition, or more generally of 'piety' or 'godliness'. 'Spirituality', then, is a new word for the Protestant faith that is engendering fresh dialogue between Protestant and Catholic traditions of discipleship.

Traditionally, the Roman Catholic Church has affirmed the religious life to be *status perfectionis acquirendae*, that is to say, a state orientated inherently towards the attainment of Christian perfection. Thomas Aquinas defined perfection as fullness of charity. This has been interpreted and defended in a twofold way. First, in permanently embracing the religious life in an institution, monks and nuns commit themselves publicly to this striving towards perfection. Secondly, the religious life includes the 'evangelical counsels', or threefold vows of poverty, chastity and obedience, which are assumed to be the means for the attainment of the perfection of charity, more easily so at least.[4] No-one can doubt that monasticism is a public demonstration of intent to take Christian discipleship seriously, even when in the history of monasticism it has also been abused and corrupted in ways that Luther, himself a former monk, had clearly recognized personally. Recently, one Catholic writer on discipleship has courageously recognized this, saying: 'The charisms of the religious life have a way of facilitating growth towards perfection. This is not enough, though, to make religious life the only "state" oriented towards the attainment of perfection.'[5]

Since this statement about perfection and monasticism can be misleading in reference to the common vocation to holiness, and the connection that all forms of Christian life have to holiness, we can understand why the Vatican Council later abandoned it in the texts especially dedicated to 'the religious life', that is *Lumen Gentium* and *Perfectae Caritatis*. At the same time, one is struck by the élitist language still used in these documents, in the frequent use of comparatives. So we read that the 'religious' who desire to derive 'still more abundant fruit' from the grace of baptism are to consecrate themselves in a more 'intimate way' to the service of God.[6] We are also told that 'the religious state of life, in bestowing greater freedom from the cares of earthly existence . . . reveals more clearly . . . the heavenly goods which are already present in this age . . . preluding our future resurrection . . .'.[7] It is a way of life that comprises 'a closer imitation . . . of the form of life which the Son of God made His own . . .'.[8] Indeed, according to *Perfectae Caritatis*, religious men and women are those who set out to follow Christ with great liberty, and are able to follow Jesus 'more closely'.[9] So in spite of pastoral reforms in the wake of Vatican II, there is no hint whatever that monasticism, and the dualism of Christian living implicit in its practice, will be faced or abolished, either institutionally or doctrinally.

Thus the dilemma of Roman Catholic spirituality today is that still too much focus is being placed upon 'the religious' to the detriment of the 'ordinariness of lay living', as the Jesuits, Gannon and Traub, reflect in their book, *The Desert and the City*:

The Christian life is seen to have a double movement. It is a life of dying with Christ, a life of the cross, a life beyond the aims and purposes that belong to this world alone. But at the same time Christian life is an incarnation, an acceptance of the world for its transformation by faith, a hopeful witness to the victory of the risen Christ made visible in history by his power of healing, preservation, and redemption – a witness carried on in the world.[10]

So they add: 'to speak of a spirituality, especially a spirituality for our time, thus involves an option not for the desert *or* the city, but the desert *and* the city – withdrawal and involvement'.[11]

This still leaves the issue: Do we opt to choose one of two forms of spirituality, to remain a 'lay' person or a 'religious' person? Or are the 'lay' and the 'religious' one person, with one spirituality? Lozano, whom we quoted earlier, puts it more bluntly:

By going to the root of the question it becomes clear that a hierarchical order of life styles is founded on the concept of a dichotomy between God and the world which is common to all Hellenistic spiritualities, but has nothing to do with the Bible. All forms of Christian life are founded on a relationship with God and all are oriented toward the world, although in different ways.[12]

Perhaps then it is more to meet psychological than truly spiritual needs of man, that we have to divide 'religious' from 'lay' forms of spirituality. Perhaps such institutional need is more centred upon man than upon God, so that it requires us to identify our spiritual seriousness.

Is evangelical piety in decline today?

If dualism has been the besetting issue of the Roman Church, pluralism has evidently been the weakness of Protestant spirituality.[13] While Protestants generally have never regretted the passing of monasticism, a few like the pietist Gerhard Tersteegen have done so, on the grounds of needing some institutional shelter for the practice of devotion.[14] Instead, Protestant spirituality has been left with a set of actions, normative for living such a life. But they have been intangible, dependent upon the spirit of the culture in large part. Once the culture changes, the piety seeks new forms in which to stabilize its spirit. Such patterns of piety have tended to become increasingly unstable, so that today, in an era of massive changes, the format of previous piety is dying, or at least is of much less relevance than before. This is the thrust of Edward Farley's book, *Requiem for a Lost Piety*, where he asserts: 'Most of the pieties that made up traditional Protestant piety are now meaningless to the contemporary Christian. The language and the vocabulary of such piety have become empty and hollow.'[15] It is not the Christian faith itself that is dying, but the historical embodiments of it. As evangelicals, we have largely inherited a Victorian form of piety: of family prayers, morning and evening; a strict observance of the Sabbath; a rigid tabooism of all that has been defined as 'worldly', such as dancing, card-playing and alcohol; a strong focus upon evangelism, at home and abroad; and a style of religious leadership, not dissimilar to colonialism, in its psyche.

Clearly, these practices have worn thin or become superseded. Bible study has become less 'devotional' and more 'inductive' study. Family prayers have almost gone out of practice as timetables within the family have become more mobile and family life itself has generally become less cohesive. Paternal authority has been eroded away with new peer pressures. The phenomenon of 'the teenager' has been socially invented, largely for the commercial market. Working mothers and feminism have brought new rules and attitudes into family life.

The Protestant passion to understand the Scriptures, rather than the Catholic posture of Mary's attitude of 'receiving' the Word of God, has made Protestant theology much more vulnerable to the impact of the rationalism of the Enlightenment.[16] Reformation theology played a central role in Reformed piety, such as we see in the insistence of Puritan 'practical divinity', which is a serious study of theology combined with a serious application of it in the daily walk with God. But Protestant theology today has become largely secular and even atheist.[17] Hence the decline of Protestant theology in public life has influenced the decline of its piety commensurately. Nor is the vacuum of true piety being filled by evangelical faith, for activism rather than piety is the way of life in modern evangelicalism. Respectability has become the hallmark of contemporary living. As Reinhold Niebuhr observed astutely: 'The Church does not seem to realize how unethical a conventionally respectable life may be.' Rather, the daily decisions of life are much more likely to be those of the advertising industry and of the secular mind-set around us. Biblical faith is not married to a way of life that expresses the central message of the gospel. Indeed, one of the great weaknesses of many evangelicals is the easy assumption that the whole content of the gospel is already known, so the main focus is therefore communication of it to others. This arises out of an emphasis upon a once-for-all-conversion, that is now behind the convert, so henceforth it is simply a matter of its promotion to others.

There is a certain falsity about this, because our transformation of life never ceases. In this sense, the medieval monks had more realization that the process of conversion was lifelong. As *conversi*, they had been, were and would still be, converted. Conversion should then be parsed in three tenses: past, present and future. The 'born-again' emphasis tends to express, however, one singular experience of God's Spirit in all of one's life, and to ignore the need of any radical changes of personality and of natural temperament thereafter.[18] Since 'Functional Man' describes much of the character of our contemporary culture, what we 'do' defines most people's definition of life, and personal identity. 'Being' a Christian is overlooked, in the concentration of what is 'done'. The dominance of 'doing' over 'being' leads those who assume they know the gospel then to promote many wares on its behalf. Perhaps it is this that helps explain the emptiness that some of us feel about all the 'packaging' of evangelical promotionalism. Church services or para-church organizations are busy promoting what needs to be 'done', without much scrutiny about what is actually happening. Religious organizations often exist like fraudulent companies that really are not in business, other than in the minds of shareholders who have not yet discovered that they are financially supporting non-existent companies. Such 'talk' without a close 'walk' with God is the reason why so many today are getting hungry for reality, and therefore for spirituality.

Recent books being written by evangelicals who have moved over to Rome often express their frustrations with evangelicalism. Ultimately they have moved for personal reasons, not always very convincing to others. Yet two explanations do stand out. One is the hollowness of what they hopefully have left behind them. So, Tom Howard writes, 'Evangelical is not enough.'[19] What is 'not enough' is really the way in which the Christian life has been presented 'evangelically'. The confusion about knowing the will of God, the distrust about the use of symbolism, the shallowness of worship, the inadequacy of prayer, the over-reaction in the total ignoring of Mary, Mother of Jesus, the loss of a liturgical sense, the ahistorical absence of a sense of tradition and the loss of the historical continuity of the church, either in the liturgical year or in the communion of saints – these are some of the motives given for default in evangelicalism. Many converts to Rome express their appreciation of the *Magisterium* that gives them a sense of authoritative continuity from the early church onwards, and of an ultimate frame of authority.[20] Not all of these are fully expressed, nor can they always rationally be communicated. Often the deepest causes are only convincing at a more subliminal level, of a more intimately personal story, that may not be too convincing to others.

Such reasons for leaving Protestantism to embrace Roman Catholicism may signify not so much a change of doctrine, as a response to a felt personal need, to nurture a deeper, more satisfying piety than the former, discarded mode seems capable of providing. This is a concern for spirituality, by which we mean the lived experience of the Christian faith, so that it reflects upon the conception that doctrine arouses in the religious consciousness and practice. There is a new sense today that the gospel cannot merely be described and known about cognitively. It needs to be personally experienced in such a manner that the life of the gospel is not only personally observed, but goes on being experienced incrementally. Thus spiritual life is seen to be an ongoing growth and maturation. So when we read a history of an evangelical movement, such as George Marsden narrates in his *Reforming Fundamentalism*,[21] and we sense a mere political triumphalism, or when we experience yet more hucksterism and commercialism in para-church organizations, or when we witness the secular spirit in which things are often done in the name of the Lord, then we may indeed become convinced that evangelical piety is dead in many areas of the church today. Why else would so many contemporary North American evangelical leaders be using the help of Roman Catholic spiritual directors for their own personal guidance, if this were not so? At least this has been my own observation, that many evangelical leaders have few insights into how to guide their own interior lives, let alone that of their flocks.

The challenge of the post-modern world

Since the 1980s, there has been a broad interest in the effects of Enlightenment thinking upon modernity. It began in the wake of the technological excesses of the arms race, and the global fears of atomic warfare. Is there a future for a society based solely upon science and technology? The answer has been a resounding 'No!' The modern world of reason and science is now being rejected by post-modernity, simply because the promises given by autonomous thinking have failed to provide the security and happiness mankind was looking for. The Enlightenment was a necessary step to correct the errors of superstitious dogmas, but it could not pull all aspects of human life into another strait-jacket of 'scientific explanation'. Reason itself needs to be kept within reasonable bounds. As Lesslie Newbigin has said: 'The liberation of our rational faculties from the control of "dogma" has not, apparently, led us into a world which is rational, which is "meaningful". We are once again at a point where accepted "explanations" no longer explain.'[22] The total explanation of life by science, or indeed the explanation by Enlightenment theology of the Christian life, have fallen down like false idols from their perches. Yet it is this peaceful co-existence of biblical faith and Enlightenment culture within the church that has created a dichotomy between a privatized faith and a publicly acceptable way of thinking, that has left the church anaemic, worldly, and helpless to change the lives of men and women to grow in godliness.

So what is required today is a new fiduciary framework of knowledge that is both publicly and privately seen and accepted. 'The self-evident truths of autonomous reason' must be challenged on a broad level of society. This is where Newbigin and others are calling for a new 'Augustinianism' that will turn the mode of thinking, 'I understand in order that I may believe', on its head and reassert, 'I believe that I may understand', as Augustine, Anselm and all true theologians have always recognized. The church needs no more apologize for its faith than science, which also has to learn to do so. Writers like Michael Polanyi, in his important book *Personal Knowledge*, are seeing this fiduciary basis as necessary for all knowledge. Polanyi observes:

> We must now recognise belief once more as the source of all knowledge. Tacit assent and intellectual passions, the sharing of an idiom and of a cultural heritage, affiliation to a like-minded community: such are the impulses which shape our vision of the nature of things on which we rely for our mastery of things. No intelligence, however critical or original, can operate outside such a fiduciary framework.[23]

Even the belief that our minds can somehow correspond to the reality of things outside of us is faith indeed, without which science could never operate.

The refusal to recognize the primary rôle of belief over knowing is what causes such alienation of our modern culture. It is, observes Colin Gunton, 'the tearing apart of belief and knowledge'.[24] From this over-esteemed capacity for mental detachment there comes the exaggerated rôle of the mind in the organization of knowledge. Immanuel Kant added a further cause of alienation when he insisted that knowledge, to be knowledge, must have certainty, with no ways of indulging in the uncertainties of belief. For rationalistic Christians, there is no way they can therefore rely upon a deep, Johannine abiding in Christ, since their faith can be only a set of propositional truths that are dependent upon cold logic. Such proponents of 'truth' act as if they did not recognize what Arthur Holmes has asserted: 'All truth is God's truth.'[25]

The result is an alienation within the Christian community itself, of those who have a deep relational repose in the truth of God from those who have an impersonal rationalistic faith. It is a tragic rift between believers, even in the same theological school. For it leads to another level of alienation, where there is a divorce between natural reasoning and moral reasoning. It is then that being and doing, thinking and knowing, knowing and acting are alienated from each other. The seriousness of this in our society is apparent when lawyers are merely technicians of the law, not concerned with being executives of justice. Likewise in our 'information society', it becomes so natural for theological education to be merely the purveyor of theological 'talk', not schools for the nurture of godly persons. Likewise, so much of the focus of evangelical para-church organizations is descriptive of need, or the promotion of information, not the actualization of felt need. Hence we sense the shadowy character of so much Christian life today, a playing with the faith, instead of living its embodiment.

The intensification of this alienation between mind and spirit shows signs of disintegration in our culture. The great philosophers of our century, Martin Heidegger and Ludwig Wittgenstein, have each in his own way been telling us that we are confused, fragmented, inauthentic beings, separated from reality by an impenetrable wall. Wittgenstein takes away the illusions to leave us with a new void. Heidegger creates a new language to expose our illusions. Both show that man lives neither by logic nor by mind alone, and that these are a small part of the human soul. Indeed, we may note that if 'Feudal Man' influenced so much the medieval consciousness, and 'Rational Man' has been so characteristic of the Newtonian world-view of modernity, 'Psychological Man' now challenges post-modern consciousness. The human person is now being psychoanalysed in such depth that human communication is likewise being taken into such nuances of the subliminal. A rationalistic, factual level of communication no longer touches the deep issues of human consciousness, anymore than the recovery of a drug addict can be effected by middle-class social conventionalism. Those living in the shallows of social conventionality cannot reach out to those living in the depth of psychic hurt and enquiry. How Christians can communicate without being anti-intellectual, and yet not merely rationalist, is a new challenge of Christian life. A Christian spirituality, then, needs to take into account the range of human emotions, affections, sensitivities, human individuation, and indeed the whole range of insights of what it means to be 'human' and a 'person'.

Unfortunately, such challenges only make the rationalists the more defensive, and assume that their hold upon reason and truth has to be held at all costs, against what they see threatening them as being anti-intellectual. 'New Age' gnosticism only adds to the cultural disintegration that is occurring. The legitimate fears of this contemporary mood of consciousness as heretical, as indeed it is, is causing over-reaction. For much interest in spirituality is also being assessed as 'New Age'. This is a tragic misunderstanding that only intensifies disintegration in Christian communication as well.

It is easy to caricature today the deep spirituality of the Christian as 'being out for lunch', even 'a deviation' from biblical faith, without any examination of the doctrinal faith attested by those who, as simply lovers of God, have personally experienced the presence of God in their lives. Are the theophanies of the Bible also to be written off, so that Jacob did not wrestle mysteriously with the stranger at the brook Jabbok? Did Moses not experience the presence of God at the burning bush? Did Isaiah not hear the call of God in the midst of his holy presence in the temple? Indeed, was Saul of Tarsus not struck down by the light in the heavens? Have not many of God's people had striking and arresting conversion experiences, or others felt God's presence in the shadow of death in serious illness, that we cannot investigate empirically, though we see great transformation of their lives afterwards?

What proposals then should be made for a renewed effort to integrate spirituality and Christian truth for post-modern man? This we can never programme nor indeed plan. It must be the manifestation of God's own Spirit working in our midst. Yet we may see certain signs of what we need in our own orientation towards the truth of the gospel in our times.

Knowledge of God and knowledge of ourselves

One disintegrating feature of modern man is that it is assumed that human beings can achieve self-knowledge without any reference to God, as secular psychology now practises. Unfortunately, much theology gives the opposite impression that knowledge of God can be discussed without much or any reference to man. A new integrative approach is needed that makes either of these clearly impossible.

Neo-platonism was comparable to modern psychology in the ancient world. It assumed that human self-knowledge was achievable. A conversion to one's self and then a conversion to God is what characterizes the teachings of Plotinus and Porphyry that Augustine, in turn, was challenged to refute. 'Let me know Thee, O Lord, who knowest me: let me know Thee as I am known', was his prayer.[26] True, Augustine admits in his *Confessions* that he read the works of the Neo-platonists, and at one stage of his search was much influenced by them. 'Admonished by these books to return to myself, I entered into the intimacy of myself under your guidance, and I was able to do so because you have become my helper. I entered, and I saw, with whatever eye of my soul, above the same eye of my soul, the unchangeable light.'[27] Like the light that struck down Saul of Tarsus, Augustine was forced to see that his conversion was wholly the gift of God's grace. So he meditates on Psalm 70:2: 'From which I am converted to you, made new by you – I who was made by you, reformed – I who was formed; no merit of mine can be said to have preceded my being converted, but your grace has gratuitously come to me, so that I might be mindful of your justice alone.' Today, too, we need a renewed Augustinian confrontation with secular psychology, to challenge man's own efforts to know himself, without God's grace and revelation.

Consistently throughout the history of the church, its great leaders have recognized the intrinsic nature of this twofold knowledge, of God and of self. Bernard of Clairvaux in the twelfth century refuses to separate this twofold knowledge. 'Know yourself and you will have a wholesome fear of God; know Him and you will also love Him.' 'You must avoid both kinds of ignorance, because without fear and love salvation is not possible.'[28] Humility stems from the fear of God and pride arises from its ignorance. Likewise, argues Bernard, despair arises from ignorance of God. Many other medieval Christian writers maintained this insistence upon the twofold knowledge of God and of self. Then, impressively, John Calvin begins the *Institutes* with the same emphasis: 'Without knowledge of self there is no knowledge of God. Nearly all the wisdom we possess, that is true and sound wisdom, consists of two parts: the knowledge of God and of ourselves.'[29] Calvin implies by this that we are not autonomous beings, so that to think of ourselves is to think of the creator who made us first. Moreover our very poverty, he recognizes, 'better discloses the infinitude of benefits we receive from God'.[30] Again, 'it is certain that man never achieves a clear knowledge of himself unless he has first looked upon God's face, and then descends from contemplating Him to scrutinize himself'.[31] For pride always deceives us to see ourselves better than we really are. All of us are prone to self-deception and hypocrisy. What Bernard calls 'fear of God', Calvin calls 'reverence for God', which, combined with love of God, are pre-requisites for piety, and for any knowledge of God. In a well-known statement, Calvin defines true religion as 'faith so joined with an earnest fear of God that this fear also embraces willing reverence, and carries with it such legitimate worship as is prescribed by law'.[32] Knowledge then, is interlaced with piety, in such a way that we can never separate godliness from true knowledge, nor can we really know ourselves without reference to God. For God is the giver of rationality about the world that he has made.

How we know ourselves in the sight of God introduces us to the Law of God, the Scriptures. Calvin uses the analogy of our human need of glasses by which to see properly. 'So Scripture, gathering up the otherwise confused knowledge of God in our minds ... clearly shows us the true God.'[33] In our sinful condition our minds are too perverted to see clearly without the Scriptures. They point us to an eschatological perspective, that is itself essential to give meaning to the present and the past. As Paul states: 'For now we see in a mirror dimly, but then face to face. Now I know in part; then I shall understand fully, even as I have been fully understood' (1 Cor. 13:12, RSV). The Holy Spirit is now already enlightening us, so an openness to the future, in God's hands, is leading us forward into more knowledge of God's ways. The same God in the narrative of the Bible, in times past, is still leading his people forward into the future.

Yet it is this scriptural focus on knowing God that keeps in balance a God who hides himself as *Deus Absconditus* with a God who chooses to reveal himself as he will in his world, *Deus Revelatus*. So man is clearly limited by *what* he can know of God, and in *how* he can know God. This cannot be theological speculation then, neither in the philosophy of religion, nor in an intellectual curiosity that does not unite mind and heart under the influence of the Spirit of God. Likewise, Scripture itself must be allowed to speak from its own authority. It can neither be reduced to a series of propositional statements, nor can it be accepted or rejected selectively, according to the prevailing intellectual climate. For that reason, it must be interpreted afresh, in each new generation. For faith is needed personally by each generation to assimilate its unchanging truth in their own context.

The meaning of being human challenges our spirituality

If we challenge our age by holding a unity of self-knowledge with divine knowledge, then our understanding of what it means to be human is also contrasted with the views of the world. The view of John Locke that belief is a lesser form of knowledge has been radically challenged by the re-emplacement of fiduciary knowledge. But also challenging the Enlightenment view of man as 'the autonomous knower' is the Christian acknowledgment that man is to surrender himself to God, and to depend upon God for all aspects of his existence and relationships.

The personalness of God takes on new meaning when we acknowledge that an 'individual' is man alone, one of an aggregate, without personal relationships. But becoming a 'person' is intrinsically progressive, as we grow in relationships with other real people. For our relational wounds arise from childhood onwards, when others have not known how to treat us as unique beings. Indeed, we learn to realize that only God knows and loves us adequately, as unique persons. We do not even know how to handle our own uniqueness, other than in anxiety, by comparing ourselves inadequately with others, or in pride in comparing ourselves arrogantly before others. In the same manner, children are early wounded in parenting, when their unique persons are not adequately accepted, or appreciated, or nurtured. Ultimately, we are all cast back upon God, our creator and redeemer, who alone can give fullness and redemption to our wounded personalities.

Recently, Glenn Tinder asked, 'Can we be good without God?', showing that many of the virtues of liberal democracy, such as belief in the dignity and equality of all people, have strong roots in the union of the spiritual and the political, achieved in the vision of Christianity.[34] Likewise, I have recently written elsewhere of the uniqueness of the Christian faith in a personal God to uphold the personal being of man.[35] No other religion has this foundation of man's personalness being posited in the personal of God himself. The Greeks could conceive of the person as merely a mask-bearer, playing a brief rôle on the tragic stage of life, before being crushed by the inscrutability of the impersonal fates. The Romans could only give the head of the family the legal status of a 'person', but as *paterfamilias* this was a right of property, not an intrinsic relationship. Only Christian faith has upheld and made intrinsic the creation of man to be a person, primarily because he is made in the image and likeness of God, and secondarily as reaching out to love of neighbour as well as love of God.

We may well doubt if any philosophy, left to its own devices, could ever have developed a concept of the person, except it be in the context of Christian faith. The nearest word the Greeks could have for it was the pronoun *autos*, like the Latin *ipse*, that is expressive of an attitude which leads us rather into the isolation of the self, inwardly convoluted up on the self. This is our classical heritage, as our secularized Western world is now reaping, in its own narcissism.

Augustine was the first great Christian thinker to study seriously the doctrine of the person. Significantly, he does so in his treatise *On the Holy Trinity*. He wrote this against the Arians, who had argued that only God is substance. The Father is Unbegotten, the Son is Begotten; each are clearly different. Therefore the Son is different in his substance from that of the Father. Augustine counters this by arguing that relation transcends substance, so that the Father is related in his whole substance with the Son, standing in living relation with the Son. This leads Augustine to declare that a Divine Person is at one and the same time a Reality identical with Itself, *in se* an Absolute, and yet also a Reality *ad alium*, directed essentially towards others. That is to say, God's essence is also relational, so that God alone is personal, constituting in his tri-personal Being a network of mutually inclusive relationships. Absolute unity, and yet distinction in love, becomes then the divine prototype for that independence, sympathy and originality that man has also as a person-in-relationship. God is the Lover, the Loved and Love. So man, too, can have that existence, understanding and life which proceed from God as Father, Son and Holy Spirit.[36]

Trinitarian spirituality alone is Christian

As we interpret our personhood as that of the image and likeness of God, we see our openness, not to live instinctually for ourselves, but relationally for others, and in communication with others. The incommunicability of pride makes it such an evil, in denying man's openness, above all towards God. This attitude is exhibited by Augustine, profoundly so, in his *Confessions*; a classic indeed, of both God and man. Likewise, *The City of God* is a classic of the communion between God and man, both now and in eternity. Both point us strongly towards the centrality of the doctrine of the Trinity in our faith. Contemporaneously with these works, the Nicene Creed (AD 325) had established centrally that theology and godliness went inseparably together, so that it was God's own character that defined the nature and content of godliness. As Hilary of Poitiers was to say in his great work, *On the Trinity*: 'in faith a person takes his stand on the ground of God's own being', and again 'God cannot be apprehended except through himself'.[37] 'Godliness', then, may be properly interpreted as expressive of a lived relationship in the triune God, personally experienced. As

Athanasius was also to affirm: 'He who believes in God is not cut off from godliness, and he who has godliness really believes.'

Of course, this teaching itself was warrant in the apostle's affirmation: 'Beyond all question, the mystery of godliness is great: He appeared in a body, was vindicated by the Spirit, was seen by angels, was preached among the nations, was believed on in the world, was taken up in glory' (1 Tim. 3:16). Such an affirmation of the incarnation lays the basis then for worship of the true God, which in turn unites theology with ethics, so that there is a continuum from faith through truth, to behaviour and to worship. This is in keeping with Paul's further teaching: 'What you heard from me, keep as the pattern of sound teaching, with faith and love in Christ Jesus. Guard the good deposit that was entrusted to you – guard it with the help of the Holy Spirit who lives in us' (2 Tim. 1:13–14). This trinitarian faith is the true test of Christian spirituality when it is being questioned by rationalistic brethren, who may question if it has the age-long Neoplatonist flavour, or the 'New Age' influence of today. Trinitarian spirituality is incompatible with either one or the other. As H. P. Owen has pointed out in his essay on the orthodox English mystics, experience and dogma are united. For they did not experience some unidentified reality, which they conveniently labelled God, but their conscious faith informed their personal experience of God. So looking at much of their writings Owen makes the reflective conclusion:

> The God whom these mystics worship and with whom they claim to be united is not a nameless Absolute; he is the God who has revealed himself in the three persons of Father, Son, and Holy Spirit. In these writings there is no suggestion of belief in a supra-personal Godhead that lies behind this triune form. The Trinity (it is assumed) expresses the whole of God's nature.[38]

Likewise the Christian doctrines of creation, incarnation, atonement, grace, the church as the body of Christ, are all upheld, so that they do not enunciate new dogmas concerning God and Christ on the basis of their experiences. Nor do biblically-minded believers today, who likewise affirm the great need for deepened spirituality.

Why then are some evangelicals so suspicious of 'spirituality' today? Is it because it is critical of the politics of evangelicalism? Because wherever power and status are defended, indeed needed, the human spirit will become more apparent than the Spirit of God. Is it because of the hidden desire to be personally in control of one's life, which a rationalistic, fundamentalistic type of person tends to portray? Is it because some of us are ill-equipped to deal with our emotions, so they get suppressed, along with the great upwelling of desire that God has implanted within us? So we tolerate addictive types of ministry that reflect more about our temperaments than the divine calling. Is it possible that we have faith about doctrine, but little faith about personal transformation of our own persons in Christ? Is it because we place a much higher emphasis upon external actions of 'ministry' than upon the life of prayer? Is it because our public 'persona' matters more to us than our life that is 'hid with Christ in God'? Our resistance to true spirituality can therefore be as personally varied and distinct as our own will.

As we reflect upon the trinitarian framework of our calling as Christians, however, we listen to Jesus' prayer to his Father: 'As you sent me into the world, I have sent them into the world' (Jn. 17:18). Such an apostolate, or 'sending' (*apostello*), conveys with it all the plenipotentiary authority and power representative of the One who sends them. Our own parents 'sent' us into the world, wounded and sinful, so that our eidetic emotions from childhood, and our fallen nature by birth, still handicap us emotionally before others, and keep us sinners before God. But to be 'sent' into the world as Christ was 'sent' into the world is an awesome mystery, equipped with all the relational life of the divine community of Father, Son and Holy Spirit; not in any tritheism, but in the One God, manifest to us in 'the grace of our Lord Jesus Christ, and the love of God, and the fellowship of the Holy Spirit' (2 Cor. 13:14). If this quality of life, in trinitarian spirituality, is our biblical mandate, then clearly it is not optional for the Christian that some should seek it and others be indifferent to its claims.

Conclusion

Just as *accidie* was the affliction of boredom with a feudalized and monastic way of life, and *melancholia* left 'Renaissance Man' and 'Rational Man' depressed in the sixteenth and seventeenth century, so *alienation* leaves post-modern man isolated and lacking community and friendship. Christian spirituality today has to address this challenge with a revitalized trinitarian faith. For alienation implies much more than loneliness; it is expressive also of the separation between being and doing, between faith and thought, between the individual and the community. Nor is it all attributable to the Enlightenment, though this has had profound impact. In reacting to its infuence we now speak of 'post-modernity'. But, most basically, we can trace throughout the history of Western thought the low emphasis of biblical and therefore trinitarian spirituality, in contrast to the compelling influences of Roman pragmatism in organization and control, and of Greek visualization in mental detachment and speculation. Instead, the following convictions need to be given redirection and focus in the shaping of the Christian life and ministry for our future.

1. We cannot separate prayer from theology, nor theology from prayer. If the triune God is personal and communicative in self-revelation, as we believe from the biblical evidence and from our own encounter with him, then prayer is not just one of the spiritual disciplines we may adopt, as perhaps a substitute for jogging in the morning, but the heart of our faith. The early Greek Fathers interpreted *theologia* as the knowledge of the triune God in the contemplation of God as he is in himself. Thus *theologia* is primarily the realm of prayer, and of the personal walk of the believer and worshipper before God, not of scholarly disputation and abstracted description of his ways. Prayer needs therefore to be placed once more in the centre of Christian life, as communing with the communing God. As all personal knowledge is participatory of prayer and worship, 'doing theology' will then take on new understanding.

2. So much of church life and Christian ministry is like a great publishing house that is turning out maps for the expert to read, but it leaves the uninitiated emotionally lost in the mountainous terrain of life. When our life is split between the great chasms of 'being and doing', between the public masks of official action and of public rôle-playing and the inner lack of personal assurance and of identity in Christ, then we all need mountain guides as well as maps. It is the personal giving of ourselves, of becoming 'epistles of Christ, known and read of all men', that is desperately needed, not just more 'talk', more public promotion, more entrepreneurs for organized ministry. However, the giving of our own persons on behalf of others demands freedom from our own emotional addictions, even freedom from addictive ministries. That is why spiritual direction is so much needed today, and why there are so few available to practise it. Indeed, it contradicts much of what purports to be ministry, and undermines what purports to be 'successful'.

3. Relationships lie at the heart of our Christian faith and practice. For clearly we can only know God as his Holy Spirit reveals his truth to us, through his living Word, and as Christ is our one Mediator between God and man. Crucial to this awareness are the words of

Jesus: 'No-one knows the Son except the Father, and no-one knows the Father except the Son and those to whom the Son chooses to reveal him' (Mt. 11:27). 'Now they know', prays Jesus to the Father, 'that everything you have given me comes from you' (Jn. 17:7). Friendship lies at the heart of God, not as we tend to use and abuse friendships, but as God's Holy Spirit would transform our friendship.[39] Yet the notion of friendships in ministry today is still viewed with much suspicion, because of their 'exclusive' or 'divisive', or simply 'indiscreet' connotations. Yet it is one of the attractive qualities of great thinkers like Augustine that his spirituality is so much associated with his fearless joy in spiritual friendship. Such examples teach us that without a friend, nothing is friendly, not even the church and its ministry. So we do not talk of a Ciceronian version of friendship when we speak of the desperate need of our alienated society for Christian friendship as a reflection of the triune God in our lives. As Augustine would teach us, 'Friendship cannot be true unless you [God] solder it together among those who cleave to one another by the charity poured forth in our hearts by the Holy Spirit.' Again he says, 'You did not look down . . . on being the friend of the humble and returning the love that was shown to you. For what else is friendship but this? It gets its name from love alone, is faithful only in Christ, and in Him alone can it be eternal and happy.'[40]

4. Having a heart for God, with affections graciously directed by him, also lies centrally in the Scriptures. 'My son, give me your heart' (Pr. 23:26). A spirituality of the heart before God thus represents the mystery of the whole being of the human person, in a redemptive and unitive manner. It expresses our openness to the transcendent grace of God in every aspect of our daily lives, so that the lordship of Christ is felt and accepted in the depth of our emotions as well as in the heights of our greatest thoughts. Yet today we live in much fear and ignorance of our emotions. *Affectus*, in its centrality in the life and teachings of Augustine and Bernard of Clairvaux, implied the constant inclination, disposition and consonance of mind, will, desire and love for God. Jonathan Edwards, in his profound treatise on *The Religious Affections* (1746), saw deeply that the greater the measure to which we respond to divine truth by gracious affections, the more we are witnessing authentically the truth that is in Christ. How serious a matter it is then to cultivate affections appropriate to the truths we know, so that they clothe us as truthful witnesses of the gospel.[41]

5. Essentially, then, the Christian life is 'the common life' that we can and should share in the trinitarian life of Father, Son and Holy

Spirit. There can be nothing élitist about this. So it gives us all profound incentive, whether lay or ordained, to live in the communion of saints. This should encourage us all to have a deep awareness of the rich heritage we have in the history of spiritual movements, of life at the grass-roots of the church, which in terms of traditional church history requires a reformed epistemology, so set is it in its worldly fascination with councils, cardinals and courts. The desperate need of community life today will not simply be resolved by community projects, pilots though they may be. It will arise when we see that our own personhood remains impoverished as long as we remain individualistic in our ministry and in our inner motives. Only as persons-in-relationship, recognizing that life is both ultimately and immediately relational, can we give hope for a fragmented, alienated society. To listen to the hurts of others, to place a premium on the uniqueness of each person, to see our identity in the heart of Christ and not simply held in our own grasping hands, these are some of the radically contrasted ways in which we stand against the world. Trinitarian spirituality alone can give us a motive for such a way of living and sharing together.

We pray with the apostle Paul:

> that out of his glorious riches he may strengthen you with power through his Spirit in your inner being, so that Christ may dwell in your hearts through faith. And I pray that you, being rooted and established in love, may have power, together with all the saints, to grasp how wide and long and high and deep is the love of Christ, and to know this love that surpasses knowledge – that you may be filled to the measure of all the fullness of God.
>
> (Eph. 3:16–19)

Authority in preaching

J. I. Packer

John Stott is a minister of the Word of God – that is, a preacher of it: expository, didactic, faithful, clear, weighty, masterful, exemplary. He has written two books on the preacher's role and function, and his style – his intonation, even – has constantly been the object of that imitation which, for better or for worse, is in truth the sincerest form of flattery. In celebration of his world-wide eminence as a preacher, I offer now some footnotes on the theology and spirituality of the preaching enterprise. 'I solemnly charge you, Timothy, in the presence of God and of Christ Jesus who will judge the living and the dead, by his appearing and his kingdom, to preach the Word of God. Never lose your sense of urgency, in season or out of season. Prove, correct, and encourage, using the utmost patience in your teaching.' Thus J. B. Phillips, that prince of paraphrasts, renders the first two verses of 2 Timothy 4. Here, for our learning, are the aspects of the communicative action that Paul prescribes (they are all there in the Greek): proclamation, demonstration, correction, instruction. Here also is the commitment to the preaching ministry that Paul requires: press on, he says, with utmost energy and stick-to-it-iveness (a fine North American word that catches the force of *makrothymia* better than Phillips' 'patience'). Here, too, is the motivation that Paul himself felt: those called to be preachers must one day give account to their Master of their preaching; woe, then, to any who have not preached the gospel! And finally, here is a pointer to the authority that preaching is meant to convey: namely, the authority of God's message, relayed in God's presence by one who is seen himself to acknowledge the authority of what he is relaying. But I am running ahead of myself. Let us begin at the beginning.

The concept of preaching

First, I focus the concept of preaching the Word of God as I think it ought to be focused. Preaching, I urge, should not be defined institutionally or sociologically, but theologically and functionally. An institutional definition would present preaching in terms of buildings, pulpits and pews.[1] A sociological definition would view preaching as a special kind of monologue fulfilling specific corporate expectations on the part of the group being addressed. Both types of definition are no doubt useful in their place; but if one is, or hopes to be, a preacher oneself, and wants to know what fulfilling the ministry that Paul urged upon Timothy really involves, then a theological definition that shows what should happen when preaching takes place is what one needs. Here, then, is my attempt to formulate this concept in normative theological terms.

Christian preaching, I affirm, is *the event of God bringing to an audience a Bible-based, Christ-related, life-impacting message of instruction and direction from himself through the words of a spokesperson.* Observe the following points about this definition. First, it is *theological*: it conceptualizes preaching in terms not of human performance but of divine communication. Also, it is *prophetic*: it views God as speaking his own message via a messenger whose sole aim is to receive and relay what God gives. Furthermore, it is *incarnational*: for it envisages God embodying his communication in the person of the messenger who both delivers it and, in delivering it, models response to it. Phillips Brooks' famous delineation of preaching as 'the bringing of truth through personality'[2] points to the way in which personal attitudes to God and man come through in the course of declaring God's message. In the messenger-rôle of preachers as bearers of God's truth and wisdom to people whom God loves, their demeanour will always, for better or for worse, become part of their message, and affect the impact that they make. Jesus himself, God's incarnate Son, is of course the paradigm case here. Finally, this normative definition of preaching has a *critical* function to fulfil; for it obliges us to test pulpit utterances, and to say of any that was not Bible-based, Christ-related and life-impacting, in a sufficient sense, that, whatever else it was, it was not preaching in the full and proper meaning of that word.

So I do not equate preaching with what is called sermonizing or pulpiteering. Not every performance from the preacher's podium is preaching. It is notorious that some sermonizing produces only bitter wisecracks about the pulpit as coward's castle, and preachers as standing six feet above contradiction, talking at rather than to their hearers, climaxing invisibility during the week with incomprehensibility on Sunday, and so on. But such sermonizing, which is certainly bad preaching, may by my definition not be preaching at all, though the institutional and sociological definitions would compel us to call it that. From my theological standpoint, what is said from the pulpit is only preaching if its content conforms to the specifications stated above. Conversely, any communication that fulfils these specifications ought to be categorized as preaching, wherever and however it is done – as when Philip sat in the Ethiopian eunuch's chariot and 'told him the good news about Jesus' (Acts 8:45, NIV; KJV had 'preached unto him Jesus' – the Greek word is *euangelizomai*, one of the two main New Testament terms for declaring the gospel). For the New Testament, a Christian spokesman preaches (*kērysso*) only when some aspect of the God-given message concerning Christ (the *kērygma*) is the content of the utterance. This is not our usual modern way of looking at the matter, but it is the biblical way, and it is always best to follow the Bible.

Preaching as described is necessary for a healthy church. Without a regular diet of Bible-based, Christ-related, life-impacting messages from God, the mind-set of a congregation will become either institutionalist and sacramentalist (as in old-style Roman Catholicism where there was no effective preaching), or moralistic and legalistic (as in liberal Protestant congregations where the agenda is social service and God is expected to accept one for doing it). Where there is preaching of the type described, however, the Bible will be received as the Word of God, because it will constantly be impacting people as just that. Jesus Christ will be known and loved, because he will constantly be projected as lover and saviour of our souls; and Christians will grow and flourish through being fed on true spiritual food. Surely it is beyond dispute that a church made and kept healthy by authentic preaching must ever be our goal.

Today's evangelicalism has behind it a noble heritage of preaching.

The Reformation itself grew out of practical biblical preaching with Christ at the centre. The great Puritan movement (and it was great) was sustained on both sides of the Atlantic by preaching of this kind. The eighteenth-century revival in Britain and the Great Awakening in New England were profound spiritual movements with powerful evangelical preaching at their heart. In the nineteenth century, men like Charles H. Spurgeon sustained magnificent ministries by preaching in this fashion, and more recently men like Donald Barnhouse and Martyn Lloyd-Jones, and certainly John Stott himself, have done the same. But the great tradition is currently tapering off. Why is this? we ask. What has happened to eclipse the grand-scale presentations of the works, ways and will of God, through which evangelicalism once grew lively and strong? It is not, I think, that preachers as a body have stopped caring about preaching or trying to do it properly; the problem goes deeper, and arises in the first instance from the drift of our culture. We live in days in which the credibility of faithful biblical preaching is radically doubted, not only outside but also inside the churches, and misguided but insistent expectations on the part of listeners put many difficulties in the way of faithful preaching that were not there before. Five factors in particular operate in this way. We need to be aware of them, so I propose to review them now.

Factors behind the eclipse of preaching

1. *The prevalence of non-preaching in Christian pulpits has eroded awareness of what true preaching is.*

Lack of good models tends always to lower standards, and unfortunately good models have been in short supply throughout this century. Far too many pulpit discourses have been put together on wrong principles. Some have failed to open up Scripture; some have expounded biblical doctrine without applying it, thus qualifying as lectures rather than preachments (for lecturing aims only to clear the head, while preaching seeks to change the life); some have been no more than addresses focusing the present self-awareness of the listeners, but not at any stage confronting them with the Word of God; some have been mere statements of the preacher's opinion, based merely on his own expertise, rather than messages from God carrying avowed divine authority. Such discourses are less than preaching, as was stated previously, but because they were announced as sermons they are treated as preaching and people's idea of preaching gets formed in terms of them, so that the true conception of preaching is forgotten.

It is often said, and truly, that sermons must teach Bible truth, and that the renewal of preaching needed today will take its rise from a fresh awareness that this is so; my slighting reference to some content-laden sermons as lectures rather than preachments may therefore have seemed perplexing. But the truth is that preaching is more than teaching – not less, but more! Preaching is essentially teaching *plus* application (invitation, direction, summons), and where that *plus* is lacking something less than preaching takes place. Study of printed sermons from past generations reveals that older evangelical preachers kept a careful balance between doctrinal content as such (biblical orthodoxy) and practical and experiential applications (biblical ortho-praxy) – something like half and half in most messages.

In our day, however, the balance has been largely lost, and sermons tend to be either all doctrinal content without application, or all exhortation without doctrinal content; and to the extent to which either form of imbalance prevails, both types of utterance become instances of non-preaching, and very inadequate models, therefore, of what pulpit work ought to be. Many in our churches have never experienced preaching of the historic evangelical sort at all.

2. *Topical as distinct from textual preaching has become common.*

For sermons to explore announced themes rather than biblical passages is a twentieth-century development, and hardly a happy one. Why should it have occurred? Partly, I suppose, to make preaching appear interesting and important to a generation that has largely lost interest in the pulpit. Partly, too, I am sure, because many topical preachers do not trust their Bible enough to let it speak for itself and utter its own message through their lips. Whatever the reasons, how-ever, the results are unhealthy. In a topical sermon any text taken is reduced to a peg on which the speaker hangs his own line of thought. The shape and thrust of his message thus reflect no more than his own idea of what is good for people, and then the only authority that the sermon can have is the human authority of a knowledgeable person speaking with emphasis (raising his voice, perhaps, and even banging the pulpit). To my mind, topical sermons of this sort, no matter how biblical their component parts may be, cannot but fall short of being preaching in the full sense, just because in them the authority of God speaking is dissolved, more or less, into the authority of human religious expertise. Many in our churches have only ever been exposed to topical preaching of this kind: no wonder then that they do not appreciate what real preaching might be.

3. *Low expectations become self-fulfilling. Where little is expected from sermons, little is received.*

Many moderns have never been taught to expect sermons to matter much, and so their habit at sermon-time is to relax, settle back and wait to see if anything the preacher says will catch their interest. Most of today's congregations and preachers seem to be at one in neither asking nor anticipating that God will come to meet his people in the preaching; so it is no wonder if this fails to happen. According to your unbelief, we might say, be it unto you! Just as it takes two to tango, so ordinarily it takes an expectant, praying congregation, along with a preacher who knows what he is about, to make an authentic preaching occasion. A century ago, in Reformed circles in Britain, the regular question to a person coming from church was how did he or she 'get on' under the preaching of the Word: this reflected the expectancy of which I am speaking. Nowadays, however, on both sides of the Atlantic the commoner question is how did the preacher 'get on' in his stated pulpit performance. This shows how interest has shifted and the mental attitude has changed. It is now assumed that those who sit under the preaching are observers, measuring the preacher's performance, rather than participants waiting for the Word of God. Many in our congregations do not know that there is any other way of listening to sermons than this way of detached passivity, and no-one should be surprised to find that those who cultivate such passivity often dismiss preaching as an uneventful bore. Those who seek little find little.

4. *The power of speech to communicate significance has in our Western culture become suspect, so that any form of oratory, rhetoric, or dramatic emphasis, to show the weight and significance of stated facts, tends to alienate rather than convince.*

This development is due mainly to the media. On radio and television, strong expressions of feeling sound and look hysterical; cool and chatty intimacy is required if one is to communicate successfully. This standard of communicative sincerity is now applied everywhere. Prior to this century a preacher could use words dramatically and emphatically for up to an hour to set forth the majesty of God the king, the glory of Christ the saviour, the greatness of the soul, the momentous importance of eternity, and the significance of present reactions to the gospel message for determining personal destiny. Congregations appreciated the manner as being appropriate to the matter. Nowadays, that kind of utterance is widely felt to be false, as if passionate speech as such argues a purpose of browbeating and bludgeoning the mind, pulling the wool over the eyes, and carrying through a confidence trick. To avoid this suspicion, many preachers nowadays talk of spiritual life and death in a style better fitted to reading the sports results, and their cosy intimacy makes the theme itself seem trivial or unreal. The discrediting among us of grand-scale public speech puts preachers into what might well be felt to be a no-win situation.

It was my privilege, forty years ago, to spend a winter under the preaching ministry of the late Dr Martyn Lloyd-Jones, and to enjoy a working relationship with him for twenty years after that, so that I was able to observe from many angles his approach to the preacher's task. His gifts fitted him for grand-scale ministry, and his sense of spiritual reality told him that great things must be said in a way that projected their greatness. He could fairly be described as a nineteenth-century preacher born out of due time, and though he was fully aware that the older type of preaching had become suspect and unfashionable, he continued to practise it and to encourage others to do the same. Combining the electric energy of the orator with the analytical precision of the courtroom or the clinic, and focusing his businesslike rhetoric on the inner drama of the hound of heaven graciously capturing and changing sinners' benighted hearts, he communicated an overwhelming sense of the greatness of God and the weight of spiritual issues, and left behind him a large body of hearers, myself among them, who will for ever be thankful that as a modern man he deliberately swam against the stream and did the old thing. The vision of preaching that I gained from him stays with me, and what I am saying now reflects, I am sure, my experience of the power of preaching under his ministry. From the vantage-point that this experience gave me, I urge that the only real way forward for preachers today is to follow Dr Lloyd-Jones in cultivating an honesty with words that earns us the right to fly in the face of our laid-back culture and to dwell passionately, urgently, dramatically and at appropriate length, on the desperately important agenda of the relationship between God and man. In this, as in so much else, the old paths constitute the good way. But how few today, preachers or people, know it!

5. *Spiritual issues themselves are felt to be irrelevant by many church attenders.*

These are issues of radical repentance, self-despairing faith, costly cross-bearing as central to discipleship, spending and being spent in order to do others good, putting holiness before happiness, and keeping the world out of one's heart.

The problem that preachers face here is that church attendance for many has little or nothing to do with the quest for God. Why then are they in church at all? The answers are all too familiar. Because church-going is the mark of a respectable and trustworthy citizen; or because the genial and relaxed regularities of Sunday worship help to stabilize a hectic life; or because faithful church-going is thought to guarantee some kind of happy lot in the next world; or because one likes the people one meets at church; and so on. There are many such reasons, but none of them has anything to do with knowing and loving God and none of them, therefore, fosters any spiritual interest in preaching. So when preachers point the way to a richer relationship with God, this type of hearer feels a sense of irrelevance. His or her heart is inclined to say: here is a religious professional talking about the things he is paid to talk about; I am not a religious professional, so none of that is really my business; however, I will sit through it patiently, as good manners require. Preachers, for their part, know that this is how many of their hearers are thinking, so they strain every nerve to speak in a way that will lead persons without spiritual interest to rate them fascinating, relevant and smart. (How we love to be rated smart!) But this preoccupation makes against faithful spiritual preaching, and results in congregations not experiencing such preaching for long periods together.

All these factors tend to set up wrong standards and thus constitute obstacles to the kind of preaching that I seek to commend. However, difficulties are there to be overcome; so I proceed.

Restoring authority in preaching

In what I have said so far I have been clearing the ground for discussion of my main concern in this essay, which is to show what authority in preaching means, and to suggest how it might be reestablished in today's churches. My interest at this stage centres not on homiletics, that is, the technical procedures whereby preachers bring to us what they have to tell us about God, but rather on the theology of preaching, that is, the supernatural process whereby God through his messenger brings to us what he has to tell us about himself. Preaching as a work of God, mediating the authority of God, is my theme, and the rest of my space will be devoted to its development in a direct way.

My first step in opening up my theme must be to outline what I mean when I speak of the authority of God. Authority is a multi-faceted relationship with a moral and intellectual as well as a given mental side: the basic idea is of a claim to exercise control that is founded on having the right, power and competence to do it. The authority that belongs to God springs from his sovereign domain over us as his dependent creatures, linked with the moral perfection of all his dealings with us. Holy Scripture, 'God's Word written' (Anglican Article 25), is the instrument of God's authority; our Lord Jesus Christ exercises and embodies that authority; and the Holy Spirit induces acknowledgment of it by making us realize the reality of the Father and the Son as they address us in all their awesomeness, holiness and graciousness. God speaks through his Word, written and preached, and our preaching of the Word should match the Spirit's strategy – that is, we should always be seeking to bring home God's reality and authority to human minds and hearts by elucidating and applying Holy Scripture. Encounter with the living, authoritative Lord brings spiritual understanding and life as we hear and respond to his call for trust and obedience, praise and worship, and the preacher's aim should ever be to occasion this edifying encounter. The discussion on which we now enter seeks to show something of what this means, and so to help us set our sights as preachers more effectively.

I now ask three questions:

1. *What does it mean for preaching to be marked by authority?*

The answer I propose is that authority in preaching is a reality in every situation in which the following things are true:

a. There is no doubt about the *nature* of what is happening: *the Bible is doing the talking.* The preacher is treating himself as a mouthpiece for the biblical Word of God, and that Word is coming through. He has resisted the temptation to stand in front of his text, as it were, speaking for it as if it could not speak for itself, and putting himself between it and the congregation; instead, he is making it his business to focus everyone's attention on the text, to stand behind it rather than in front of it, to become its servant, and to let it deliver its message through him. As the Westminster Directory for Public Worship put it, three and a half centuries ago, what the preacher presents must be 'contained in or grounded on [his] text, *that the hearers may discern how God teacheth it from thence*'. Preaching has authority only when the message comes as a word from God himself. That only happens when what is said is perceived as, in the words of the *Westminster Confession*, 'the Holy Spirit speaking in the Scripture';[3] and that perception only occurs as the preacher labours to let the text talk through him about that with which, like every other text in the Bible, it is ultimately dealing – God and man in relationship, one way or another. If what is presented appears as the preacher's ideas, it can have only human authority at best; when, however, the preacher serves the written Word in a way that lets it speak for itself, its divine authority is felt.

b. There is no doubt about the *purpose* of what is happening: *response to God is being called for*. The preacher, as spokesman for the text, is seeking not only to inform and persuade, but to evoke an appropriate answer to what God through the text is saying and showing. Man's answer will consist of repentance, faith, obedience, love, effort, hope, fear, zeal, joy, praise, prayer, or some blend of these; for such are the dispositional qualities, springing from the heart into devotional and doxological expression, that God everywhere requires. The preacher is hoping, under God, to reproduce the state of affairs that Paul looked back to when he wrote to the Romans, 'you wholeheartedly obeyed the form of teaching to which you were entrusted' (Rom. 6:17). The teaching is God's testimony, command and promise; the preacher entrusts his hearers to it by begging them to respond to it and assuring them that God will fulfil his promises to them as they do so; and in this process the divine authority of the message is felt.

c. There is no doubt about the *perspective* of what is happening: *the preaching is practical*. This point is an extension of the last. What is being said would not be preaching at all were it not life-centred. Communication from the text is only preaching as it is applied and brought to bear on the listeners with a life-changing thrust. Without this, as was said earlier, it would merely be a lecture – that is, a discourse designed merely to clear people's heads and stock their minds, but not in any direct way to change their lives.

I must confess that I do not think that the present-day evangelical pulpit is strong here. Reacting against the kind of preaching that too often marks the liberal pulpit, in which the speaker offers personal reflections on human and religious life, too many of us preach messages that suffer from what might be called 'doctrinal overload'. With twenty or thirty minutes in which to preach, we spend eighteen or twenty-eight of them teaching general principles of divine truth from our text, and only for the last minute or two do we engage in any form of application. But there is little sense of God's authority where so much of the message is lecture and so little application is found.

A wiser way of proceeding, and one that mediated a very vivid sense of divine authority, was that followed by Dr Martyn Lloyd-Jones in the greatest days of his preaching ministry. The introductions to his pastoral and evangelistic sermons were very cunningly conceived. Having announced his text, he would spend the first few minutes of the sermon talking about some widely-felt perplexity of modern life, pointing out in everyday language that no adequate solution or remedy seemed to be in sight. In this he was operating on the wise principle, 'scratch where it itches', and involving his hearers in a realization that this was their problem, pressing and inescapable. When he had secured their interest at this level, he would begin to demonstrate that his text gives God's angle on the problem and his answer to it, and the demonstration would be applicatory all the way. Not everyone who experienced the authority of God in the preaching of 'the Doctor' discerned its source. Certainly, Dr Lloyd-Jones's personal power as a speaker and his humble, insightful submission to his text had much to do with it, but much of the authority flowed from the fact that he was applying the truth in a searchingly practical way throughout to remedy the need that he had already brought his hearers to face and own. The more explicit the practical perspective, and the more overtly it involves the listeners, the more the divine authority of the preaching will be felt.

d. There is no doubt about the *impact* of what is happening: *the presence and power of God are being experienced.* The preaching mediates an encounter not merely with truth, but with God himself. A staggering throw-away line in 1 Corinthians 14 illustrates this. Paul is showing the superior usefulness of prophecy (speaking God's message in intelligible language) over tongues, and he says: 'If the whole church comes together and everyone speaks in tongues, and some who do not understand or some unbelievers come in, will they not say that you are out of your mind?' (Expected answer: 'Yes.') 'But if an unbeliever or someone who does not understand comes in while everybody is prophesying, he will be convinced by all that he is a sinner and will be judged by all, and the secrets of his heart will be laid bare. So he will fall down and worship God, exclaiming, "God is really among you!"' (1 Cor. 14:23–25). Whatever else in this passage is uncertain, four things at least are plain. First, prophecy as Paul speaks of it here corresponds in content to what we would call preaching the gospel: detecting sin, and announcing God's remedy. Secondly, the expected effect of such prophecy was to create a sense of being in the presence of the God of whom it spoke, and of being searched and convicted by him, and so being moved to humble oneself and worship him. Thirdly, in the experience of both Paul and the Corinthians what Paul describes must have actually occurred, otherwise he could not have expected the Corinthians to believe his assertion: for that which never happened before cannot be predicted with such certainty. Fourthly, Paul is anticipating a situation in which a divine authority in and through the preaching would be felt.

To sum up, then: preaching is marked by authority when the message is a relaying of what is taught by the text, when active response to it is actively sought, when it is angled in a practical, applicatory way that involves the listeners' lives, and when God himself is encountered through it. So much for the first question.

2. *What are the hindrances to authority in our preaching?*
I can be brief here, since the points are so obvious.

Lack of a clearly Bible-based, applicatory message, summoning its hearers one way or another to a deeper relationship with God in Christ, precludes the possibility of authority.

Imprecision, confusion, and muddle in presentation, so that the message and its application cannot be clearly grasped, has the same effect.

Self-projection also undermines and erodes authority. If by his words and manner the preacher focuses attention on himself, thus modelling some mode of self-absorption or self-satisfaction rather than humble response to the word that he proclaims, he precludes all possibility of his channelling any sense of divine authority: what he does not feel himself he cannot mediate to others. James Denney said somewhere that you cannot convey the impression both that you are a great preacher and that Jesus Christ is a great saviour; he might have added: or that the Lord is a great God. God-projection and Christ-projection rather than self-projection is the way to communicate and engender in one's hearers a sense of divine authority in one's preaching.

Self-reliance in the act of preaching is a further hindrance to true authority in preaching, just as self-projection is. It too has the effect of inducing the hearers to attend to the messenger rather than the message – in other words, to man rather than to God – and authentic authority is eliminated when that happens.

So to my final question:

3. *What are the conditions of authority in our preaching?*
To this question I offer first a general and then a specific answer.

The general answer is that preaching has authority when both its substance and its style proclaim in a transparent way the preacher's own docile humility before the Bible itself and before the triune God whose word the Bible is. It is as the preacher himself is truly under, and is clearly seen to be under, the authority of God and the Bible that he will have authority, and be felt to carry authority, as God's spokesman. It needs to be obvious to the hearers that he has put himself whole-heartedly under the authority of the God as whose emissary he comes; of Christ the chief shepherd, whom he serves as a subordinate shepherd, and to whom he must one day give account of his service; and of the Holy Spirit, whom he trusts each moment as he preaches actually to communicate the divine message to his hearers' hearts at that moment. A preacher who has authority will come across as one who consciously depends on the Holy Spirit to sustain in him vividness of vision, clarity of mind and words, and freedom of heart and voice, as he delivers his message, just as he trusts the Holy Spirit to be the agent of conviction and response in the lives of his hearers. It is those under authority who have authority; it is those whose demeanour models submission to the Scriptures and dependence on the Lord of the Word who mediate the experience of God's authority in preaching. 'Unlike so many,' writes Paul, 'we do not peddle the word of God for profit' – that is, we do not preach with mercenary motives, nor do we modify the message in order to please hearers who, if pleased, will smile on us, but if displeased, might become obnoxious to us. 'On the contrary, in Christ we speak before God with sincerity, like men sent from God' (2 Cor. 2:17). Only those preachers who can say the same, by reason of their conscious and conscientious fidelity to the written Word, are likely ever to be able to say, as Paul elsewhere said: 'We also thank God continually because, when you received the word of God, which you heard from us, you accepted it not as the word of men, but as it actually is, the word of God, which is at work in you who believe' (1 Thes. 2:13).

Specifically, and looking at the matter directly from our own standpoint as preachers, the conditions of authority are four in number, each of which we should now recognize as a summons and a directive to us from the Lord himself.

a. The heart of our message on each occasion must be an *application of biblical material* to the heart and conscience, to lead folk to know, love, worship and serve God through Jesus Christ. Is this our constant purpose when we preach?

b. The way we preach must display *a transparent whole-heartedness of response* to our own message, as well as a thoroughgoing commitment to persuade our hearers to trust, love, honour and serve the Lord as we ourselves seek to do. Constant self-scrutiny is therefore required of preachers in particular, to make sure that our own hearts are right before we attempt to speak in the Lord's name. Do we practise this self-scrutiny?

c. We need *the unction of the Holy Spirit* for the act of preaching itself.[4] Richard Baxter, the Puritan, in his classic volume, *The Reformed Pastor* (which every would-be pastor-preacher will be wise to read once a year), spoke of 'a communion of souls' that takes place in preaching, whereby the hearers catch the preacher's mood.[5] This being so, it is vital that the preacher should be full of the Holy Spirit for his appointed task, so that he is clear-headed, warm-hearted, ardent, earnest, and inwardly free to concentrate on the task of instruction and persuasion that each message imposes. An anointing of the Spirit, therefore, giving *parrhasia* – uninhibited freedom to say from one's heart what one sees with one's heart – is to be sought every time we preach. Beethoven wrote on the score of his Mass in D (*Missa Solemnis*): 'From the heart it comes, to the heart may it go,' and these same words should express the preacher's desire and prayer every time he ventures to speak. But it is only as we receive the divine unction, sermon by sermon, that it will be so. Do we seek unction as we should?

d. Finally, we need *grace to be spontaneous* when we speak: that is, easy and free-flowing in appropriate expression. This, too, is a gift from God – it is in fact an aspect of the *parrhasia* that this Spirit bestows – but it does not come without hard work in preparation, preparation both of the message and of the messenger. The right word here comes, I believe, from W. H. Griffith Thomas, and runs thus: 'Think yourself empty; read yourself full; write yourself clear; pray yourself keen; then into the pulpit – and let yourself go!' That is the formula of preparation that produces spontaneity. Is this how we prepare to preach?

It is beyond question that the greatest and most fruitful pulpit ministry in last-century Britain was that of Charles Spurgeon. It was he who observed, at the time of his silver jubilee with his 6,000-strong Metropolitan Tabernacle congregation, 'to speak your heart out every time [twice a Sunday!] and yet to have something fresh to say for 25 years, is no child's play'.[6] Shortly after the jubilee, the following was written of him:

> Mr Spurgeon's . . . views of the Word of God, and his manner of preparation for the pulpit . . . secure *the inexhaustible variety* which so strikingly characterizes his sermons. It is not his manner to spin the web out of himself . . . He never preaches from a topic. He always has a text. His text is not a mere motto, but *in it* he finds his sermon. He uses the text with as much apparent reverence and appreciation as if those few words were the only words that God had ever spoken. The text is the germ which furnishes the life, the spirit, and the substance of the discourse . . .
>
> The Word of God is to him a thing of life and power . . . He sees God in the very words of the Bible. Like the bush on Horeb, a chapter, or a single verse, at times, glows with celestial splendour, and, to use his own words, 'hundreds of times I have as surely felt the presence of God, in the page of Scripture, as ever Elijah did when he heard the Lord speaking in a still small voice.' He seems never to be satisfied, in his study of the Scriptures, till every single verse is thus verified by the Spirit, and becomes to him a living word.[7]

On almost the last two pages of *I Believe in Preaching*[8] John Stott hints at Spurgeon's significance for him personally as a model of preaching with the humility that mediates authority. Surely no preacher ever did, or could, choose a better model.

God empower all of us who are called to this ministry to preach with authority – as we ought to preach!

The Christian faith: context, communication and content

Michael Nazir-Ali

To speak of the content of faith, without also mentioning the context in which such a faith is set, as well as ways in which it is to be communicated, would be rather like a medieval school-man asked to speak on substance without reference to accidents. Medieval schoolmen, of course, were capable of doing so. I cannot pretend to such facility myself, and it is not possible to talk about the content of our faith without also talking about the work, the witness, and the worship where this faith is expressed.

The context of faith

The form of divine revelation is given to us in particular contexts, and is not given apart from those contexts. The normative record of divine revelation in the Bible cannot be encountered precisely as revelation until the worshipping and witnessing and reading community has come to grips with the contexts of the Bible. It is necessary for us to come to grips with the language, with the thought forms, with the idiom, and with the culture of the periods in which the biblical revelation was first given. But the horizon of the Bible – its culture and idiom – has to be related to the contemporary world, to *our* horizon. Our context too is therefore exceedingly important if we are to encounter the revelation of God in a living and immediate way.

Different communities, individuals and groups of people find that they have particular affinities with particular themes of the Bible. Biblical scholars nowadays call them trajectories. Our particular upbringing, culture, maybe even our language, equip us to have a special insight about a particular theme, a trajectory, in the Bible.[1] The renewal that the church has experienced through the reading of the Bible in context cannot be overemphasized. In all sorts of ways, all kinds of Christians, with all sorts of commitment, have come to a realization that when they allow the Bible to interact with their context, then new, strange and wonderful things happen. Some people have come to the conclusion that the ways in which the Bible speaks of the experience of the Holy Spirit almost as an invasive experience is something that speaks to them. They find that the prophets in the Old Testament are led to do strange and wonderful things for God because of this kind of experience of the Holy Spirit. They find this confirmed, of course, in the experience of the early church at Pentecost.[2] They discover that in their situation this is the way that God is speaking to them. They can see that this kind of experience of the Holy Spirit is right for themselves and their community.

This discovery has happened across a wide range of Christian traditions. I remember visiting an old church in the middle of Manila *intra muros*. It was very depressing to see this church, because it was traditional Roman Catholicism at its worst. Immediately afterwards I was taken to the Roman Catholic cathedral in Manila. There I found that the charismatic movement in the Roman Catholic Church had taken hold of the congregation and the clergy. It was nothing like the other church at all.

There are others who have found the passionate concern for justice in the prophets as something that has spoken to *them* in their situation. These people have found that the God who is just, and who justifies sinners, is also a God who demands justice in his world. Again this phenomenon has occurred over an extremely wide range of Christian commitment and tradition. We cannot say that it is only radicals in Latin America who are into this kind of thing, because it makes an impact on people in strange ways and at different times. A recent testimony to this was given to me by a friend of mine who is a Jewish

Rabbi, and teaches at the University of Kent in Canterbury. He has written a book called *On Earth as it is in Heaven*, on how liberation theology in Latin America has alerted him to his own prophetic tradition, and made it come alive for him.[3] There are yet others who find the theme of liberation in the Bible, the exodus narrative for example, as something that speaks to them. The American blacks in the nineteenth century, groaning under the burden of slavery, found that the exodus narrative was something with which they could identify. So it is not surprising that many 'Negro spirituals' are about the exodus. Today, the modern 'slaves' of urban Latin America and Asia also identify with the exodus narrative, as a way of release from the captivity that notions of development forced upon them have brought about in urban areas of the two-thirds world.

Now, for each context, the insight a community has into the Scripture is ultimately valuable for that community and yet at the same time for all of us, as we need each other. Private judgment, the Reformers' recovery of the insight that the reading of the Bible can speak in an immediate way to us, is something that we must not lose. I do not always agree with Dr David Samuel, until recently Director of Church Society. But he speaks of the immediate, felt authority of Scripture. This is something that we need to relearn. There is a place for private judgment. There is a way in which Scripture makes itself felt in an authoritative way for us as individuals, as communities, as churches. That doctrine of private judgment, however, has to be complemented by a doctrine of the church. In other words, we need to complement and supplement each other's insights. So there is a sense in which no particular context can dictate to others about what is ultimate in the Christian scheme of things.

Communication of the faith

If the essentials of the gospel are to be found anywhere, it is in the act of communicating the gospel. This has been so from the very beginning. The essential message of the gospel was known in the preaching, so it is no accident that *kērygma* and *kērysso* are cognate. We should not have needed Marshall McLuhan in the 60s and 70s to tell us that the medium is the message, because in a very real way the medium has been the message wherever the gospel has been proclaimed. If you want a theological statement of this, then Romans 10 is quite a good place to begin!

The content of our faith

God's love and the Trinity

Now I must apply Ockham's razor to the substantial matter before us, the content of our faith.

'God is love' is about the briefest proposition there is in the Bible. This proposition is not just about the relation of the Godhead to us. It also concerns the mystery of the Godhead itself. It is about the heart of the Godhead, the internal relationships within the Godhead. The Father loves the Son, the Son loves the Father. St Augustine, in a famous remark that has never been forgotten, said that the Holy Spirit was the *vinculum amoris*, the bond of love between the Father and the Son. Of course, the Holy Spirit is, and has always been, understood by the church and in the Bible as communal, as the communion not only between the Father and the Son, but between God and human beings, and among believers. Bishop John Taylor, in his wonderful book *The Go-between God*, reminds us that when we say the Grace, as we so often do, we say: 'The grace of our Lord Jesus Christ, the love of God and the fellowship (or the communion) of the Holy Spirit.'[4] Augustine has been criticized by some who have asked whether his understanding does not reduce the Holy Spirit, doing injustice to his personality and reducing him to a relation. Bishop John sees the Holy Spirit not so much as a bond but as a medium in which love can take place – the love that the Father has for the Son, and the Son has for the Father, that God has for human beings, and the love that they can have for each other.[5] But whether as bond or as medium, does this not to some extent depersonalize the Holy Spirit?

Augustine's reference to the Holy Spirit as the bond of love is not all that he has said about the Holy Spirit, of course. In his work on the Trinity, and in the latter part of his *Confessions*, he elaborates what has come to be known as the psychological analogy. In this analogy, Augustine compares the human self with God the Father, the fount, the source of the Godhead. He compares the human mind with God the Eternal Word, and the human will (or the human capacity of love) with the Holy Spirit. Augustine insists again and again that the three persons of the Godhead, the Father, the Word and the Spirit, are in the most intimate union with each other. For this reason he is very reluctant to refer to them even as persons. He says that he uses the word 'person' because there is no better word to hand. Augustine is very strong on what came to be called the doctrine of co-inherence. According to this, the persons of the blessed Trinity share in each other's qualities, and in each other's work, so what can be said of the Son can also be said of the Father, and what is said of the Son can also be said of the Holy Spirit, and so on. The important point is that this doctrine of co-inherence for Augustine only makes sense because he is willing to use the analogy of a single person for the Godhead.[6]

The Western Christian tradition in its thinking on the Trinity has always begun with the oneness of God, and then gone on to consider how there could be diversity in this unity. The Christian Orient agrees with the West on this point. (By the Orient, I mean those churches that did not accept the Council of Chalcedon.) But the East – the Greek and the Russian East – have always begun with the plurality of experience of God, with God experienced as Father, Son and Holy Spirit, and then gone on to ask the question: 'How can these three be one?' The most orthodox expositions of the Eastern tradition safeguard the oneness of God by laying heavy emphasis on co-inherence. But this is very difficult to do. So, quite often in the East, the danger is of slipping into a kind of tritheism. I believe that the Western theological tradition has been faithful to the biblical faith in beginning with the oneness of God, and then going on to ask how diversities are possible within that divine unity, a unity which is given, and which the church has inherited from Israel.

There is a lamentable tendency these days to use the doctrine of the Trinity, and particularly the social analogy as it was used by the Eastern Fathers, to build all sorts of houses of cards. So the cause of ecumenism is commended because there is diversity, they say, in the unity of the Godhead; diversity in the community is commended because of an alleged diversity in the Godhead. I have even heard the family being described in terms that were analogically taken from the doctrine of the Trinity! Now as someone who has lived and worked in a Muslim culture, I have found this quite disturbing, because most of our apologetic work for Muslims has been to show precisely that we do not believe in three Gods, but that we believe in one God who is nevertheless experienced in these diverse ways.[7]

The love of God is creative and boundless. It is not limited, therefore, to the Godhead itself, but it spills over into creation. We see the Trinity active in creation. The Father wills creation; the pattern, the design, and the order of creation reflects God the Word, the *Logos*; and the power, the energy and the personality which we encounter in creation all reflect God the Holy Spirit. We must remember, however, that because of co-inherence, what is said of the one can also be said of the others.

God's love and creation

If science is possible because the human mind encounters design, pattern and order in the world, then there is a way in which we can develop an apologetic to the scientific community properly based on a theology of the Word. There are, of course, scientists who are now beginning to see that design and pattern are not just about breaking things down into their constituent parts. There is such a thing as end, as final cause, which determines what a thing is. They are now talking, for example, about the so-called anthropic principle, according to which the evolution of the universe, and the wonderful checks and balances that we encounter in this world, can only make sense if we posit a human being at the end of the process. That is, the process can be seen from this end as leading up to the emergence of rational, self-conscious, moral and spiritual beings. Now, though scientists are not drawing any theological conclusions from this, I think we are free to do so.[8] The order, design and pattern of the universe reflect God the Word. If science has most to do with God the Word, then perhaps it is poetry that has most to do with God the Holy Spirit as he is encountered in the universe. It is our response to the Holy Spirit that makes poetry possible.

From creation in general we get to what is perhaps the climax of creation – the creation of human beings. It is here that we find divine love bringing about the creation of a being able to respond in love. But to be able to respond in love, one must be free; there can be no coercion in love. The freedom of the human being is involved in the eliciting of this free response of love. So human beings are created *posse non peccare* with the possibility of not sinning, but that implies *posse peccare*, the possibility of sinning. Love cannot be something that is compelled. We know as a matter of fact that human beings have refused to respond to the invitation of divine love, so the *posse peccare*, the possibility of sinning, has in fact become actual. Nor is it episodic, it is not something that has happened once for all. It is something that has happened, happened again, and continues to happen; it is, in short, endemic. It has become endemic to the human situation. Since the coming of sin, the human situation is one of *non posse non peccare*, the inability not to sin. There is no way in which human beings cannot sin. It is here that in the divine revelation we find a wholly new trajectory introduced, if you want to use that fashionable word, and so divine love is now not only about creation, but about redemption. It is very easy to separate, rather artificially, creation and redemption. There is, however, a very real sense in which a new sort of discussion begins in the Bible after the introduction of the theme of human sin.

218

God's love and salvation history

The history of redemption has been more often termed 'salvation history'. Let us begin with the exodus, and God's choice of a people for himself. Why did he choose them? They were not a beautiful people, wealthy and powerful. They were in fact exploited, oppressed, and rejected slaves in a very large imperial context. I'm not an Old Testament scholar, and I stand to be corrected, but I believe that the *Habiru* people, of whom the Israelites were a part, were a despised social group in ancient Middle-Eastern societies.[9] Why did God choose them? The answer is found in the Bible itself. He chose them so that they could be a light to lighten the nations (Is. 49:6; 62:6; Lk. 2:32). Even in the particular choice of a specific people, God's purposes were universal.

While the perception of the Israelites during the ages, from time to time, was rather less than perfect about why they had been chosen, that cannot limit us from seeing why they were chosen, and what the purpose of God was. Sometimes the Israelites thought that they had been chosen to bring judgment on the world. I think there is an element of truth in this. There was a kind of judgment that the Israelites brought to the nations of Canaan, for example, where the city states were organized around an axis of priests and kings. The advent of the Israelites, the tribes of Yahweh as they have been called, destroyed the system in Canaan, and introduced what is widely recognized by sociologists of the period as social and political egalitarianism. One sociologist of the period has said that Yahwehism can be defined as a function of social and political egalitarianism at that time in Canaan.[10] John Goldingay, in a marvellous response, has pointed out that one could also say that social and political egalitarianism in Canaan at that time was a function of Yahwehism.[11]

Very quickly the Israelites, and particularly the prophets among them, began to see that if their God was universal, if he was truly the God of the whole world and of all human beings, then their choice must mean something in the context of the history of the world. They could not reduce Yahweh to being a tribal God. This is why you see, scattered throughout the Old Testament, different models of understanding what can be called biblical universalism. You find, for example, the great visions in Isaiah and Micah, where Israel is shown as understanding its cultic focus, Zion, as the centre of the world. All the different nations stream there. We are all familiar with those wonderful prophecies we read at Christmas-time. But the same prophets very often saw that this marvellously centripetal view of history was not adequate. They began to see that God was at work in the nations where they were. So we have the eschatological visions in Isaiah 19, where Israel sees that a time will come when Egypt will be the people of God, Assyria will be the work of his hands, and Israel will be his heritage. Now some people say: 'All that's in the future. You cannot build too much on it.'[12] In the Bible itself, however, we have evidence that the biblical writers were beginning to see that the history of God's work among the nations goes back to their very origin. It is not just an eschatological vision for the future. So we have the recognition that the God who brought the Israelites out of Egypt is also the God who has made the Ethiopians a nation, who has brought the Philistines out from Crete, and the Syrians from Kir (Am. 9:7). When the prophet Malachi is rebuking the Israelites for offering polluted sacrifices to Yahweh, he acknowledges at the same time that there are sincere seekers after truth in the nations roundabout (Mal. 1). This does not mean, however, that the prophet necessarily endorses the *cults* of these nations.

Already in the Old Testament, then, we have a situation of many salvation histories, where God is working among people, cultures and groups. Now this in no way reduces the need for having normative salvation history, because, if we do not have a touchstone, a paradigm, how are we to determine what is authentically salvation history in a particular people? In India, or in Pakistan, or among pagan Europeans, or whoever it may be, how are we to determine, without a paradigm, what it is that authentically prepares them for the gospel, or encounter with God? Salvation history in the Bible is our touchstone for determining whether it is the dominant religious tradition of a people that prepares them for encounter with God, or whether it is a counter religious movement. In many cases the dominant religious tradition is merely oppressive. In such cases, is it the forces for social and political change that are the salvation histories of these people? We cannot determine these matters without reference to a paradigm. This is illustrated by Oscar Cullmann's diagram which incorporates the shape of the St Andrew's cross cutting across the biblical line of time.[13] Salvation history begins with Israel, narrows down to Christ, and then goes out again to the world. Christ paradoxically is the most particular act, where God's choice is concerned, and yet the most universal – because he includes all that is to come. I have always been very impressed with Karl Barth's exegesis of Ephesians 1:4, where it talks about God having chosen us in Christ before the foundation of the world. Barth's point is that it is only Christ who has been chosen eternally; all of us are chosen by virtue of our incorporation in Christ. In this way Barth saves both the doctrine of predestination and also that of human choice.[14]

God's love and the atonement

Salvation history comes to its climax in the incarnation of God the Word. Ever since the publication of *Lux Mundi*, Anglicans have been rather good at a theology of the incarnation, taking seriously the doctrine of the incarnation.[15] Sometimes I have wondered whether this is not because the English Anglican tradition finds itself incarnate in the parochial system! There is no choice in the matter. The church has to be present in the inner cities, in the villages, and in the suburbs. It is easy, therefore, to take incarnation seriously. The Anglican tradition is deeply committed to it and, at the same time, is rightly suspicious of hit-and-run evangelism and pastoral work. But has Anglican incarnation been kenotic? At about the same time as *Lux Mundi* was being written, Bishop Gore and others were also developing their views on kenosis, on the self-emptying of the divine Word in his human condition.[16] While we can say of Anglicanism that it can be incarnational in its structure and its forms, we have to ask how far this incarnation is kenotic.

The incarnation, and kenosis, which is a giving-up, an emptying ('our Lord Jesus Christ, . . . though he was rich, yet for your sakes he became poor', 2 Cor. 8:9), bring us all to alertness about sacrifice. Most people in the West these days know very little about sacrifice. They may talk about it and may even preach about it, but how many have actually seen a sacrifice? Every year in Pakistan we are all treated to this spectacle, and I cannot pretend that it is a pleasant occasion, but you do see sacrifice. I have begun to realize how deeply rooted the biblical writers are in the metaphors of sacrifice because of their familiarity with the Hebraic system of sacrifice. Kenosis brings us to sacrifice, to atonement, which, of course, means at-one-ment, reconciliation. I would not limit atonement simply to the cross. It is part and parcel of, and integrally related to, the incarnation itself. The whole of the incarnation may be understood as sacrifice, and as atonement; the whole of it has to be understood as reconciliation. Again and again I find that all kinds of people are reconciled to God because of something in the life of Christ. It may be his teaching. For Muslims very often it is his healing power. It may be an appreciation of the cross and the resurrection. But often it is not just one thing. The cross may rightly be regarded as the climax to this work of atonement, reconciliation and sacrifice, but it cannot be separated from the rest of Christ's life.

The atonement is objective because God has set forth a way of reconciliation in Christ. It is objective because, in Christ, God has begun a new humanity. The beginnings of a new humanity occur in this reconciling, atoning, sacrificial life and death. It has a representative character because, if our situation is truly *non posse non peccare*, the inability not to sin, then we need rescue; a way has to be set forth to rescue us from our predicament. There is a subjective element also about the atonement because, unless we respond to what God has set forth, the atonement remains meaningless to us. It is not, of course, meaningless in itself. We do not know what the atonement means for those who do not respond to it; only God in his wisdom knows. But for us it must remain meaningless unless we decide to follow Christ, to follow the way of the cross, to be incorporated into this new thing, into this new life. It remains meaningless unless we decide to forego our solidarity in the sin of the old Adam, and to forge our solidarity in this new life, this new Adam – the last Adam as the New Testament sometimes calls him (1 Cor. 15:45).

From the very earliest times, both Scripture and the Fathers have strongly denied that the incarnation could be merely a semblance. I've been re-reading recently the Epistles of Ignatius, which he wrote on his way to martyrdom. I have been struck how often Ignatius insists that Christ has truly come in the flesh, and truly died in the flesh. Docetism is not an option for Christians; the incarnation was not a semblance. The resurrection of Jesus Christ from the dead is part of the apparatus of the incarnation. I find it very difficult to believe people who claim to have a strong doctrine of the incarnation, but have a weak doctrine of the resurrection. If docetism is not possible at one end, it is not possible at the other. Now, of course, the fledgling Christian community was called with reason 'the Easter community' because it was the Easter faith that had brought them together. It was Pentecost, however, the coming of the Holy Spirit, that empowered them for their mission to the world. So we are back to the first verses of the book of Genesis, the Spirit creatively brooding over the void and bringing creation out of nothing. It is the same with the creation of the church. Pentecost makes the church out of nothing, as it were, and sends the church out for mission, for communicating the faith to those whom God has created and wants to save.

> 'Tis Love, 'tis Love! Thou diedst for me!
> I hear Thy whisper in my heart;
> The morning breaks, the shadows flee,
> Pure, universal Love Thou art;
> To me, to all, Thy mercies move:
> Thy nature and thy name is Love.[17]

Evangelism in the local church

Michael Green

John Stott has taught the contemporary church so much about evangelism through his own example, primarily at All Souls, Langham Place in London, that it occurred to me that I could usefully approach this subject by examining some of the principles his work has embodied. He will maintain that the embodiment has been imperfect. That is as may be. The principles his work has embodied are a beacon to us all. My approach to them here is deliberately immediate and impressionistic, rather than carefully weighed and researched. I have tried to provide the latter in my book *Evangelism through the Local Church*.[1]

Perhaps the most important lesson of all is the truth that *the local church is the primary agency in evangelism.* John Stott was himself raised in para-church circles, Christian houseparties for boys in Dorset, and then the Christian Union at Cambridge. He would be the first to express his admiration for them and the nourishment he drew from them. Nevertheless his study of the Bible as well as his innate sense of strategy, convinced him that the local church is the key to ongoing, incarnational evangelism which really makes a lasting difference in the market-place of life. When the local church is on fire for God, the need for para-church work is much reduced. John Stott set about making All Souls just such a church. And he succeeded.

It is instructive to see some of the principles in that success. The church, to whose leadership he succeeded at a remarkably young age, had a superb location in the heart of London's West End, a magnificent building, and an excellent predecessor. But it was far from the church it is now. I do not know it intimately, but to an outsider's gaze John has brought together a number of emphases which make a church a continuing resource for outreach in loving, vibrant evangelism. They are emphases which are important, irrespective of the location of the church or the ability of its pastor. They are universal requirements in a local church that is set for evangelism.

The church must be *a loving, welcoming church*. John has gone to great lengths to bring this about. Attractive publicity is displayed on the steps outside. Friendly faces greet the newcomers. It is not difficult to follow the services.

There is a weekly bulletin advertising a whole gamut of activities. Lunch or coffee is provided. Homes are opened up. No wonder people come from afar! A warm welcome awaits them. And this is a chilly world, where unselfish love is rare. Our churches need to embody the love of God and his welcome to those who are not yet members of his family. A church is, in a sense, intended to be a maternity ward. And maternity wards need to be warm.

An important part of that love is nurtured in small home groups, meeting on a regular basis. Here hurts can surface, the implications of the Christian life be talked through, prayer be offered, friends be made. A good home group is an extended family. The solitary (and there are plenty of them in central London) feel loved. They belong. Such groups become powerful agencies for ministry in the local church, like platoons in a regiment. Their leadership needs to be trained and encouraged. Their members need to grow, and to have an opportunity to discover and use their talents for Christ. Such home groups are now commonplace in the churches of our land. But they were not in the days when John began. He realized that the church in the home was not merely a historical accident in New Testament times, but a statement of principle.

The church must be *under the Word of God*. That is clearly taught in the New Testament, recognized in the formularies of most denominations, and most certainly the Anglican; and yet it is honoured more in the breach than the observance. Not so at All Souls. The preaching of Scripture, at length and in depth, proved itself not only in drawing hungry people in, but in building them up into effective Christian workers. The devotional reading of Scripture was strongly encouraged and largely carried out. As a result, All Souls became a church of instructed Christians, who knew the good news of Jesus, and were able to give good reasons for their faith.

The church needs to be *under the guidance of the Holy Spirit* and open to his leading. This will often result in doing things that have not been done before. All Souls under John Stott has demonstrated that a conservative attitude to Scripture, so far from making for dull predictability, opens up a church to very fresh and radical action in all sorts of areas. The innovative Christian initiatives that have sprung from All Souls are too numerous to mention, even if I knew them all. They sprang, and still do spring, from a radical openness to God the Holy Spirit. It is his church, not the rector's. And he, the living Lord, must be allowed to have his way with his church.

That is why *prayer* is so vital. Nothing is achieved of any substance without it. It is in prayer that the mind of the Spirit is discerned. It is prayer that, in some strange way which we do not fully understand, binds principalities and powers of darkness and frees the hand of God to act. The midweek prayer meeting at All Souls became a major institution for the congregation before many churches in the country had got round to having one at all. Its prominence in the life of the church drew attention to the primacy of prayer. It is a praying church which is an evangelizing church. There is good reason for this – God himself is the evangelist. We cannot bring any person whatever to faith in Christ; only the Spirit of God can do that. In prayer we confess as much; we ask him to do his sovereign work, and he does. Evangelistic methods without prayer are as useless as a car without petrol.

The leadership team is another very important aspect of the church which is equipped for mission. It was so from the first. The Antioch church which spawned the first missionary journey, an outreach which transformed Christianity from being a subculture within Judaism into becoming a counter-culture in the whole world, was led by a team. There was no one 'pastor' at Antioch, but five very assorted men, coming, as they did, from different backgrounds and different countries. John Stott, gifted as he is, might well have become a prima donna, of which there are many examples in the church leaders in the USA. He refused the temptation, and surrounded himself with a team. A team like that is mutually corrective and supportive. It is able to address a spread of issues which no one man ever could, and it is the best way in the world of equipping the next generation of leaders. Any church can do it – not, to be sure, with paid ministers, but with gifted

225

members of the congregation – if only the will is there. It will mean a repudiation of the one-man syndrome: 'I am the rector, and what I say goes.' Vigorous Christians will not want to belong to a church with a monarchical leadership like that. They want to be part of a living body where the contribution of every limb is valued. They want to be part of a team, and they need to see this modelled before their eyes in the leadership of their church.

If 'every member ministry' like this is the avowed aim of the church, as it should be, then this will involve *training*. All Souls was, under John's leadership, producing training courses for lay people in the congregation, and getting them commissioned by the bishop, at a time when most churches had not even grasped the idea that training was important. He pioneered this area, vital for evangelism, as he pioneered so many others. You cannot expect a congregation to get involved in evangelism if they are not helped to understand the essence of their faith and how to communicate it to others. John provided this help, systematically, carefully, and with as much attention to the personal growth of the worker as to the content of the faith he was being equipped to share.

All of this suggests the need for *an informed Christianity*, which is able to hold its head high in the midst of the surrounding scepticism. John Stott has an equal determination to reach the head and the will. He has no time for emotional evangelism that has little intellectual content. Your mind matters, and he knows it. His intellectual assault on unbelief is as much a part of his evangelism as is his challenging assault on the will. As a result, those who come to faith through such preaching tend to stand. They have been introduced to a holistic Christianity, where there is no dichotomy between head and heart.

In many circles new believers are either left to fend for themselves as best they can, or to fit into the existing structures of the church, however different a culture it may be. John Stott has shown us how wrong that is. He was one of the first in contemporary England to follow through on an evangelistic address or an evangelistic conversation by *a course for new believers* called, if I recall aright, a Nursery Class, and lasting for some three months. The name may not have been the most flattering, but the concept was invaluable. New believers *are* spiritual babes, and need milk, company and tender loving care. That is what is provided in the Nursery Class. Any church which is going to take seriously the Lord's commission to make disciples is going to need some such group for the nourishment of new lives as they come into contact with the Life-giver.

The final characteristic of the church God uses in evangelism that I want to mention now is this: *a passion for excellence*. All Souls embodies this. There is a careful attention to detail, so that everything is done to the highest possible standards for the glory of God. Whether you look at the bookstall, the catering, the quality of music in worship, the care taken in the leading of prayers, the training for those who are to read the lessons – everything is given the utmost attention. It is a mute but powerful message. It says 'Our God is great. Nothing but the best is good enough for him.'

Reaching out

Those seem to me to be some of the important characteristics of the church God uses in its locality. They are well embodied in the church John Stott has led for so long. But if those are in place, at least to some extent, how is a local church to begin to reach out in evangelism to the increasingly secularist mind-set of the people who live within its area?

Here again, the work which John inaugurated at All Souls gives us many pointers. They are not necessary: there are, after all, manifold ways to spread the gospel. They are not exhaustive: the work at All Souls has itself been developing over the years. They are certainly not foolproof techniques: for one thing none such exist, and for another the methods we employ are almost irrelevant compared with the recognition of the plight of people all round us who are strangers to God, and the passionate determination to try to introduce them to him. But nevertheless the methods they employed at All Souls are suggestive, and will prove fruitful in many circumstances as different from London's West End as chalk from cheese. So I shall mention ten, as a sample.

First, *the guest service.* It was John Stott who pioneered these services in England, so far as I know. This is simply a service in church which is totally given over to a single aim: helping those who do not know Christ to find him. That one aim governs the publicity, the visiting beforehand, the invitations from friend to friend, the choice of music, the nature and the ambiance of the service, the content and manner of the address, the use of testimonies, the challenge to commitment, and the signing-up of people for nurture groups. It is a very well tried procedure, which is highly effective, and particularly valuable because it is an exhibition of body life. All the members of the church are encouraged to bring a friend. All can engage in heartfelt intercession at a half-night of prayer beforehand. All can turn to their friend when it is over and ask 'How did you enjoy that?', a question which may well lead to personal conversation about Christ, and eventually to conversion. To have such services three or four times a year, after careful preparation, good publicity, and a detailed shaping of the service for the unchurched, would be a marvellous start in the direction of evangelism through the local church. It is particularly useful at drawing in those who are on the fringe of the church: they may be married to a member, or may come two or three times a year on cultic occasions like Christmas and Harvest Festival. Such lingering memories of a religious past can be built on, and turned to good purpose by a guest service.

At the opposite extreme from the preaching to large numbers in a service is *the conversation* you can have *with just one individual.* This is normally, but not necessarily, a friend with whom you have shared many experiences over the years. The time will come when you are presented with an opportunity to talk about the one who means most to you, Jesus Christ. John Stott has not only been outstanding in the clarity and cogency of his personal evangelism, but he has modelled it for others and made sure that the ordinary members of his church know that it is their privilege and responsibility. It is when members of the congregation get to the stage of speaking with humble confidence about Jesus Christ, and helping their friends to encounter him for themselves, that real excitement about evangelism ignites in the congregation. The fire begins to spread throughout the church and to give out warmth to all who approach it.

The New Testament makes it very plain that all Christians, not just some, are called to be witnesses to Jesus Christ and the fact that he is alive. It is not given to everyone to have the gifts of an evangelist, but a great many more people have that gift than realize it. Part of John Stott's own gifting has been to discover the evangelists among the congregation of witnesses, and give them freedom to use their gift for Christ. There is of course enormous value in personal evangelism, 'one beggar telling another beggar where to get bread'. It means that the message can be directed in the most appropriate way to the actual concerns and needs of the enquirer. In a sermon this is rarely possible: it is necessarily too general, and designed for general consumption. The sermon is like spraying the lawn with a sprinkler, while personal work is like taking a watering can to a very special plant. Personal evangelism has enormous advantages, too, and can be done anywhere, and by anyone. It is the sort of thing Philip did with the Ethiopian official in Acts 8, or Jesus with the Samaritan woman in John 4. If personal work can become normal in the local church, one thing is certain. That church will be more effective in evangelism than any major thrust, be it a crusade or an area mission, could achieve.

Nevertheless, *specific planned outreaches from the local church* are not to be despised. They may occur either at the single church level or, better still, at a townwide level, supported by co-operating churches across the denominational and doctrinal spectrum, thus emphasizing that the things which unite Christians are far more significant than those which keep us apart. John Stott has been outstanding both in supporting major ventures of this kind (such as the many occasions when Billy Graham has been in this country conducting crusades) and in initiating them himself. He has led missions in many parishes, as well as at university and city levels. It could be argued that if the local churches were operating as they should, such special efforts would be rendered otiose. True, but which of us, either individually or corporately, lives consistently up to our responsibilities? In a fallen world, such special efforts from time to time provide a focus for the imagination, dedication and involvement of a great many Christians. Moreover, they bring many people to a living faith, and this is not only very valuable in itself, but it is an encouragement to the church to persevere in reaching out to those who are strangers to God's love, knowing that hard though evangelism is, it is not at all impossible, and not at all unfruitful.

Not every local church is equipped to launch a mission. It would be better to begin by inviting a team to come and lead a mission in your own area, to learn from it, and then to go and bring fresh life to another church. Many churchmen are disillusioned with 'missions', feeling that they touch only the fringe, that they win few people to faith, and are expensive and time-consuming. There is something to be said for such hesitations, particularly when directed against the traditional one-man mission. But they are far less valid when directed against the sort of mission where a number of Christians from another church, be they ten or a hundred, come to the receiving community as guests who give their time and ministry free. And the speaking is not done from a pulpit six feet above contradiction in an ecclesiastical building, but in a multiplicity of homes, restaurants, saunas, clubs, bars maybe – anywhere where a few Christians can invite a few friends to meet with two members of the visiting team in a context where everyone is at ease. The visitors are invited to explain why they are there, and say something of what Christ means to them. There is then a free-for-all, and out of the open discussion it is not difficult to see who is being touched, and to help that person, then or subsequently, to face up to Christ and to join a nurture group.

There may well be a few, big central meetings in such a mission, but I have found that taking a large team with me and building on the friendships of members of the church or university so that twenty or more small meetings can go on, simultaneously if necessary, is far more effective in reaching people who are not yet Christians than the older method of trying to get people to come to church to hear a preacher. There is still a lot of mileage in the running of missions if done sensitively, imaginatively and corporately. There is another great advantage. The shared ministry draws the team together in a wonderful way. The receiving community is struck by the way these enthusiastic Christians love one another and pour themselves out, while the team themselves return home absolutely thrilled to have seen God at work and to have been a small part of it. The subsequent life of the sending church is enhanced in a big way as a result.

But we do not need to go away to engage in a venture of this kind. Opportunities abound on our doorstep. A little imagination will show ways in which the local church can host *some event of general interest where the Christian gospel can be communicated.* A concert, given by a talented Christian singer, is one such way. In between songs it is all too easy for such a person to explain why he or she is a Christian, and the difference this has made to his or her whole perspective on life. At the end of the evening either the singer, or someone with the appropriate gift, can draw the event to a conclusion by making Christ's offer personal to the hearers, and by inviting them to respond to the Lord and to join a group for further nurture and growth. A dinner provides a similar opportunity. It is in fact rather easy for three or four Christian friends who have a large number of contacts to invite them for an evening where a Christian judge, traindriver, or whatever, is advertised to speak on some attractive topic. It is overtly Christian: this must not be concealed, or people will feel they have been got there on false pretences. But it sounds quite interesting, it is in a private home with refreshments, and the invitation comes from a friend. The result is that a very high proportion of those invited actually come, and are keen to come on a subsequent occasion. Before long some of them have quietly come to Christian faith, and are looking for nurture.

A fifth method of outreach which is not beyond any local church is running *an Agnostics Anonymous Group.* People will be intrigued by the title. Fringe members of the church who come perhaps three times a year, but really believe little or nothing, can often be persuaded to join. This is especially true if the course is by invitation only, for a short period of, say, two months, and is conducted in a private home with a meal, where they are promised that they will not be preached at. Under such circumstances, many people who have serious problems with the Christian faith can be persuaded to come along and air their difficulties.

There are all sorts of ways in which such a group can be run, and All Souls pioneered several of them. A short video outlining the Christian claim, and leaving many loose ends to be taken up in debate afterwards, is a possible approach: David Watson's *Jesus Then and Now* is an

excellent tool in this respect.[2] Alternatively one can ask the participants to say what is the stumbling-block in Christianity as far as they
are concerned, or to state what they do in fact believe. If the leaders
are wise and positive in giving deep respect to each participant, however wild their views, and keep drawing the discussion back to Jesus
and the resurrection, people will feel they have freedom to say what
they like, while at the same time being increasingly magnetized by
Jesus. It goes without saying that the Bible needs to be freely used
from the start – not as an authoritative religious judiciary (they will
react against that) but as the record by honest contemporaries of
Jesus of the one they knew and began to follow. Alternatively, the
leaders can find out what are the major sticking-points of their group,
and tackle one a week, culminating in an evening on the challenge of
Jesus to every person. Those groups are some of the most exiting and
worthwhile undertakings you can ever engage in. They bring new
believers into the church, believers who are all the more committed
because they are genuinely convinced, and have come over to the
faith from a contrary position.

A sixth way of evangelism which any local church can undertake is
provided by *the occasional services*. By this I mean weddings, baptisms,
funerals and the like. These are often something of a formality, but
what marvellous vehicles for the gospel they can become! John Stott
made superb use of these regular pastoral opportunities. One of his
early books, *Your Confirmation*, springs out of leading young people
(and older ones as well) to personal faith by means of the confirmation preparation for full church membership, which in other hands
has often proved ineffective or merely formal. He made it his aim to
bring each such person not only to the church for membership, but to
the Lord for all eternity. Nobody would be allowed to be confirmed
without a personal interview, to see if the teaching had gone home
and if there really was something to confirm – a genuine trust in
Christ. Having been through wedding preparation at his hands, I
know that he made regular use of such occasions to press the claims
of Christ on the couple. What has the Christian minister to offer to
the bereaved if it is not a relationship with the only person who has
overcome death, and brought life and immortality to light through the
gospel? In the visiting beforehand, and in the address at the funeral
service itself, as well as in the aftercare, there is a prime opportunity
to bring people, sensitively and gently, face to face with the risen
Jesus. Such opportunities come to meet us: we do not even have to
go out to look for them. They are there in the experience of every
local church. The only question is whether those opportunities are
taken or not.

A seventh area of outreach which was signally grasped by John Stott in the parish was *ministry directed towards special groups*. Here are three of which I know; there were certainly others.

One was a St Luke's Day service for the medical profession. Since Harley Street lay in the parish, it goes without saying that there were plenty of doctors. So All Souls had a regular, well-planned, well-publicized outreach service for them, and John preached the gospel in terms appropriate to them, or sought to bring a biblical insight into a pressing area of their professional concern.

John Stott also inaugurated a remarkable work among the big stores which were, and are, a feature of the city-centre parish. He even got the stores to appoint a chaplain, who was one of his staff. I have reason to be particularly grateful for this, having managed to persuade the big stores in the parish where I was starting my ministry to believe that they lacked one thing – a chaplain! So began a ministry among the stores in my small patch. Had All Souls not pioneered the way, I would never have thought of it. Once the chaplain has won respect and trust, he is called upon in times of need and crisis by members of the staff, and often has the joy of marrying them and entering into their joys and sorrows. I found, in my amateur way, that it was possible to start a lunchtime Christian fellowship in the store, and there was a large turn-out at the special Stores Harvest Festival or Carol Service. These were, naturally, evangelistic opportunities, and quite apart from the people who came to Christ through them, the flavour of the gospel became widely known in the business community. In the work at All Souls it was a much more far-reaching and professional ministry, of course. But it was a work of Christian initiative from which I personally gained a valuable insight, and it taught me right at the outset of my ministry the important lesson of looking at every situation in which I was placed as a gateway for ministry, not a roadblock on progress.

A third example of Dr Stott's initiative was the installing of a chaplain in the London Polytechnic, which also lay within the parish. The influence of a dynamic man of God in such an environment is obvious. The chaplain was able to influence enormous numbers of young lives at a critical stage in their development. I fear that I would have felt 'There's nothing much we can do about the Poly. It is a self-governing institution and there is no way in which I can get in there and influence it.' I am sure that it was not easy to 'get in there'. But John succeeded – how, I do not know. It was a ministry towards a special group, in this case students, simply because they were part of the geographical area for which he had responsibility. So he did not rest until he had found an appropriate way to reach them.

Clearly not every community will have three such specialized areas for ministry within them. But each has some special group or groups which characterize it. If the local church is alert evangelistically, it will not spare any effort to make appropriate inroads with the gospel.

The media often appear to have little time for the church and its doings. I do not suppose the BBC, which was situated across the street from All Souls, had any initial prejudice towards building a relationship with the young rector of the adjacent church. But by the time he left the rectorship to become head of the London Institute for Contemporary Christianity, which he himself inaugurated, he had achieved a position of honoured trust in the BBC. They used his church to record their daily radio service on the air. They frequently broadcast from his church. He often walked across to the studio to do the 'Thought for the Day' at 7.50 a.m. That seems to me to be a fine example of making good use of the opportunities presented to him to build good relationships with the media, and to use those for the gospel. Another form of the media is writing. In his case it has not so much been in magazines, as in books and booklets. His booklet *Becoming a Christian* has been in print for very many years, and has been instrumental in leading thousands, probably hundreds of thousands of people, to take the initial plunge of commitment to Christ. What power there is in the pen! It is indeed mightier than the sword.

Here again, not every local church will have the BBC within its boundaries. Not every minister will have the talents for frequent appearances on the air. Not every pastor can write a booklet like *Becoming a Christian*,[3] or a book like *Basic Christianity*. But all churches have some form of regular publicity, and most have a church bulletin or magazine which goes into many an unbelieving home. Some could write a simple tract specifically prepared for their area. Some could work themselves into a position where they could write a column in the local newspaper on an occasional or regular basis, or else encourage a member of the congregation who happened to be gifted with the pen to do so. It needs a bit of nerve to accost the editor and tell him that he will not have an adequate product until he lets you write a regular piece! But it is just that sort of cheek that speaks volumes to some editors, and they may well be willing to give you a try. You could not ask for more.

A ninth expedient which John Stott has taken is to recognize *the opportunity provided by the large number of overseas students* in central London. All Souls is a church which supports many missionaries overseas, and it might well have rested satisfied with that situation. It did not, however, but set about actively befriending, through its members, the visitors from overseas who lived nearby. In these days of fast travel, when we live in a global village, it is easy to forget that the mission field is all around us. People from a variety of nations live in our street. On the whole, the Christian churches regard this as a bane rather than a blessing: 'We find it very hard in our area, because so many Chinese have come to live here.' In point of fact, of course, this mobility of population, this mixture of races in our cities, is a magnificent challenge to us to go that extra mile and get to know them and befriend them – and to do so with no hidden motive, but simply to embody among them the love with which Jesus has loved us, and to do it whether they will respond to him or not. I recall once being at All Souls when there was an international lunch which was very well attended. My guess is that different nationalities from time to time put on their favourite national dish for the rest. Accommodation could sometimes be arranged, legal or administrative aid given.

There is a great deal we can do with other nationalities if we are prepared to take the trouble. I know a church which has pioneered more than twenty 'congregations' of different nationals which it has taken the trouble to find and serve in the name of Jesus. It is demanding, hard work, but also very rewarding. We are finding in Vancouver that many Chinese from the mainland come here to study, and because they are welcomed and loved by local Christians without strings attached, some of them discover a personal faith for themselves. Coming as they do from a Communist country, they are naturally inquisitive about the religion of the West of which they have heard, but know nothing. There must be endless opportunities awaiting us in the local churches up and down our land, of getting to know and serve in the name of our Master those strangers who have come into our midst. If only we could see hospitality to them, putting ourselves out for them, as ministry we are offering to Jesus himself (Mt. 25), we might be less ready to pass them by on the other side. If only we could see that although we may not, for a variety of reasons, be able to go to the 'mission field', the 'mission field' has, none the less come to us, we might notice more, and care more. Many previous generations of Christians would have given much to have such opportunities in their day: but then people rarely moved a hundred miles from their birthplace. In our day, the opportunities are overwhelming.

Finally, I cannot help being struck by the *ministry* of All Souls *to the poor and disadvantaged*. It would have been all too easy for a large, fashionable, wealthy middle-class church in the West End to go its way oblivious of the seamier side of life represented by the adjacent Tottenham Court Road area. But All Souls under John Stott took on that challenge too. The Clubhouse was designed specifically to minister to the underprivileged youth of the neighbourhood, and it was one of the most exciting and rewarding of all the aspects of outreach from

All Souls. Jesus loved the poor, the diseased, the helpless, the children. Those who love him share that love. If not, their authenticity is in doubt. There can be hardly a church in the country which does not face the challenge of ministering to the poor in its vicinity. God forgive us, but we more often treat them as a nuisance than as men and women, boys and girls for whom Jesus was content to suffer and die. As Matthew 25 sharply informs us, they will condemn us on the day of judgment. For too long, Christians in general, and evangelicals in particular, have avoided involving themselves with the poor because it was too demanding and difficult on the one hand, and because, on the other, it was the main thrust of the ministry of the 'liberals' from whom evangelicals were anxious to dissociate themselves. That is not so true today, but the challenge of the poor in our midst directs us to one of the most obvious ways of spreading the gospel, not in word only but also in deed. In this ministry we shall need to have an infinite capacity to be disappointed. But then, God has that too . . . with us!

These ten methods of outreach are only samples of the work of the lively London church which for many years had John Stott as its rector, and still has him as beloved Rector Emeritus. I am delighted to take this opportunity to honour as friend and mentor one from whom I have learned so much. Even if we were to confine ourselves to these ten examples of evangelism which he has shown us, we would be able to hold up our heads when evangelism in the local church was discussed. John Stott does not so confine himself. He keeps learning. If we ask the source of his motivation, I think the passage he spoke on at my wedding many years ago tells the tale. He 'died for us', wrote Paul to the Thessalonians, 'so that whether we wake or sleep we might live with him' (1 Thes. 5:10, RSV). Christ did not die for us so that we might be forgiven. The forgiveness of sins was only to be a preliminary to our full enjoyment of his fellowship. And so it is with evangelism. Christ did not die for the church so that it could be forgiven, but so that it could, once forgiven, share his life. That life is one of ceaseless self-giving for the unlovely. That is the love which has taken hold of the Christian individual and church. We must give it room to be lived out in our churches for the sake of those who know nothing of that love. John Stott has blazed for us a trail, and a book like this, written by many friends from all over the world, is a wonderful opportunity to say to him a heartfelt 'Thank you'.

The search for ministry effectiveness in the modern world

Michael Cassidy

It is a singular privilege to contribute to this volume honouring John Stott on his seventieth birthday. Few people have influenced me more in my own ministry, or been such a blessing ever since student days. Apart from that, he got me going on a little birdwatching (orni-theology, he calls it!) during a trip in June 1988 to some Northern Natal parks near the Mozambique border. What a delight!

And I warm to my theme, too, because I know so much of John's concern, over all these years, has related to helping Christians worldwide, both clerical and lay, to move into greater effectiveness of ministry.

For myself this has been, and remains, an ongoing odyssey of mind and spirit. One has not arrived. Indeed, the search for ministry effectiveness, or greater effectiveness, holds one ever tighter in its grip, especially as the challenges and obstacles to Christian effectiveness advance, multiply and deepen world-wide. The horizons are indeed darkening across the world as ideologies, neo-paganism, hedonism, materialism and various false gospels lay their dread clutches on the souls of humankind.

Shine as lights

This is no time for a loss of Christian nerve, though, for we know that the gospel is good news against all bad news. Moreover, we know and are assured that light has shined into the world, and the darkness has not and will not overcome it (see Jn. 1:5).

What daunts us and makes the spirit tremble, however, is that it is we, sons and daughters through Christ of the living God, yet frail creatures of dust nevertheless, who are mandated by the apostle Paul to be 'without fault' and to 'shine like stars in the universe', in the midst of 'a crooked and depraved generation' (Phil. 2:15). In fact, not only are we, who were once part of the world's darkness and now are light, to 'live as children of light' (Eph. 5:8), but we are to 'expose' the 'fruitless deeds of darkness' (Eph. 5:11), 'demolish strongholds' (2 Cor. 10:4), 'take captive every thought to make it obedient to Christ' (2 Cor. 10:5), 'arguing persuasively about the kingdom of God' (Acts 19:8) and generally to be rather effective in ministry!

Paradoxically, the Calvary paradigm, and the eschatological pessimism about the Lord's home-straight of history (see Mt. 24), also alert us to the fact that we are destined at another level to be a non-triumphalist, failing community who will neither usher in Utopia, nor restore the kingdom of God, nor produce a millennium. Rather, we will hover tantalizingly between the 'already and the not yet', with our best achievement being to manifest a rather mottled outcrop of the kingdom 'midst a dreadfully wicked world' (see 2 Tim. 3), and probably midst a largely apostate church; a church full of 'counterfeit faith' (2 Tim. 3:8, RSV) where 'impostors' and 'deceivers' (v. 13, RSV) ply their trade and 'oppose the truth' (v. 8), 'having a form of godliness but denying its power' (v. 5).

Beyond that, we will know that any ministry we have, we have 'through God's mercy' (2 Cor. 4:1) because we are weak and sinful. In fact we are so sinful that we have to be kept weak and earthen, if need be through a thorn in the flesh, so that his strength might be 'made perfect in weakness' (2 Cor. 12:9), and it be shown that 'the transcendent power belongs to God and not to us' (2 Cor. 4:7, RSV).

This is why we embrace the paradoxical posture whereby, midst our personal weakness and our pessimism about human history, we nevertheless move as people of power, hoping to search for greater ministry effectiveness in helping the kingdom to come.

In this reflection, I first want to focus on three pre-requisites to ministry effectiveness, and then look at two spheres of ministry effectiveness, evangelism and social concern. These are my selected areas for this essay, knowing of course that there are many others.

I. Three pre-requisites to ministry effectiveness

1. A clear conversion

In the nine months prior to going up to Cambridge, I taught in a small prep school. Along with having to inflict my impoverished Latin and French on all those little boys, I was, *mirabile dictu*, given Divinity! Poor things! All they got from me were the muddled mumblings of the blind seeking to lead the blind. The pit, as you might presume, was where we all landed.

Then came conversion through a man in the Cambridge Inter-Collegiate Christian Union in my first few weeks at the university. Suddenly, overnight, I had a message and could actually lead others to Christ. Ministry effectiveness had made its modest beginnings in my life because I was now a converted person, and that made all the difference. I had found Christ in a living way for myself and now longed to share him with others.

Conversion comes in many shapes and sizes (*gradual* as in St John, a *crisis* as in St Paul, a *crisis at the end of a process* as in the Ethiopian eunuch, a *series of crises* as in St Peter), and no one pattern may be declared normative for all. Nevertheless it remains true that without a definite and clear personal knowledge of Christ as saviour and Lord, no-one will have an effective ministry in the biblical sense. Indeed, it is just this lack which presents us world-wide with the pitiful spectacle of certain clergy, and even some theologians, trying to ply their trade and reproducing in others the barren spiritual confusions and wastelands which characterize their own lives and ministries.

John Wesley stands as a prime precedent. All his first efforts to evangelize Indians and Colonists in Georgia in the years 1736–38 produced what one biographer calls his 'American Fiasco'.[1] The Moravians rightly discerned his problem, hence August Spangenberg's insistent question to him, 'Do you know Jesus Christ?' – in fact the very same question that Robert Footner put to me in Cambridge in October 1955.

In despair and ignominy Wesley left Georgia after a fruitless and abortive ministry. In his journal en route for home (24 Jan 1738) he could write: 'I went to America to convert the Indians: but oh! who shall convert me? . . . I have a fair summer religion.'[2]

Then came Aldersgate (24 May 1738). The man whose heart was there 'strangely warmed' now bolted from the new starting-blocks to become a mighty flame of evangelistic and discipling fire whose life still touches and blesses the world daily.

The difference between ministry ineffectiveness and effectiveness lay for John Wesley in a clear conversion.

Mildred E. Whitcomb put it this way: 'When once I took fright at God's Name, I now understand why there are people who stand on street corners shouting the Good News about God and His Son. The Church calls it conversion. The Bible calls it New Birth. I call it miracle. For that is what happened to me.'[3]

2. A good theological training

There are those who have effective ministries without good theological training. It would in my view, however, always hugely enhance a called person's effectiveness to get a good formal, theological training under Bible-honouring lecturers. In my own experience, although I am no theologian, I nevertheless remain deeply grateful for my four years at Fuller Theological Seminary.

The other side of the coin is evidenced when good people are sent to bad theological colleges. A prominent Anglican leader told me of some twenty-five ministers once in his charge. 'About 23 out of 25,' he said, 'had had a reasonable conversion years previously but *had been ruined by their theological colleges*.' I have seen this sort of thing again and again.

The unbelieving theologian. This ruin usually starts with that chief menace and scoundrel, the unbelieving theologian, who has got ensconced in a theological college where he can permanently imperil the ministry effectiveness of countless students committed to his charge. Such 'pervasive unbelief', which has made 'its way into ecclesiastical circles', is rightly described by USA theologian Martin Marty as one of the chief 'enemies of theology'.[4] I would add that this person is probably the chief enemy of the church as a whole.

The trouble is that this teacher produces after his or her kind. German theologian Helmut Thielicke, who could both lecture in theology and fill a church, describes the young person who could at one time lead an effective Bible study in his youth group, and who then goes off to theological college. When he returns after his third semester, he and his theological friends are invited once again to lead a Bible study. A question is raised. The young man and his other young theological 'pro's' feel summoned to the lists:

> With lances lowered and at a rattling gallop, with their jaws painfully locked, hardly repressing a howl of triumph, they pounce upon him. Then the technical terms fly around the uninitiated ears of the unhappy laymen. They rattle upon him words like 'synoptic tradition', 'hermeneutical principle', 'realized eschatology', 'prophetic fore-shortening of the time perspective', . . . so that he hastily runs for cover, with one hand held up to protect his face and the other raising the white flag.[5]

They, poor things, imagine they have engaged in a piece of 'effective ministry'. But how far from the truth are they! Adds Thielicke:

> They easily suppose that this truce, owing to helplessness, is victory and that they have convinced the other man. But in fact, instead of winning him over, they have merely applied a kind of shock therapy – only it was never 'therapy'. They have smothered the first little flame of a man's own spiritual life and a first shy question with the fire extinguisher of their erudition.[6]

The student with the question – now 'smothered and strangled' – replies: 'Although my fate and my life were at stake, those others came at me with their routine. I found in them no trace of life or truths learned by experience. I smelled only corpses of lifeless ideas.'[7]

Diabolical theology. This, says Thielicke in a later chapter, is 'diabolical theology'. It has become a coat of mail which 'crushes' people and 'freezes them to death' along with the theologian who has thus trafficked his wares. And what makes the difference between 'sacred theology and diabolical theology' is the 'hands and hearts which further it'.[8] If these be proud, unbending, sceptical, naturalistic or even irreverent, then the damage is done.

Pari passu with this theological arrogance comes the undermining of scriptural authority and the uniqueness of Jesus as God incarnate. As the reliability of Scripture is torpedoed, Jesus becomes ranged as part of a pantheon of religious options. Take your pick. Any will do. They all lead to the same place. Sincerity is all that counts. But try that on your medicine cupboard or in the cockpit of a 747! Yet the bad theologian will try it in his classroom and then the young pastor, having tried it in his congregation, wonders why he suffers from 'ministry ineffectiveness'.

In the foreword to his little classic *The Ring of Truth*, New Testament translator J. B. Phillips castigates those theologies and seminary teachers who have given the ordinary laymen 'the impression that the New Testament is no longer historically reliable'. He says:

> What triggered off my anger against some of our 'experts' is this. A clergyman, old, retired, useless if you like, took his own life because his reading of the 'new theology' . . . finally drove him, in his loneliness and ill-health, to conclude that his own life's work had been founded upon a lie. He felt that these highly-qualified writers and speakers must know so much more than he that they must be right. Jesus Christ did not really rise from the dead and the New Testament, on which he had based his life and ministry, was no more than a bundle of myths.
>
> That made me angry, and I remembered the terrible words of Jesus which, in effect, say that a man would be better off dead than cause one of 'his little ones to stumble'. For many years it has been my solid purpose to communicate the truth of the Christian Gospel. I am *not* concerned to distort or dilute the Christian faith so that modern undergraduates, for example, can accept it without a mumur. I am concerned with the truth revealed in and through Jesus Christ. Let the modern world conform to him, and never let us dare to try to make him fit into our clever-clever modern world. I am no anti-intellectual, any more than St Paul, who wrote so penetratingly that 'the world by wisdom knew not God'. But I say quite bluntly that some of the intellectuals (by no means all, thank God!) who write so cleverly and devastatingly about the Christian faith appear to have no personal knowledge of the living God.[9]

Modernity. In my own observations of the wrong sort of theological teachers, I feel their guilt lies in a false bowing at the shrine of modernity which produces this damage. Of course, the pastor's concern to reach modern people must on the one hand mean that theology can never be too modern, in that it must be packaged and repackaged to reach each new generation of contemporaries. But the whole endeavour aborts if modernity for its own sake is made the chief criterion and becomes an end in itself.

Following on from this false modernity comes the catastrophe of theological students hearing from their lecturers that they may set aside any aspects of New Testament teaching which do not fit modern man's naturalistic presuppositions.

Interestingly enough, Helmet Thielicke once again feels this is nothing new:

> It goes back two thousand years. Again and again the package of divine truth has been opened and everything which didn't suit was laid aside. Over and over, the figure of Jesus has been horribly amputated until he fit the Procrustean bed[10] of what one particular age held to be 'modern' concepts. In the first centuries he was shaped according to the Greek logos concept and made to square with philosophy. During the Enlightenment he was made into a rational being, under idealism an idea, in liberal protestantism a teacher of morality, and by the existentialists a Socrates who reveals the depths of human existence to us. Through the whole history of the church Jesus Christ has suffered a process of repeated crucifixion. He has been scourged and bruised and locked in the prison of countless systems and philosophies. Treated as a body of thought, he has literally been lowered into conceptual graves and covered with stone slabs so that he might not arise and trouble us any more.[11]

The German theologian then puts this shattering question:

> Isn't the history of Christianity the sum of the fatal misunderstandings which have arisen over Jesus Christ? Isn't the history of the church to the present day one vast experiment gone awry, a dreadful victory of the currently 'modern' over the Nazarene who must bear it all helplessly and silently?[12]

All this being so, the fact that so much thinking of this sort emanates from our theological seminaries and university departments of religion, means that those who would seek greater ministry effectiveness for the ministers of the church today must take long hard looks at the matter of theological training and at the kind of theologians into whose hands they are entrusting the rising generation of clergy and Christian workers. Thankfully there are men like John Stott who have done this. But many more senior leaders in the church need to give the matter urgent attention.

3. A well-discipled personal life

Ah! Here now comes the rub. Which of us in ministry does not know Paul's lament within our own souls? 'I do not understand what I do.

For what I want to do I do not do, but what I hate I do. . . . For I have the desire to do what is good, but I cannot do it' (Rom. 7:15, 18).

We know, however, that we can never rest with our personal lives in disarray, nor can we ever have any effective ministry if they are not right. Even as 'the Word became flesh' in Jesus, so must every word in Christian ministry become flesh if effectiveness is to be achieved. No wonder Paul could first exhort Timothy 'Take heed to yourself', before he pressed on him to take heed of what he taught (1 Tim. 4:16, RSV). Personal life preceded doctrinal faithfulness. Yet what struggles beset each one of us here! We long for greater effectiveness in ministry but we know that again and again we torpedo that coveted reality by the sinfulness and undisciplined nature of our personal lives.

Over the years 1971 to 1980, I had the huge privilege of several brief periods of study under the late and great Bishop Stephen Neill. Whenever I saw him after a spell away he would sit me down and ask me to mark myself out of 20 in: (1) *devotion*, (2) *diligence*, (3) *study*, (4) *priorities*, and (5) *personal relations*. A score of over 16 produced a grunt of approval, while any score below 12 was accounted weak, and produced strong rebuke. A score of 9 or below earned one a verbal flagellation, and I got a few!

For Stephen Neill it mattered not how many missions Africa Enterprise had lined up, or how many conferences one was speaking at, if one was failing in these areas of discipleship and personal life. Ministry effectiveness began in these hidden places, he believed.

Devotional life. Significantly enough, pride of place went to one's *devotional life*. He deplored the minister, evangelist, missionary or theological lecturer whose ministry was not born and daily nourished on the Bible, prayer and the enabling power of the Holy Spirit.

One great churchman once said: 'If I wished to humble anyone, I should question him about his prayers. I know nothing to compare with this topic for its sorrowful self-confessions.'[13] Yet curiously most of us, even those seeking an effective ministry, have a curious aversion to prayer, even though we know that

> Prayer moves the arm
> That moves the world
> To bring deliverance down.

In any event, what delights and what fresh power descend upon us when we conquer our reluctance and keep a strong prayer-life in motion!

Thus could the biographer of the great Samuel Chadwick record:

He was essentially a man of prayer. Every morning he would be astir shortly after six o'clock, and he kept a little room which was his private sanctum for his quiet hour before breakfast. He was mighty in public prayer because he was constant in private devotion ... When he prayed he expected God to do something. 'I wish I had prayed more,' he wrote toward the end of his life, 'even if I had worked less; and from the bottom of my heart I wish I had prayed better.'[14]

Could we not each one echo such a lament? May I add here that to travel with John Stott, as I did round South Africa in mid-1988, was to find oneself constantly challenged in this area. No matter how early I awoke to answer either the calls of nature or grace or both, John's light was always on! And I discovered that by 5 a.m. daily he was with his Lord in prayer and study of the Word. Then later in the day I would observe the effectiveness of his ministry, and while others wondered how and why, I knew!

Diligence and study. These were Stephen Neill's next two litmus tests for ministry effectiveness.

By *diligence* he meant serious and dedicated application to the task in hand. There was no place in the ministry for laziness or slackness. Effective ministry for him came forth from those who would work while others frittered, pray while others played and *study* while others slept. I generally found with the bishop that my study scored lowest, and he would fulminate on this.

I recollect in Nairobi in 1976 having a chat one evening with Billy Graham in his hotel room during PACLA (Pan African Christian Leadership Assembly). 'If I had my life over again,' said the great evangelist, 'I would study more – and I would cut out everything secondary.' Then he added with a twinkle: 'You know, laying foundation stones and all that sort of thing!' Donald Grey Barnhouse (of Tenth Presbyterian Church in Philadelphia) once said: 'If I had only three years to serve the Lord, I would spend two of them studying and preparing.'[15]

Again in this regard John Stott has been exemplary to us all and we salute him for this. Thus in his superb volume, *I Believe in Preaching*, he writes:

If we are to build bridges into the real world, and seek to relate the Word of God to the major themes of life and the major issues of the day, then we have to take seriously both the biblical text and the contemporary scene. We cannot afford to remain on either side of the cultural divide. To withdraw from the world into the Bible (which is escapism), or from the Bible into the world (which is conformity), will be fatal to our preaching ministry. Either mistake makes bridge-building impossible and non-communication inevitable. Instead, it is our responsibility to explore the territories on both sides of the ravine until we become thoroughly familiar with them. Only then shall we discern the connections between them and be able to speak the divine Word to the human situation with any degree of sensitivity and accuracy. Such exploration means study.[16]

Clearly for both Neill and Stott, those who would be effective ministers of the Word need to remain students all their lives, and subscribe to Calvin's dictum that 'None will ever be a good minister of the Lord unless he is first of all a scholar.'[17] C. H. Spurgeon put it this way: 'He who no longer sows in the study will no more reap in the pulpit.'[18]

Our diligence and study, however, dare not move directly from the isolated ivory tower of the study or lecture room into the pulpit. That only produces the ministry of the purely cognitive and cerebral against which liberation theologians in Latin America and Africa have so justifiably reacted. Our study of the Word should take us to the noisy street, the hospital bed, and the coal-face of political, social or physical need and thence via the place of prayer and further reflection back to the pulpit of proclamation.

Priorities and relationships. Stephen Neill's next test was *right priorities* – a category we can take with his fifth concern, for *right relationships*. By this he meant the need to manifest a properly ordered life, with a carefully synchronized balance between the demands of one's God-given calling and the importance of having all life's basic relationships rightly working.

Though I never discussed it with him, I think he would have approved of the priority line once presented to me by a friend in Washington, DC. 'We need', said my friend, 'to put our relationship with Jesus first, with our spouse and families second, and with our friends and colleagues third. Only fourth comes the work of witness, and finally one's organization.'

Most of us get close to getting this all the other way round. In fact one frenzied and frustrated minister to whom I put that line replied: 'You could inverse that order exactly for me and that would be my life. The church and its committees come first, then my preaching and teaching work, then my friends and colleagues, then my family, who get the dregs of my time, and finally the Lord with whom I spend almost no time.'

Shortly after sharing his lament with me he died of a heart attack.

Perhaps out of this tale one might highlight three things:

Calling. First, each person in ministry needs to be true to his or her calling and not come aside 'to serve tables' (Acts 6:2, RSV), unless the serving of tables or its equivalent is one's calling. Most in Christ's work lead inordinately busy lives. Nothing is easier than to be side-tracked from the ministry of the Word and prayer into endless committees and organizational wheel-spinning. Says Paul to Timothy: 'Fulfil your ministry' (2 Tim. 4:5, RSV), and be careful, like the soldier, not to get 'involved in civilian affairs' (2 Tim. 2:4). For Jesus, his joy was being able to affirm to the Father: 'I have brought you glory by completing the work you gave me to do' (Jn. 17:4). If God gives us the cabbage patch to work, we must not spend and be spent on the rose garden. I can't think of anything worse than finally facing the Lord and hearing him declare one's labours misfocused and therefore, in terms of his 'Plan A', to be pronounced 'wood, hay or straw' (1 Cor. 3:12).

Family life. Point two from the tale of the upside-down minister relates to family life. He just could not give his family adequate time. Most of us know the problem. Yet it need not defeat us. To plan our year, our week and our individual days to make room for family time and recreation is the starting-point. This allocated time needs to be diarized, guarded and fought for like a tigress for her cubs. Even with this there will be failure. But without it there will be potential disaster. For nothing torpedoes an effective ministry more lethally than a home which at one level or another is falling apart.

Management. Point three from the upside-down minister lies in the need all of us have in Christian ministry to know something of the art of management. He was being kindly killed off by committees. At Seminary, few of us are ever told we will need any executive or management skills if we are to have an effective ministry. Nor are we taught any. So we struggle along, learning here and there, and coping by trial and error – mainly error! The problem is that the minister or Christian worker who lacks executive ability to any marked degree, however spiritual he or she may be, will not be able to translate vision into action.

Lord Macaulay once noted of John Wesley that he had a genius for government not inferior to that of Cardinal Richelieu:

> The genius of his organization is still seen in the church which he founded. It is owing to his superb executive ability and powers of organization that the movement remained unshaken even

when deprived of his presence and guidance. His judgment of men, his skill in using them, his power to employ them to the best advantage and to attach them to himself in loyal submission to his authority amounted to genius and saved the movement from the most serious dangers.[19]

While we can't all be Wesleys, at the least we need to develop some administrative skills (see Pr. 11:14). This will also call for 'a post-Jethro' ministry in which we learn the art of delegation. In fact, one definition of leadership is 'the ability to recognize the special abilities and limitations of others, combined with the capacity to fit each one into the job where he [or she] will do his [or her] best'.[20]

The indispensable requirement. Perhaps overarching all these qualities, the effective minister of the gospel needs what J. Oswald Sanders calls 'the indispensable requirement', namely the fullness of the Holy Spirit. Says Sanders simply: 'Spiritual leadership can be exercised only by Spirit-filled men.'[21] Then he adds:

Appointment of men with a secular or materialistic outlook prevents the Holy Spirit from carrying out His programme for the church in the world. The Holy Spirit does not take control of any man or body of men against their will. When He sees men elected to positions of leadership who lack spiritual fitness to cooperate with Him He quietly withdraws and leaves them to implement their own policy according to their own standards, but without His aid.[22]

In this regard, the heated charismatic and anti-charismatic debates over proper vocabulary relating to the Spirit's work will often be futile. The thing is to press through to the reality (whether it be labelled the Baptism in the Spirit or the fullness of the Spirit) so that our ministries gain new effectiveness as we seek to be marked by the Spirit's walk and way. Along with that will also come a manifestation of both his fruit (Gal. 5:22) and his gifts (1 Cor. 12, 14, *etc.*). Otherwise we end up illustrating the lament made by Patriarch Athenagoras of the Orthodox Church: 'We have made the Church an organization like any other . . . it goes, more or less, really mostly less, but it goes. Only it goes like a machine, not like something alive.'[23] This being so, the person who seeks ministry effectiveness will register some great words spoken in 1968 at the Ecumenical Council of Churches meeting in Uppsala by Metropolitan Ignatios of Latakia:

Without the Holy Spirit, God is far away,
    Christ stays in the past,
    the Gospel is a dead letter,
    the Church is simply an organisation,
    authority a matter of domination,
    mission a matter of propaganda,
    the liturgy no more than an evocation,
    Christian living a slave morality.

But in the Holy Spirit:
    the cosmos is resurrected and groans with the birth-pangs
        of the Kingdom,
    the risen Christ is there,
    the Gospel is the power of life,
    the Church shows forth life of the Trinity,
    authority is a liberating service,
    mission is a Pentecost,
    the liturgy is both memorial and anticipation,
    human action is deified.[24]

In sum, ministry effectiveness is a good which is much to be desired. But it does not fall from the high heavenlies into the lap of every sincere soul who would casually covet it. It comes to those who qualify and pay some price for it. In my own judgment, at the least this will generally involve (though some glorious exceptions challenge the rule) a *clear conversion*, a *good theological training* and a *well discipled personal life*.

With these in place, the Lord's servant will seek ministry effectiveness in the spheres of mission, evangelism, worship and service. However, I want now to highlight two dimensions, namely evangelism and socio-political concern, and the battle for balance in these two areas. BBC (Balanced Biblical Christianity) is always John Stott's plea.

II. Two spheres in which to seek ministry effectiveness

1. Evangelism

It is sad to say, but true, that many in the modern church are happy to be fixated in a hopelessly unbalanced way on everything under the sun except evangelism. Thus it is relegated to the category of the irrelevant, or the pious, and set on one side while more pressing matters of social concern hold sway.

This being so, we must cry out vigorously to one section of the modern church that evangelism must yet retain pride of place in our witness if we would be true to our Lord and his Great Commission. On the other side we call on more conservative Christians who are strong on evangelism to embrace a biblical socio-political concern as part of a holistic ministry and witness.

Turning to the Old Testament we find the powerfully pregnant word of Proverbs: 'He who wins souls is wise' (Pr. 11:30). In the New Testament there is the command of Jesus to 'Go into all the world and proclaim the good news to all creation' (Mk. 16:15) and the word of Paul, 'Do the work of an evangelist' (2 Tim. 4:5). Of course, the whole book of Acts is also a story of evangelism.

Evangelism is not there only as the labour of the professional. It was the primary task laid upon the whole early church, and it still is. Canon Michael Green puts it this way:

> Evangelism is not an optional extra for those who like that kind of thing. It is not an acceptable pastime for the person who likes making a fool of himself on a soap box in the open air, or titillating his ego by addressing a large gathering in a public hall. Evangelism is sharing the good news of what God has done for us all. It is the sacred duty of every Christian.[25]

Then he adds:

> Evangelism is not the task of the ordained ministry alone. It is not primarily their task at all. They are meant to preach and teach the faith, but by the very nature of things they are not in such close contact with agnostics as most members of their churches are from Monday to Saturday. There is no hint among ancient records that the early church saw evangelism as the task of the leadership alone. All were called to pass on the good news. It was too good to leave to the professionals.[26]

In other words, whoever would seek to be true to Christ and to seek a more effective witness, whether in the ordained ministry or out of it, cannot and dare not bypass this holy obligation. In order to do it more effectively we need to begin by knowing what evangelism is – and isn't.

First of all, it is not everything the church is sent to do. That we subsume under the rubric of 'mission'. Teaching, counselling, protesting, liberating, caring, pastoring – all are part of mission. But, secondly, evangelism is that unique dimension of mission geared to the proclamation of the Evangel (Gk. *euangelion, e.g.* Gal. 1:11) to those who have not heard it, or not responded to it, or not understood it, or forgotten it.

The gospel is preached. Speaking in the South African Congress on Mission and Evangelism in Durban in 1973, Canon Douglas Webster, then of St Paul's Cathedral, noted: 'In the great majority of the seventy-six instances of the word "gospel" in the New Testament, the verb that goes with it is "to preach" . . . Just as a game is something you normally play, so the gospel is something you normally preach.'[27]

I believe that to be so. Indeed Helmut Thielicke, if we may come back to him, affirms that the critical criterion of every theology is that 'it must be preachable, because its very origin is in preaching'.[28] But, as Thielicke also notes, 'the gospel must be preached afresh and told in new ways to every generation, since every generation has its own unique questions. This is why the gospel must constantly be forwarded to a new place, because the recipient is repeatedly changing his place of residence.'[29]

There is here, then, a fixed deposit of truth (Gk. *kērygma, e.g.* 1 Cor. 1:21) which is communicated to the seeking person, and there is also the context or 'new address' at which the seeker resides. The preaching produces an interplay between text and context, on which more in a moment.

As to the kerygmatic messsage it could, I believe, be summarized in a simple outline. It involves the comunication of:

1. *One event*: The Jesus Event (Acts 8:35) – his life, death, resurrection and return. Interestingly even C. H. Dodd included the Parousia within the kerygma;[30]

2. *Two offers:* ● the forgiveness of sins (Acts 2:38a)
   ● the gift of the Holy Spirit (Acts 2:38b);

3. *Three demands:* The kingdom is at hand (Mk. 1:15a) – therefore
   ● repent (Mk. 1:15)
   ● believe (Mk. 1:15)
   ● follow (Jn. 1:43);

4. *Four relationships:* ● with God (Eph. 2:4–6; 1 Pet. 2:9–10)
   ● with oneself (Mt. 22:39)
   ● with the church (Acts 2:47)
   ● with the world (Mk. 16:15).

Differently and more simply, we could say that we present a historical proclamation, a theological explanation and an ethical summons.
We present the story of Jesus, we explain it, and we urge response to it.

While many of us know the message of evangelism, however, we
battle to get it through effectively. To be sure, I know I do. Perhaps the
reason for this lies in failure to understand our context adequately and
adapt not the '*esse*' of the message, but its wrapping and packaging.

In this adaptation we will at some time have to grapple with *two types
of mega-shift*, the one relating to how and what we know and how we
experience life, and the other relating to where we live (no longer in
the rural areas but in the mushrooming mega-cities of the world). Both
these issues were ably addressed in the 1989 Lausanne II Congress on
World Evangelisation in Manila, by Os Guinness (see chapter 4) and
Ray Bakke respectively.

Modernity. At Lausanne II, Os Guinness noted apropos of modernity that it is not basically the idea of modernization in the sense of
change and development. Nor is it a description of new philosophical
attacks on the faith. Rather it is the result, in the first instance, of three
revolutions – the capitalist in the fifteenth century, the industrial and
technological beginning mainly in the early nineteenth century, and
the ideological in the eighteenth and nineteenth centuries.

Another way of putting it, says Guinness, is:

> Modernity is the result of a whole constellation of forces work-
> ing together. The capitalist economy, the modern centralized
> bureaucratic state, the new industrial technology going every-
> where, rapid population growth, urbanization, the mass media,
> and as a certain stage is reached, but only then, globalization, so
> that all these things happen together and their tentacles reach
> to the furthest corners of the world.[31]

The problem with all this, observes Guinness, is that it leads to
information overload, and then a state of 'unknowing' brought on by
the hankering for 'happiness in a small circle where each person wants
to know and care as little as possible'. Television, advertising and pop
culture (the 'terrible trio') have thus produced a shift in the way people
experience and understand the world. This change produces a huge
challenge in our search for greater ministry effectiveness because we
find ourselves dealing with 'The shift from words to images; the shift
from action to spectacle; the shift from exposition to entertainment;
the shift from truth to feeling; the shift from conviction to sentiment'.
This shift results in our knowing 'all about the immediate and nothing

about the ultimate, because the explosion of information (facts without a framework) is leading to knowledge without obedience, wisdom or action'.[32]

The main danger here is that modernity has produced a hostility to the ideas of transcendence and truth. By increasing choice and change we decrease 'in committment, continuity and conviction'. We downplay the either/or, life or death dimensions of the gospel and 'up-play' a generalized syncretism. As in the supermarket, we can pick and choose bits and pieces of religion here and there but ignore the lordship of Christ which says 'give all to me, for all is mine'.

If then we are to deepen our evangelistic commitments and become more effective in ministry, this shift in the way people think, feel, understand and protect themselves from serious commitment to the lordship of Jesus Christ is going to have to be faced more resolutely than ever.

Urbanization. The second big shift we have to grapple with relates to the massive move of the planet's peoples to the city.

In our Africa Enterprise ministry we have understood our calling to be the evangelization of the cities of Africa. But our effectiveness in doing this has been exceedingly modest, relative to the magnitude of the task. We have focused on 'event-type', short-term evangelistic happenings. I am convinced now that if we are to make better progress we need to hear the kind of challenge Ray Bakke brings. We will have to wrestle much more fully with urban issues if we are to be ready in any way for the Africa, and the world, of tomorrow. Bakke puts it this way: 'A reflective reading of the biblical urban texts requires that we have a vision *for* the city as well as *of* the city.'[33] He goes on:

> The biblical picture of God is one that grapples with the total environment. He is the God who gets glory *in spite* of Pharaoh and *because* of Cyrus. This is the God who directed the building and occupation of cities in the past, and who integrates the creative and redemptive threads in a kingdom agenda of which the church is both sign and agent. It is this large picture of God that gives us permission, yet requires us, to get our heads and our hearts around the great cities of the world.[34]

In other words, we all need to understand the cities, where we labour not only spiritually and morally but sociologically, so that our evangelism goes to the polar points of need. It not only creates an event by which some souls are won, but triggers an ongoing chemistry of process by which the city can be changed and brought more under the lordship of Jesus.

In this understanding, our mechanisms of discipling inquirers will need fresh scrutiny. Instead of teaching people just to have assurance of salvation, plus a regular quiet time, we will have to help them bring spirit and matter more into convergence. Each Christian will need to see himself or herself as 'a power-unit', which will translate private faith into public action for the Christian transformation of the city. Indeed the whole evangelistic enterprise world-wide must grapple afresh with the ongoing mobilization of the lay person for effective witness of every sort. Interestingly enough, at Lausanne in Manila, all those won to Christ by the witness or efforts of an individual lay person were asked to stand. By far the majority of the Congress stood, thereby revealing individual personal witness as by far the most effective means of evangelization. I tested this a few weeks later in a South African group with the same result. So the use, misuse, or non-use of the lay person, along with many other challenges, face each of us who is concerned for greater ministry effectiveness in evangelism in this last decade of the twentieth century.

2. Socio-political concern and compassionate care

In terms of maintaining proper balances, the Christian faith is fraught with hazard, not least in the area of socio-political concern, and the proper Christian expression of compassionate care in all things societal.

The history of the church, certainly in more modern times, gives full credence to the perilous path the Christian is called on to follow. Thus it was in the late nineteenth and early twentieth centuries that liberal Protestantism lost its biblical balance. While cleaving to a proper social concern for the upliftment of all mankind, it abandoned and betrayed that biblical faithfulness which upheld the deity of Jesus, the supernatural dimensions of Scripture, and the primacy of evangelism and missionary outreach. While embracing the Great Commandment to love the world, liberals forsook the Great Commission to evangelize the world. They seemed to believe the kingdom of God on earth could be brought in merely by political and economic endeavours, together with social protest. As the church tends to live and theologize at the extremities of an oscillating pendulum of theological reaction, it was not surprising that evangelicals not only reacted but over-reacted, thus tossing out the baby of social concern with the bath water of liberal theology. The commitment to social action as historically embraced by evangelicals (one thinks of the Wesleys, Wilberforces and Shaftes-burys) was now jettisoned in what American theologian David Moberg called 'the great reversal', in a book of that title.[35]

This reversal was tragic but not wholly beyond understanding. For while the so-called 'social gospellers' were now neglecting the impera-tive of taking the good news of salvation for sinners to the ends of the earth, evangelicals inevitably felt with new intensity the huge burden and responsibility for world mission and evangelism. The legitimacy of their passion for world mission however did not excuse the illegitimacy of their developing neglect of societal issues.

Neo-evangelicalism. Thankfully, the pendulum began to swing again with the arrival on the scene in the 50s of men like Carl Henry in North America and John Stott in Britain. Henry and the Fuller Seminary, of which Henry was a founding faculty member, saw them-selves as a form of 'neo-evangelicalism'.

In 1947, Henry put out a volume called *The Uneasy Conscience of Modern Fundamentalism*.[36] He was not prepared to allow a comfortable spectating of all the world's ills just as 'signs of the end-times'. So he affirmed that 'while the Lord tarries, the gospel is still relevant to every problem that vexes two billion inhabitants of an apprehensive globe'.[37] More than that, he castigated the so-called fundamentalists of the 1930s for developing a 'disastrous isolation from the questions on which the future direction of civilization hung'. For, in his view, they had not only ignored the philosophical challenges that Christianity could bring against the prevailing cultural views, but they were also ready 'to fall all over each other in the rush to make it clear that they have no message which is relevant to modern political, sociological, economic and educational tensions'.[38] Said Henry, 'It is an application of, not a revolt against, fundamentals of the faith, for which I plead.'[39] Then he lamented: 'For the first protracted period in its history, evangelical Christianity stands divorced from the great social reform movements.'[40]

Thankfully, as men like Carl Henry and David Hubbard in the USA, and John Stott in the UK, began to cry for evangelical reform at this point, it began to happen through the 50s, 60s and 70s. Finally it became settled evangelical orthodoxy in 1974 at the first Lausanne Congress on World Evangelisation. Balance was returning. *Deo Gloria.* Thus the *Lausanne Covenant* could rightly express evangelical pen-itence:

> both for our neglect and for having sometimes regarded evan-gelism and social concern as mutually exclusive. Although

reconciliation with man is not reconciliation with God, nor is social action evangelism, nor is political liberation salvation, nevertheless we affirm that evangelism and socio-political involvement are both part of our Christian duty. For both are necessary expressions of our doctrines of God and man, our love for our neighbour and our obedience to Jesus Christ.[41]

Commenting on this balancing clause in a post-Congress Symposium of essays, Athol Gill of Australia wrote:

> The traditional evangelical position has been that 'the renewal of the individual also reforms society', but this tragically under-estimates the existence and the power of corporate evil. Changes in the lives of individuals do not automatically lead to changes in the structures of society. As one Congress report expressed it, 'Institutionalised evil requires institutional action.'[42]

In the 1970s and 80s, around the world, the Christian church generally, and evangelical Christians specifically, pressed on further with the battle for balance as church leaders, pastors, evangelists and missionaries struggled with how to work all this out practically.

Manila. Then, in the second Lausanne Congress in Manila in 1989, the Manila Manifesto caught the balances even more succinctly but perhaps also more explicitly. In a section on the gospel and social responsibility, it states this:

> The authentic gospel must become visible in the transformed lives of men and women. As we proclaim the love of God we must be involved in loving service, and as we preach the kingdom of God we must be committed to its demands of justice and peace.
> Evangelism is primary because our chief concern is with the gospel, that all people may have the opportunity to accept Jesus Christ as Lord and Saviour. Yet Jesus not only proclaimed the kingdom of God. He also demonstrated its arrival by works of mercy and power. We are called today to a similar integration of words and deeds. In a spirit of humility we are to preach and teach, minister to the sick, feed the hungry, care for prisoners, help the disadvantaged and handicapped and deliver the oppressed. While we acknowledge the diversity of spiritual gifts, callings and contexts, we also affirm that good news and good works are inseparable.

The proclamation of God's kingdom necessarily demands the prophetic denunciation of all that is incompatible with it. Among the evils we deplore are destructive violence, including institutionalized violence, political corruption, all forms of exploitation of people and of the earth, the undermining of the family, abortion on demand, the drug traffic and the abuse of human rights. In our concern for the poor, we are distressed by the burden of debt in the two-thirds world. We are also outraged by the inhuman conditions in which millions live, who bear God's image as we do.

Not overboard. The challenge now that socio-political concern and action is back where it belongs is not to go overboard on it. So many situations, my own South African one included, are still heavily beset with oppression and the absence of true liberation. There is therefore a ready-made danger lurking in the wings for the liberation passion to become so over-riding and compelling that in the end the whole gospel and the whole work of mission become re-interpreted in political categories. Some liberation theology exponents seem to come close to this.

No issue, of course, can or should be taken with the goal defined by men like Gustavo Gutiérrez, in his epoch-making volume *A Theology of Liberation*, when he writes of the need to act for 'liberation from all that limits or keeps man from self-fulfilment, and liberation from all impediments to the exercise of freedom'.[43] All that is well and good. Liberation theologians have been helpful in re-introducing hope for history into the Christian perspective once again. More than that, they have dared to believe that Christ is Lord, and can bring nations, groups, and governments under his righteous rule. But we cannot concede validity to any attempts to interpret salvation just in socio-political categories, or effectively to see labours for socio-political liberation as the whole task of mission in the church.

Clearly evangelical Christians have often failed by confining Christ to heavenly heights, where he only deals with individual and personal problems, and only urges us to save souls from the sinking ship of the world. Nevertheless in correcting that imbalance we will not go to the other extreme, noted by Emilio Núñez of El Salvador and René Padilla of Argentina, of reducing 'the purpose of God in history to mere humanization' and thereby 'losing sight of the ultimate cause of injustice which is within man himself'.[44]

The inimitable and ever quotable John Stott himself puts it all this way:

Although liberation from oppression and the creation of a new and better society are definitely God's good will for man, yet it is necessary to add that these things do not constitute the 'salvation' which God is offering the world in and through Jesus Christ. They could be included in the 'mission of God', . . . in so far as Christians are giving themselves to serve in these fields. But to call socio-political liberation 'salvation' and to call social activism 'evangelism' – this is to be guilty of a gross theological confusion. It is to mix what Scripture keeps distinct – God the Creator and God the Redeemer, the God of the cosmos and the God of the Covenant, the world and the church, common grace and saving grace, justice and justification, the reformation of society and the regeneration of men. For the salvation offered in the gospel of Christ concerns persons rather than structures. It is deliverance from another kind of yoke than political and economic oppression.[45]

III. Conclusion

All the above speaks of the battle for balance which is, by my lights, a major and crucial dimension in the search for effective ministry.

The pre-requisites for such ministry, we saw, were a clear conversion, a good theological training, and a well-discipled personal life. If we can add to these pre-requisites a balanced, biblical, active harmonizing of vigorous evangelism with a deep socio-political concern, part of whose expression is focused in compassionate care for Jesus' sake, then we will have made at least some meaningful strides in the search for ministry effectiveness.

Beyond that, many of us will know that few people helped us more towards this end than the one whose seventieth birthday we celebrate in this volume. To John Stott, then, we express deep gratitude and to John Stott's Lord we ascribe, as is most justly due, all might, majesty, domination and praise, now and for ever.

Notes on chapters

John Stott: An introduction

1 Henry Bett, *Studies in English Literature* (Epworth Press, 1929), p. 104.
2 Derek Beales and Geoffrey Best (eds.), *History, Society and the Churches* (Cambridge University Press, 1985), p. 1.
3 John Eddison (ed.), *'Bash' – a study in spiritual power* (Marshalls, 1983), p. 57.
4 *Ibid.*, p. 57.
5 John Stott, *Basic Christianity*, 2nd ed., p. 128. (Full publication details of all John Stott's books can be found in the list at the end of this volume.)
6 John Stott, *Men with a Message*, p. 1.
7 John Pollock, *A Cambridge Movement* (John Murray, 1953), pp. 263–264.
8 John Stott, 'World-wide Evangelical Anglicanism', in John C. King (ed.), *Evangelicals Today* (Lutterworth Press, 1973).
9 *Christian Foundations*, ed. Philip E. Hughes and Frank Colquhoun (Hodder & Stoughton, 1964–67); from the Foreword by Hugh Gough, Archbishop of Sydney.
10 Charles Smyth, *Simeon and Church Order* (Cambridge University Press, 1940), p. 9.
11 Charles Smyth, *Cyril Forster Garbett* (Hodder & Stoughton, 1959), p. 453.
12 C. René Padilla (ed.), *The New Face of Evangelicalism* (Hodder & Stoughton, 1976).
13 *Ibid.*, pp. 35–36.
14 David F. Wright (ed.), *Essays in Evangelical Social Ethics* (Paternoster, 1979), pp. 179f.
15 Quotation taken from a letter to UCCF Associates, Autumn 1989.
16 *Cf.* H. C. G. Moule, *Charles Simeon* (IVF, 2nd ed. 1965), p. xii.
17 Charles Smyth, *Simeon and Church Order* (Cambridge University Press, 1940), p. 7, quoting from Sir G. O. Trevelyan, *Life and Letters of Lord Macaulay* (1908), p. 50n.
18 John Stott, *I Believe in Preaching*, p. 15.
19 John Stott, *The Preacher's Portrait*, p. vii.
20 Charles Simeon, with Introduction by John Stott, *Evangelical Preaching: An Anthology of Sermons* (Multnomah, 1986), p. xxvii.
21 Jean Claude, *Essay on the Composition of a Sermon*; English tr. republished together with one hundred 'skeletons', being the substance of sermons preached before the university by the Rev. Charles Simeon, MA, Fellow of Kings College, Cambridge (S. Cornish, 1837).
22 Charles Simeon, with Introduction by John Stott, *op. cit.*
23 Harry Blamires, *The Christian Mind* (SPCK, 1963).
24 J. B. Lancelot, *Francis James Chavasse* (Blackwell, 1929), p. 110.

25 See, for example, the Preface to *The Cross of Christ*, pp. 7ff.
26 David L. Edwards, *Leaders of the Church of England 1828–1944* (Oxford University Press, 1971), p. 334.
27 *Essentials*, p. 1.

Chapter 1: The authority of Scripture in an age of relativism
1 Oliver O'Donovan, *Resurrection and Moral Order: An Outline for Evangelical Ethics* (IVP, 1986), p. 122.
2 Richard N. Longenecker, 'Three Ways of Understanding Relations between the Testaments: Historically and Today', in G. F. Hawthorne and O. Betz (eds.), *Tradition and Interpretation in the New Testament: Essays in Honour of E. Earl Ellis for His Sixtieth Birthday* (Eerdmans and Mohr, 1987), pp. 22–32.
3 Helpful representative articles on the ethical use of the Old Testament in the theonomic and dispensational traditions are Greg L. Bahnsen, 'Christ and the role of civil government: The theonomic perspective', *Transformation* 5.2 and 5.3 (1988), and Norman L. Geisler, 'Dispensationalism and ethics', *Transformation* 6.1 (1989).
4 Walter Brueggemann, *The Land: Place as Gift, Promise, and Challenge in Biblical Faith* (SPCK, 1978), is a most stimulating survey of the land tradition in the Scriptures, emphasizing the redemptive historical dimension and yet showing how the theme can be fruitfully applied today.
5 O. O'Donovan, *Resurrection and Moral Order*, pp. 60–61.
6 Chris Wright, 'Response to the Theological Overviews' (of the presentations in the Social Concern Track at the Lausanne II conference in Manila), *Transformation* 7.1 (1990), p. 17.
7 O. O'Donovan, *op. cit.*, p. 67.
8 H. R. Niebuhr, *Christ and Culture* (Harper and Row, 1951).
9 Christopher J. H. Wright, *Living as the People of God: The Relevance of Old Testament Ethics* (IVP, 1983). (In N. America, the same book is entitled *An Eye for an Eye*.)
10 Vern S. Poythress, *Science and Hermeneutics: Implications of Scientific Method for Biblical Interpretation* (Apollos, 1988).
11 Thomas S. Kuhn, *The Structure of Scientific Revolutions* (University of Chicago Press, 2nd ed. 1970).
12 Vern Poythress, *op. cit.*, p. 43.
13 Millard C. Lind, 'The Concept of Political Power in Ancient Israel', *The Annual of the Swedish Theological Institute* 7 (1968–69), pp. 4–24.
14 One does not need to agree with the sociological positivism and ideological motivation of Norman Gottwald to accept the thrust of his detailed analysis of the close functional relationship between Israel's social, economic and political structures and ideals on the one hand and the total shape of their religious beliefs on the other. In *The Tribes of Yahweh* (SCM, 1980) he has shown with massive evidence how distinctive the Israelites actually were from their surrounding culture, both in values and in practice. *Cf.* also Christopher J. H. Wright, 'The Ethical Relevance of Israel as a Society', *Transformation* 1.4 (1984), pp. 11–21.

15 John Goldingay, *Theological Diversity and the Authority of the Old Testament* (Eerdmans, 1987). I am thinking particularly of chapter 3, 'A Contextualizing Study of "the People of God" in the Old Testament'.

16 In *Living as the People of God*, chapter 8, 'Society and culture'.

17 *Cf.* Wright, *ibid.*, chapter 7, 'Law and the legal system' and also G. Wenham, 'Law and the legal system in the Old Testament', chapter 2 in B. N. Kaye and G. J. Wenham (eds.) *Law, Morality and the Bible* (IVP, 1978), pp. 24–52.

18 John Goldingay is again very helpful in stressing the importance of the concrete particularity of Old Testament laws and institutions. They prevent us from being content with abstract generalities. See *Approaches to Old Testament Interpretation* (IVP, 1981; 2nd ed. Apollos, 1990), p. 55:

> Thus either the Bible's statements tell us how to live, or (when they do not do this) these actual statements are the model for and the measure of our attempts to state how we are to live. This means we do not ignore the particularity of biblical commands (and apply them to our own day as if they were timeless universals). Nor are we paralysed by their particularity (and thus unable to apply them to our day at all). We rejoice in their particularity because it shows us how the will of God was expressed in their context, and we take them as our paradigm for our own ethical construction.

19 Review in the USA publication *TSF Bulletin*, March–April 1985.

Chapter 2: The obsolescence of the atonement

1 Stephen Neill, *Christian Faith and Other Faiths: The Christian Dialogue with Other Religions* (Oxford University Press, 2nd ed. 1970).

2 Wilfred Cantwell Smith, *The Meaning and End of Religion* (SPCK, 1978).

3 Hans Küng, *et al.*, *Christianity and the World Religions: Paths to Dialogue with Islam, Hinduism, and Buddhism* (Collins, 1987), p. xiv.

4 John Hick, 'The Non-Absoluteness of Christianity', in *The Myth of Christian Uniqueness: Toward a Pluralistic Theology of Religions*, ed. John Hick and Paul Knitter (SCM Press, 1988), p. 20.

5 Rosemary Radford Reuther, 'Feminism and Jewish Christian Dialogue', in *The Myth of Christian Uniqueness*, pp. 137–148.

6 See Paul F. Knitter, *No Other Name? A Critical Survey of Christian Attitudes Toward the World Religions* (SCM Press, 1985), pp. 2–14.

7 See the argument developed in Peter L. Berger, *The Precarious Vision: A Sociologist looks at Social Fictions and Christian Faith* (Doubleday, 1961), pp. 8–101.

8 This is what sociologists understand by 'privatization' and it is a phenomenon that is evident, not only in the liberal, but among the conservative as well. See James Davison Hunter, *American Evangelism: Conservative Religion and the Quandary of Modernity* (Rutgers University Press, 1983), pp. 73–101.

9 The ideal of a model is partly borrowed from Ian T. Ramsay's discussions in *Christian Discourse: Some Logical Explanations* (Oxford University Press, 1965) and *Religious Language* (SCM Press, 1957).

10 John Calvin, for example, assumed that because of God's exalted nature,

which is beyond our cognitive range, and because of our sin, an objective and divinely given revelation was necessary and indispensable. 'If we turn aside from the Word,' he said, 'though we may strive with strenuous haste, yet since we have got off the track, we shall never reach the goal. For we should so reason that the splendour of the divine countenance, which even the apostle calls "unapproachable", is for us like an inexplicable labyrinth unless we are conducted into it by the thread of the Word; so that it is better to limp along this path than to dash with all speed outside it' (Calvin, *Institutes*, I. vi. 3). See also T. H. L. Parker, 'Calvin's Concept of Revelation', *Scottish Journal of Theology* 2 (March, 1949), pp. 29–47.

11 Within the idea of a model, there is room for an understanding of the analogical function of language because the correspondence between the reality and its replica is preserved where that use of analogy works off revelation. In the discussion below of the contemporary use of analogy as a theological method, the correspondence between what is being compared – private experience of God and God's activities in the world – can only be inferred. On this general topic, see Baptista Mondin, *The Principle of Analogy in Protestant and Catholic Theology* (M. Nijhof, 1963).

12 The original title of Troeltsch's book was *The Absolute Validity of Christianity and the History of Religions*. When republished in English translation, it was given its present title of *The Absoluteness of Christianity* (SCM Press, 1972).

13 This essay, entitled 'The Place of Christianity Among the World Religions', has recently been republished in *Christianity and Other Religions*, ed. John Hick and Brian Hebblethwaite (Fortress Press, 1980), pp. 11–31.

14 Albert Schweitzer, *The Quest of the Historical Jesus: A Critical Study of Its Progress from Reimarus to Wrede* [1906; Eng. tr. 1909], trans. W. Montgomery (SCM Press, 1981).

15 Karl Barth, *Protestant Theology in the Nineteenth Century* (SCM Press, 1972), p. 537.

16 Peter L. Berger, *A Rumour of Angels: Modern Society and the Rediscovery of the Supernatural* (Penguin, 1970), p. 39.

17 Emil Brunner is an important exception to this statement for he argued for natural revelation, the presence of the *imago Dei*, and for common grace in the world, all of which were opposed by Barth. See their debate in *Natural Theology: Comprising 'Nature and Grace' by Emil Brunner and the Reply, 'No!' by Karl Barth*, trans. Peter Fraenkel (G. Bles, 1946).

18 Gustav Wingren, *Theology in Conflict: Nygren, Barth, Bultmann*, trans. Eric H. Wahlstrom (Muhlenberg Press, 1958), pp. 23–44.

19 Cornelius Van Til, *Christianity and Barthianism* (Presbyterian and Reformed Publishing Co., 1962).

20 John Hick and Paul Knitter (eds.), *The Myth of Christian Uniqueness: Toward a Pluralistic Theology of Religions* (SCM Press, 1988).

21 John Hick, *God and the Universe of Faiths: Essays in the Philosophy of Religion* (Macmillan, 1973), pp. 1–17.

22 See Hick's major study, *Death and Eternal Life* (Collins, 1976).

23 John Hick, *Evil and the God of Love* (Macmillan, 1966), pp. 381–385.

24 John Hick, *God Has Many Names* (Macmillan, 1980), p. 5.

25 Hick, *God and the Universe of Faiths*, pp. 92–93.

26 *Ibid.*, p. 14.
27 'The christian essence is not to be found in beliefs about God, and whether he is three in one and one in three, but in an attitude to man as our neighbour; not in thinking correctly about christ's two natures, as divine and human, but in living as disciples who in his name feed the hungry, heal the sick and create justice in the world. In short, the essence of christianity is not in believing rightly but in acting rightly in relation to our fellows' (Hick, *ibid.*, pp. 109–110).
28 Hick, *Death and Eternal Life*, pp. 243–250.
29 Hick, *God and the Universe of Faiths*, p. 62.
30 The common search for a world spirituality is uniting Catholics and Protestants across the older divide that once separated them. A good illustration of this is the recent volume edited jointly by Hans Küng and Jürgen Moltmann and entitled *Christianity Among the World Religions* (Concilium; T. & T. Clark, 1986).
31 Karl Rahner, *Theological Investigations* (20 vols.; Darton, Longman & Todd, 1961–81), vol. 1, pp. 297–318.
32 *Ibid.*, vol. 6, pp. 390–391.
33 *Nostra Aetate*, 1.
34 *Gaudium et Spes*, 38.
35 Christopher Butler, *The Theology of Vatican II* (Darton, Longman & Todd, 1967), p. 126.
36 *Lumen Gentium*, 14.
37 *Lumen Gentium*, 15.
38 *Lumen Gentium*, 16.
39 *Lumen Gentium*, 16. See also *Gaudium et Spes*, 19–21; Karl Rahner, 'The Teaching of the Second Vatican Council on Atheism', *Concilium* 3, no. 3 (March, 1967), pp. 5–13.
40 Butler, *op. cit.*, p. 176.
41 George Tyrrell, the leader of the English Catholic modernists, wrote toward the end of his life: 'in these days the thoughtful Catholic no longer regards his Church as a sharp-edged sphere of light walled round with abrupt and impenetrable darkness, but rather as a centre and focus from which the light of religion, spread over all ages and nations, shades away indefinitely in varying degrees with that darkness which can never wholly conquer it' (George Tyrrell, 'Beati Excommunicati', unpublished manuscript, *Petre Papers*, British Museum, MSS 52369). That Tyrrell anticipated the position with the Second Vatican Council reached on this matter may not be so remarkable; that he did so from within a movement whose theology the Pope condemned in 1907 as representing 'the quintessence of all heresy' surely is.
42 Eric Sharpe has noted that this new religious arrangement has produced new ways in which the word 'dialogue' is used. It may still be used of the kind of rational discussion by which differences are clarified, or it might be used of the meeting between different people in which their mutual relations are what is important, not their respective doctrines, or it might be used of the common effort between those who disagree religiously to join in

working co-operatively to ameliorate the world's condition. See his essay, 'The Goals of Inter-Religious Dialogue', *Truth and Dialogue: The Relationship Between World Religions*, ed. John Hick (Sheldon Press, 1975), pp. 77–95.

43 John Hick, it has already been noted, is an exception to this observation; he still believes that we can engage in that kind of discussion on religious matters whose goal is to distinguish what is true from what is false.

44 Emil Brunner, *The Mediator: A Study in the Central Doctrine of the Christian Faith*, trans. Olive Wyon (Lutterworth Press, 1947), pp. 150–151.

Chapter 3: Evangelical Christianity and the Enlightenment

1 This essay first appeared in slightly different form in *Crux*, vol. 25, no. 4 (1989). It represents the substance of a Staley Lecture delivered at Regent College, Vancouver, in April 1989. I am grateful to the editor of *Crux*, Dr D. M. Lewis, for permission to reproduce the article here.

2 G. W. McCree, *George Wilson McCree* (J. Clarke & Co., 1893), p. 20.

3 Quoted by K. R. Manley, in 'The Making of an Evangelical Baptist Leader: John Rippon's early years, 1751–1773', *Baptist Quarterly*, vol. 26, no. 6 (1976), p. 267.

4 *Hansard*, 3rd series, vol. 110 (1850), col. 713.

5 John Telford (ed.), *Wesley's Veterans* (Robert Culley, n.d.), vol. 3, p. 57.

6 Charles Simeon, *Horae Homileticae*, vol. 9 (Richard Watts, 1820), pp. 310–325.

7 Olinthus Gregory (ed.), *The Works of Robert Hall, A.M.*, vol. 5 (S. Holdsworth, 1839), pp. 73–103.

8 Max Weber, *The Protestant Ethic and the Spirit of Capitalism* (George Allen & Unwin, 1930), pp. 98–128.

9 *The Confession of Faith* (Sir D. Hunter Blair & J. Bruce, 1810), xviii. 3, p. 106.

10 W. R. Ward and R. P. Heitzenrater (eds.), *Journals and Diaries, 1 (1735–38)* (*The Works of John Wesley*, vol. 18) (Abingdon Press, 1988), p. 250.

11 Franz Hildebrandt, O. A. Beckerlegge and James Dale (eds.), *A Collection of Hymns for the Use of the People called Methodists* (*The Works of John Wesley*, vol. 7) (Oxford University Press, 1983), p. 195.

12 Thomas Scott in J. M. Pratt (ed.), *The Thought of the Evangelical Leaders* (1856; Banner of Truth, 1978), p. 257.

13 Joseph Bellamy, 'The Millennium', *Sermons*, ed. J. Sutcliff (T. Dicey & Co., 1783), p. 51, cited by W. R. Ward, 'The Baptists and the Transformation of the Church, 1780–1830', *Baptist Quarterly*, vol. 25, no. 4 (1973), p. 171.

14 Arthur Skevington Wood, *Thomas Haweis, 1734–1820* (SPCK, 1957), p. 116.

15 John Gillies, *Memoirs of the Life of the Reverend George Whitefield, M.A.* (E. & C. Dilly, 1772), p. 287.

16 'Invitation to Sinners' in George Osborn (ed.), *The Poetical Works of John and Charles Wesley* (Wesleyan Methodist Conference Office, 1868), vol. 4, p. 371.

17 Mary Raleigh (ed.), *Alexander Raleigh: records of his life* (A. & C. Black, 1881), p. 282.

18 Lesslie Newbigin, *On the Other Side of 1984* (World Council of Churches, 1983), chapter 2.

Chapter 4: Mission in the face of modernity

1 This essay first appeared in the form of a paper for the Plenary Session on The Impact of Modernization, given on 14 July, 1989, at Lausanne II in Manila.

Chapter 5: Change and decay in British society?

1 E. F. Schumacher, *Small is Beautiful* (Sphere Books, 1974), p. 34.

Chapter 6: The 'new science' and the gospel

1 Lesslie Newbigin, *Foolishness To The Greeks* (SPCK, 1986), p. 95.

2 P. Davies, *God and the New Physics* (Pelican, 1984).

3 A. Peacocke, *God and the New Biology* (Dent & Sons, 1986).

4 P. Davies, *The Cosmic Blueprint* (Unwin, 1989), contains a useful introductory discussion of chaos.

5 Lord Kelvin (Sir William Thompson), 'Nineteenth Century Clouds over the Dynamical Theory of Heat and Light', in *Philosophical Magazine* 2 (1901), pp. 1–40.

6 About 186,000 miles per second, or 300,000 kilometres per second, in a vacuum.

7 Gary Zukav, *The Dancing Wu Li Masters* (Flamingo, 1982).

8 P. Atkins, *The Creation* (W. H. Freeman, 1981).

9 Jacques Monod, *Chance and Necessity* (Collins, 1983), p. 110.

10 Thermodynamics, especially of the non-equilibrium kind, is not an easy subject for the non-expert to understand. There is a helpful introduction in the appendix 'Thermodynamics and Life' in Peacocke's book *God and the New Biology*. Those wanting more detail might start with I. Prigogine and I. Stengers, *Order out of Chaos* (Flamingo, 1985).

11 C. H. Bennet, 'On the Nature and Origin of Complexity in Discrete, Homogeneous, Locally-Acting Systems', in *Foundations of Physics* 16 (1986), p. 585.

12 James E. Lovelock, *Gaia: A New Look at Life on Earth* (OUP, 1979) and *The Ages of Gaia* (OUP, 1988).

13 Donald M. MacKay, *Science, Chance and Providence* (OUP, 1978).

14 D. J. Bartholomew, *God of Chance* (SCM Press, 1984) provides an interesting but, I think, a not fully satisfactory discussion of this.

15 See, for instance, J. Polkinghorne, 'A Note on Chaotic Dynamics', *Science and Christian Belief* 1 (1989), pp. 123–127.

16 There is a helpful brief discussion of this by Peacocke in *God and the New Biology*, chapters 1 and 2.

17 R. K. Clifton and M. G. Regehr, 'Capra on Eastern Mysticism and Modern Physics', *Science and Christian Belief* 1 (1989), pp. 53–74, give a detailed critique of Capra's use of both quantum theory and relativity.

18 R. H. Jones, *Science and Mysticism* (Associated University Presses, 1986).

Chapter 7: The gospel and Hinduism

1 Perhaps the most significant development in recent years relating to the church's mission in the world and its mission theology is the resurgence of the world religions and their global impact. A very large number of books and articles on the subject has appeared recently. To mention only a few select ones: Stephen Neill, *Christian Faith and Other Faiths* (Oxford University Press, 2nd ed. 1970); Norman Anderson, *Christianity and World Religions: The Challenge of Pluralism* (IVP, 2nd ed. 1984; 1st ed. 1970, entitled *Christianity and Comparative Religion*); Paul F. Knitter, *No Other Name?* (SCM Press, 1985); Leonard Swidler, *Toward A Universal Theology of Religion* (Orbis, 1987); and Kenneth Cragg, *The Christ and the Faiths* (SPCK, 1986). A few works specifically dealing with Christianity and Hinduism are Raimundo Panikkar, *The Unknown Christ of Hinduism* (Darton, Longman & Todd, 1981); S. J. Samartha, *The Hindu Response to the Unbound Christ* (CLS, 1974); and Harold Coward (ed.), *Hindu-Christian Dialogue* (Orbis, 1989).
2 Vinay Samuel and Chris Sugden (eds.), *Sharing Jesus in the Two Thirds World* (Partnership in Mission – Asia, 1983), pp. 202–203.
3 Sunder Raj, *The Confusion Called Conversion* (Traci, 1988), p. 130.
4 Stephen Neill, *Christian Faith and Other Faiths*, pp. 92–94.
5 Sunder Raj, *op. cit.*, p. 128.
6 P. D. Devanandan, *The Gospel and Renascent Hinduism* (SCM Press, 1959), p. 34.
7 Richard Taylor in Harold Coward (ed.), *Hindu-Christian Dialogue* (Orbis, 1989), p. 125.
8 S. Wesley Ariarajah in *Hindu-Christian Dialogue*, p. 252.
9 Ariarajah in *Hindu-Christian Dialogue*, pp. 259–260.

Chapter 8: Agreed in principle?

1 John Stott, *Issues Facing Christians Today*, p. 31.
2 Harry Blamires, *The Christian Mind* (SPCK, 1963), p. 3.
3 A. H. Birch, *The British System of Government* (Allen & Unwin, 7th ed. 1986), p. 91.
4 A. H. Birch, *ibid.*, p. 94.
5 R. Rose, *Politics in England* (Faber & Faber, 4th ed. 1985), p. 163.
6 Mrs M. Thatcher, quoted in *The Independent*, May 1988.
7 Leon Morris, *1 & 2 Thessalonians* (Tyndale New Testament Commentaries; IVP, 1st ed. 1958), p. 147.
8 Eric Heffer in John Selwyn Gummer, Eric Heffer and Alan Beith, *Faith in Politics* (SPCK, 1987), p. 85.
9 John Selwyn Gummer, *ibid.*, p. 34.
10 For example, M. Wilcock, *The Message of Luke* (Bible Speaks Today series; IVP, 1979), pp. 185–186, and R. A. Cole, *Mark* (Tyndale New Testament Commentaries; IVP, 2nd ed. 1989), p. 271.

11 Clark H. Pinnock, 'Pursuit of Utopia, Betrayal of the Poor', in *Crux*, vol. 23, no. 4 (1987), p. 6.
12 Lloyd Billingsley, *The Generation That Knew Not Joseph* (Multnomah Press, 1985), p. 18.
13 Lloyd Billingsley, *ibid.*, p. 143.
14 Lloyd Billingsley, *ibid.*, pp. 140–141.
15 Edward Norman, *Christianity and the World Order* (OUP, 1979).
16 Rachel Tingle, *Another Gospel?* (Christian Studies Centre, 1988), p. 60.
17 Rachel Tingle, in the 'Pulpit Watch' column of *Free Nation*, April 1986.
18 Clark Pinnock, *op. cit.*, p. 6.
19 Lloyd Billingsley, *op. cit.*, pp. 33–34.
20 Rachel Tingle, *Another Gospel?*, pp. 58–59.
21 Edward Norman, *op. cit.*, p. 2.
22 Clark Pinnock, *op. cit.*, p. 5.
23 Clark Pinnock, *ibid.*, p. 11.
24 B. Griffiths, *Morality and the Market Place* (Hodder & Stoughton, 1982), p. 36.
25 Clark Pinnock, *op. cit.*, p. 11.
26 T. Bottomore *et al.*, *A Dictionary of Marxist Thought* (Blackwell, 1983), p. 216.
27 D. McLellan, *Marx* (Fontana, 1975), p. 36.
28 K. Marx and F. Engels, *The Holy Family*, quoted in D. McLellan, *The Thought of Karl Marx* (Macmillan, 1980), pp. 34–35.
29 K. Marx, *The German Ideology*, quoted in D. McLellan, *ibid.*, p. 243.
30 John Stott, *Issues Facing Christians Today*, pp. 39–40.
31 Peter Broadbent, 'The Soul of the Parties', in *Third Way*, vol. 12, no. 3 (1989), pp. 20–22.
32 Peter Broadbent, *ibid.*, p. 22.
33 Richard Mouw, *Politics and the Biblical Drama* (Eerdmans, 1976).
34 Philip Wogaman, *Christian Perspectives on Politics* (SCM Press, 1988).
35 William Temple, *Christianity and Social Order* (SCM Press, 3rd ed. 1950), p. 47.
36 J. A. Kirk, *God's Word for a Complex World* (Marshall Pickering, 1987).
37 Described in J. A. Kirk (ed.), *Handling Problems of Peace and War* (Marshall Pickering, 1988).
38 Philip Wogaman, *op. cit.*, p. 123.
39 B. Griffiths, *Morality and the Market Place*, p. 72.
40 See, for example, M. Graham, *Stretching the Limits of Politics*, Jubilee Centre Paper no. 8, 1988.
41 Alan Storkey, *Transforming Economics* (Third Way / SPCK, 1986).

Chapter 9: An appropriate spirituality for a post-modern world
1 John Stott, *Issues Facing Christians Today*.
2 Francis de Sales, *Introduction to the Devout Life*, trans. John K. Ryan (Image edition, Doubleday, 1972), pp. 42–45.
3 The accusation of 'quietism' was characteristic of such intense spiritual fervour in the seventeenth century.
4 See John M. Lozano, *Discipleship: Towards an Understanding of Religious Life*,

trans. Beatrice Wilczynski (Claret Center for Resources in Spirituality, 1983), vol. 2, pp. 70–72.

5 *Ibid.*, p. 72.

6 Vatican Council II: *The Conciliar and Post-Conciliar Documents*, ed. A. Flannery, *Lumen Gentium*, 44a (Castello Publishing House, 1975).

7 *Op. cit.*, *Lumen Gentium*, 44c.

8 *Op. cit.*, *Lumen Gentium*, 46b.

9 *Op. cit.*, *Perfectae Caritatis*, 1.

10 Thomas M. Gannon and George W. Traub, *The Desert and the City* (Loyola University Press, 1969), p. 290.

11 *Ibid.*

12 John M. Lozano, *op. cit.*, p. 257.

13 See Frank C. Senn (ed.), *Protestant Spiritual Traditions* (Paulist Press, 1986).

14 Winifred Zeller, 'The Protestant Attitude to Monasticism, with special reference to Gerhard Tersteegen', *Downside Review*, vol. 93 (1975), pp. 178–192.

15 Edward Farley, *Requiem for a Lost Piety: The Contemporary Search for the Christian Life* (Westminster, 1966).

16 Hans Urs von Balthasar, *On Prayer*, trans. A. V. Littledale (SPCK, 1973), p. 73.

17 Klaus Bockmuehl, *The Unreal God of Modern Theology* (Helmers & Howard, 1988).

18 Eric W. Gritsch, *Born Againism: Perspectives on a Movement* (Fortress Press, 1982).

19 Thomas Howard, *Evangelical is not Enough* (1984; Ignatius Press, 1990).

20 Dan O'Neill (ed.), *The New Catholics* (Crossroads, 1987), in which seventeen contemporary converts tell their story.

21 George M. Marsden, *Reforming Fundamentalism* (Eerdmans, 1987).

22 Lesslie Newbigin, *The Other Side of 1984* (World Council of Churches, 1983), p. 19.

23 Michael Polanyi, *Personal Knowledge* (Routledge, Kegan & Paul, 1962), p. 266.

24 Colin Gunton, *Enlightenment and Alienation* (Marshall, Morgan & Scott, 1985), p. 5.

25 Arthur F. Holmes, *All Truth is God's Truth* (IVP, 1979).

26 Augustine, *Confessions*, x. 1, trans. Edward B. Pusey (Macmillan, 1961), p. 153.

27 *Ibid.*, vii. 10.

28 Bernard of Clairvaux, *On the Song of Songs*, trans. Kilian Walsh (Cistercian Publications, 1976), vol. 2, *Sermon* 37,1, p. 181.

29 John Calvin, *Institutes*, I. i. 1.

30 *Ibid.*, I. i. 1.

31 *Ibid.*, I. i. 2.

32 *Ibid.*, I. ii. 1.

33 *Ibid.*, I. vi. 1.

34 Glenn Tinder, 'Can we be good without God?' *Atlanta Monthly*, Jan. 1990.

35 J. M. Houston, *In Search of Happiness: A Guide to Personal Contentment* (Lion, 1990), ch. 7, pp. 137–164.

36 Augustine of Hippo, *Selected Writings*, trans. Mary T. Clark (Paulist Press, 1984), pp. 15–21.

37 Quoted by T. F. Torrance, *The Trinitarian Faith* (T. & T. Clark, 1988), p. 21.

38 John Owen, *The Grace and Duty of Being Spiritually Minded*, in *The Works of John Owen*, vol. 11, ed. William H. Goold (The Banner of Truth Trust, 1965), p. 476.

39 J. M. Houston, *The Transforming Friendship: A Guide to Prayer* (Lion, 1989).

40 Quoted by Theodor Tack, *If Augustine were Alive* (Alba House, 1988), p. 35.

41 See Jonathan Edwards, *The Religious Affections*, ed. J. M. Houston (Multnomah Press, 1984).

Chapter 10: Authority in preaching

1 Most books on preaching assume an institutional definition as their starting-point. Typical is this, from D. Martyn Lloyd-Jones:

What then is preaching? What do I mean by preaching? Let us look at it like this. There, is a man standing in a pulpit and speaking, and there, are people sitting in pews or seats and listening. What is happening? Why is this? Why does that man stand in that pulpit? What is his object? Why does the Church put him there to do this? Why do these other people come to listen? What is this man meant to be doing? What is he trying to do? What ought he to be doing? These it seems to me are the great questions . . .

From *Preaching and Preachers* (Hodder & Stoughton, 1972), p. 53.

2 Phillips Brooks, *Lectures on Preaching* (H. R. Allenson [1877]), p. 5.

3 *Westminster Confession of Faith*, I. x.

4 See Lloyd-Jones, *op. cit.*, pp. 304–325.

5 Richard Baxter, *The Reformed Pastor* (Banner of Truth, 1974), p. 149.

6 C. H. Spurgeon, *Autobiography* (Banner of Truth, 1973), vol. 2, pp. 291f.

7 Dr Stanford Holme (1879), cited in Spurgeon, *op. cit.*, p. 361.

8 John Stott, *I Believe in Preaching*, pp. 334f.

Chapter 11: The Christian faith: context, communication and content

1 John Goldingay, *Theological Diversity and the Authority of the Old Testament* (Eerdmans, 1987), pp. 29ff.

2 H. Wheeler Robinson, *The Religious Ideas of the Old Testament* (Duckworth, 1913), pp. 102ff.

3 Dan Cohn-Shabok, *On Earth as it is in Heaven: Jews, Christians and Liberation Theology* (Orbis, 1987).

4 John V. Taylor, *The Go-between God* (SCM Press, 1972), p. 17.

5 *Ibid.*, p. 44.

6 See further Leonard Hodgson, *The Doctrine of the Trinity* (Nisbet, 1943), Lecture VI, pp. 144ff.

7 See Michael Nazir-Ali, *Frontiers in Muslim-Christian Encounter* (Regnum Books, 1987), pp. 15ff.

8 See further Hugh Montefiore, *The Probability of God* (SCM Press, 1985).
9 B. W. Anderson, *The Living World of the Old Testament* (Longman, rev. ed. 1978); K. A. Kitchen, *Ancient Orient and the Old Testament* (Tyndale Press, 1966), pp. 49, 69f.
10 Norman K. Gottwald, *The Tribes of Yahweh: A Sociology of the Religion of Liberated Israel* (SCM Press, 1980), p. 611.
11 John Goldingay, *op. cit.*, p. 67.
12 See, for example, Joyce G. Baldwin, *Haggai, Zechariah and Malachi* (Tyndale Old Testament Commentaries; IVP, 1972), pp. 227ff.
13 Oscar Cullman, *Christ and Time: The Primitive Conception of Time and History* (SCM Press, 1951), pp. 82, 117–118.
14 Karl Barth, *Church Dogmatics* (Eng. tr., T. & T. Clark, 1959), vol. 2, *The Doctrine of God.*
15 See Geoffrey Wainwright (ed.), *Keeping the Faith: Essays to Mark the Centenary of 'Lux Mundi'* (SPCK, 1989); Robert Morgan (ed.), *The Religion of the Incarnation: Anglican Essays in Commemoration of 'Lux Mundi'* (Bristol Classical Press, 1989).
16 Charles Gore, *Dissertations on Subjects Connected with the Incarnation* (1895), pp. 69–226.
17 Charles Wesley, 'Come, O Thou Traveller unknown'.

Chapter 12: Evangelism in the local church

1 Michael Green, *Evangelism through the Local Church* (Hodder & Stoughton, 1990).
2 David Watson, *Jesus Then and Now*, a video by Lella Productions, sponsored by the Trinity Trust; the book *Jesus Then and Now* is by David Watson and Simon Jenkins (Lion, 2nd ed. 1987).
3 John Stott, *Becoming a Christian* (IVP booklet, 2nd ed. 1972).

Chapter 13: The search for ministry effectiveness in the modern world

1 Garth Lean, *John Wesley – Anglican* (Blandford Press, 1964), p. 24.
2 P. L. Parker (ed.), *The Journal of John Wesley* (Moody Press, 1974), p. 53.
3 From David Wesley Soper, *These Found the Way* (Westminster Press, 1951); quoted in Stanley Jones, *Conversion* (Hodder & Stoughton, 1966), p. 48.
4 Helmut Thielicke, *A Little Exercise for Young Theologians* (Eerdmans, 1962), p. xii.
5 *Ibid.*, pp. 13–14.
6 *Ibid.*, p. 14.
7 *Ibid.*, p. 14.
8 *Ibid.*, pp. 36–37.
9 J. B. Phillips, *The Ring of Truth* (Hodder & Stoughton, 1967), pp. 7–8.
10 Procrustes, according to Greek legend, was a robber who laid travellers on a bed and made them fit it by cutting off their limbs or stretching them! Hence 'Procrustean': 'seeking to enforce uniformity by violent methods' (*Concise Oxford Dictionary*, 7th ed.).
11 Helmut Thielicke, *How Modern Should Theology Be?* (Fontana, 1970), p. 18.
12 *Ibid.*, p. 19.

13 Quoted in J. Oswald Sanders, *Spiritual Leadership* (Marshall, Morgan & Scott, 1967), p. 75.
14 Quoted in Sanders, *ibid.*, p. 76.
15 Quoted in John Stott, *I Believe in Preaching*, p. 181.
16 *Ibid.*, p. 180.
17 Quoted in Stott, *ibid.*, p. 180.
18 Quoted in Stott, *ibid.*, p. 180.
19 Sanders, *op. cit.*, p. 69.
20 *Ibid.*, p. 127.
21 *Ibid.*, p. 70.
22 *Ibid.*, p. 71.
23 Quoted in O. Clement, *Dialogues Avec Le Patriarche Athénagoras* (Fayard, 1969), p. 154.
24 Léon Joseph Cardinal Suenens, *A New Pentecost?* (Fount, 1974), pp. 19–20.
25 Michael Green, *Evangelism Now and Then* (IVP, 1979), p. 14.
26 *Ibid.*, p. 15.
27 Canon Douglas Webster, 'What is Evangelism?', in Michael Cassidy (ed.), *I Will Heal Their Land* (Africa Enterprise, 1974), pp. 87–88.
28 Thielicke, *op. cit.*, p. 86.
29 *Ibid.* p. 10.
30 C. H. Dodd elaborated the kerygma as follows:
  1. The age of fulfillment has dawned.
  2. This happened in the ministry, death and resurrection of Jesus.
  3. Jesus has been exalted to God's right hand as the head of the new Israel.
  4. The gift of the Holy Spirit is the sign of Christ's present power.
  5. There will be a consummation of the age in the return of Christ.
  6. The preaching ends with an appeal for repentance and faith, the offer of forgiveness, salvation and the promised Holy Spirit.
  From C. H. Dodd, *The Apostolic Teaching and Its Development* (Hodder & Stoughton, 1963), p. 17.
31 Os Guinness, speaking at Lausanne II Congress on World Evangelisation in Manila, on *The Impact of Modernization*, July 1989. His actual paper is reproduced here as chapter 4.
32 *Ibid.*
33 Ray Bakke, 'A Theology As Big as the City', in Harvie Conn (ed.), *Urban Mission* (Westminster Theological Seminary, 1989), p. 8.
34 *Ibid.*, p. 9.
35 David O. Moberg, *The Great Reversal: Evangelism and Social Concern* (revised ed., Lippincott, 1977).
36 Carl Henry, *The Uneasy Conscience of Modern Fundamentalism* (Eerdmans, 1947).
37 Quoted in George D. Marsden, *Reforming Fundamentalism* (Eerdmans, 1987), p. 77.
38 *Ibid.*, p. 77–78; see also Carl Henry, 'The Vigor of Evangelicalism', in *Christian Life*, Jan. 1948, pp. 30–32; March 1948, p. 35; April 1948, p. 32.
39 Carl Henry, *The Uneasy Conscience of Modern Fundamentalism*, p. 14.

40 *Ibid.*, p. 36.
41 *Lausanne Covenant*, Clause 5.
42 Athol Gill, 'Christian Social Responsibility', in C. René Padilla (ed.), *The New Face of Evangelicalism* (Hodder & Stoughton, 1976), p. 101.
43 Gustavo Gutiérrez, *A Theology of Liberation* (Eng. tr., SCM Press, 1974).
44 Emilio Núñez, *Liberation Theology* (Moody Press, 1985), p. 80.
45 John Stott, *Christian Mission in the Modern World* (Falcon, 1975), p. 95.

Books by John Stott

Books are listed in chronological order according to publication date. The *Bible Speaks Today* series of expositions is listed separately. Where a book is published in Britain and America, the British publisher is named first. Small booklets, and those derived from larger books, are not included.

Men with a Message (IVP, 1954), published in USA under the title *Basic Introduction to the New Testament* (Eerdmans/IVP, 1964). An introduction to the principal New Testament authors and the distinctive message of each.

Fundamentalism and Evangelism (Crusade Booklet, 1956; Eerdmans, 1959).

Basic Christianity (IVP, 1958, revised 1971; Eerdmans, 1959). An evangelistic book outlining the evidence for the deity of Christ and the way of salvation. Translated into thirty-six languages.

Your Confirmation (Hodder & Stoughton, 1958, revised 1991). An elementary treatment for confirmation candidates of Christian beginnings, belief and behaviour.

What Christ Thinks of the Church (Lutterworth, 1958; Eerdmans/IVP, 1959). Expository addresses on the Letters to the Seven Churches in Revelation 2 – 3. Revised and illustrated edition published in 1990 by Word (UK) and Harold Shaw (USA).

The Preacher's Portrait (Tyndale, 1961; Eerdmans/IVP, 1961). Some New Testament word studies. The 1960 Payton Lectures at Fuller Theological Seminary. Reissued by IVP in 1991.

Confess Your Sins. The first volume in the *Christian Foundations* series, published under the auspices of the Evangelical Fellowship in the Anglican Communion (Hodder & Stoughton, 1964; Word, 1974). An appeal for secret, private and public confession, and a reasoned rejection of auricular confession.

The Epistles of John (Tyndale, 1964; Eerdmans, 1964; revised edition based on the NIV text published by IVP/Eerdmans, 1988). A volume in the *Tyndale New Testament Commentaries* series.

The Canticles and Selected Psalms (Hodder & Stoughton, 1966). One of the *Prayer Book Commentary* series, expounding all the Canticles and about fifty psalms. Illustrated and modernized edition published in 1988 by Word (UK) and Moody (USA) under the title *Favourite Psalms*.

Men Made New (IVP–UK, 1966; IVP–USA, 1967; Baker, 1984). An exposition of Romans 5 – 8.

Our Guilty Silence. The last book in the *Christian Foundations* series, published under the auspices of the Evangelical Fellowship in the Anglican Communion (Hodder & Stoughton, 1967; Eerdmans/ IVP, 1969). An examination of the four main hindrances to, and essentials of, biblical evangelism.

One People (Falcon, 1969; IVP, 1970; revised edition Revell, 1982). The 1968 Pastoral Theology Lectures in Durham University on the relation between clergy and laity in God's church.

Christ the Controversialist (Tyndale, 1970; IVP, 1972). A study in some essentials of evangelical religion as taught by Jesus in his public debates with religious leaders. Reissued by IVP in 1991.

Understanding the Bible (Scripture Union and Gospel Light, 1972; Zondervan, 1980). An introduction to the Bible's purpose, setting, history, authority, interpretation, message and use.

Your Mind Matters (IVP in UK and USA, 1972). The place of the mind in the Christian life.

Balanced Christianity (Hodder & Stoughton/IVP, 1975). A call to evangelical Christians to avoid unnecessary polarization.

Christian Mission in the Modern World (Falcon/IVP, 1975). A study of five words ('mission', 'evangelism', 'dialogue', 'salvation' and 'conversion') in the forefront of contemporary debate. The 1974 Chavasse Lectures at Wycliffe Hall, Oxford.

Baptism and Fullness (IVP in UK and USA, 1975). The revised and enlarged version of *The Baptism and Fullness of the Holy Spirit* (1964). A biblical study of the promise, fullness, fruit and gifts of the Holy Spirit, in the light of the charismatic movement.

The Lausanne Covenant: An Exposition and Commentary (Worldwide Publications, USA, 1975). Published in UK as *Explaining the Lausanne Covenant* (Scripture Union, 1975). The Covenant was composed and adopted at the 1974 International Congress on World Evangelisation in Lausanne, Switzerland.

Focus on Christ (Collins in UK and USA, 1979; also Zondervan, 1981, under the title *Understanding Christ*). 'An Enquiry into the Theology of Prepositions' – a devotional study of the Christian's personal relationship to Christ.

The Bible: Book for Today (IVP in UK and USA, 1982). First published in USA as *God's Book for God's People*; reissued by Discovery House as *You Can Trust the Bible* (1991).

I Believe in Preaching (Hodder & Stoughton/Eerdmans, 1982, but published in the USA under the title *Between Two Worlds: The Art of Preaching in the Twentieth Century*). A defence of and call to expository preaching as the church's greatest contemporary need.

Issues Facing Christians Today (Marshalls, 1984; Revell, 1985, but published in the USA under the title *Involvement*. Revised edition published in UK and USA, 1990). An appraisal of contemporary social and moral questions.

The Authentic Jesus (Marshalls/IVP, 1985). A response to current scepticism in the church.

The Cross of Christ (IVP–UK, 1986; IVP–USA, 1987). The implications of his death for him and for us.

Essentials (Hodder & Stoughton/IVP, 1988. USA title *Evangelical Essentials*). With David L. Edwards. A liberal–evangelical dialogue.

Expositions by John Stott in
The Bible Speaks Today series

(All published by IVP in UK and USA.)

The Message of Galatians (1968). Original title *Only One Way*. The first volume in the *BST* series.

The Message of 2 Timothy (1973). Original title *Guard the Gospel*.

The Message of the Sermon on the Mount (1978). Original title *Christian Counter-Culture*.

The Message of Ephesians (1979). Original title *God's New Society*.

The Message of Acts: To the Ends of the Earth (1990). Published in USA under the title *The Spirit, the Church and the World*.

The Message of Thessalonians: Preparing for the coming King (1991). Published in USA under the title *The Gospel and History*.

About the contributors

Saphir P. Athyal, who has a PhD in the Old Testament from Princeton, served as the Principal of Union Biblical Seminary, Pune, India, for fifteen years. He is a member of the Lausanne Committee, and was the Programme Director for Pattaya 1980 and Programme Chairman for Lausanne II, 1989, in Manila. He was the founder and first Chairman of the Asia Theological Association, and has been teaching in a number of seminaries in North America for short periods as guest professor.

D. W. Bebbington is a historian specializing in British history since the eighteenth century. He is completing a study of W. E. Gladstone for the *Library of Religious Biography* series to be published by Eerdmans, and researching a monograph on the mind of Gladstone. Other particular interests include the history of evangelicalism in Britain and abroad. He is helping to organize a conference on Transatlantic Evangelicalism, and to plan an international association for the study of Christianity and history. His *Patterns in History* is published by Apollos.

Michael Cassidy is the founder and South African team leader of Africa Enterprise, a pan-African evangelistic association. He has ministered in many countries across the world, and has a special concern for evangelism and reconciliation in Africa generally, but South Africa in particular. He graduated from Cambridge with an MA in modern and medieval languages, and from Fuller Seminary with a BD. He is an Anglican, and is married with three children.

Timothy Dudley-Smith was Secretary of the Church Pastoral-Aid Society from 1965 to 1973, before moving to Norfolk to become Archdeacon of Norwich and then Bishop of Thetford. He is President of the Church of England Evangelical Council and of the Evangelical Alliance, and is widely known as a writer of hymns.

Martyn Eden is Secretary for Home Affairs for the Evangelical Alliance of the UK. Prior to that he was first Dean of the London Institute for Contemporary Christianity and then Director of Research and Publications, Christian Impact. Formerly, he was Principal

Lecturer in Public and Social Administration at Southampton Institute of Higher Education. With Ernest Lucas he wrote *Being Transformed* (Marshalls, 1988).

Michael Green. After being the first Principal of St John's Theological College, Nottingham (1969–75), and for twelve years rector of St Aldate's Church, Oxford (1975–87), Michael Green is now Professor of Evangelism at Regent College, Vancouver. He speaks widely in Canada and internationally, and has written many books, including most recently *Evangelism through the Local Church* (Hodder & Stoughton). He teaches New Testament and Apologetics, but his main academic and practical commitment has been to evangelism.

Os Guinness is a speaker and writer. An Englishman born in China of missionary parents, he is a graduate of the Universities of London and Oxford, gaining his DPhil from the latter. Married, with one child, he makes his home in Virginia. He is author of *The Dust of Death* (IVP), *Doubt: Faith in two minds* (Lion), and *The Gravedigger File* (Hodder & Stoughton).

James M. Houston is Professor of Spiritual Theology and former Chancellor of Regent College, Vancouver, and a writer.

Ernest C. Lucas. As a former research chemist with theological training, Dr Lucas has a long-standing interest in the science–religion interface, as well as in Old Testament Studies. He is Education Director of Christian Impact, which seeks to help and encourage Christians to apply biblical thinking to contemporary social, spiritual and cultural issues.

Michael Nazir-Ali is General Secretary of the Church Missionary Society, and holds both British and Pakistani citizenship. He has studied at Karachi, Oxford and Cambridge, in economics, sociology, theology, comparative literature, and comparative philosophy of religion. He tutored at Karachi Theological College for some years, and, in 1984, was made Bishop of Raiwind. In 1986 he returned to Britain, involved in the Lambeth Conference. Bishop Michael is also a director of the Oxford Centre for Mission Studies, and does much speaking and writing.

J. I. Packer is a writer and teacher of theology, and Sangwoo Youtong Chee Professor of Theology, Regent College, Vancouver.

ABOUT THE CONTRIBUTORS

Elaine Storkey lectures in Social Science with the Open University, and is a writer. She is a member of the Anglican General Synod, and is married, with three sons.

David F. Wells is Andrew Mutch Professor of Historical and Systematic Theology at Gordon-Conwell Theological Seminary, and previously taught at Trinity Evangelical Divinity School. He studied at London, Manchester and Trinity, and was Research Fellow at Yale Divinity School, 1974.

Chris Wright is an Ulsterman, lecturing in Old Testament at All Nations Christian College. Previously, he taught at Union Biblical Seminary, Pune, India. He is a graduate of Cambridge, where he also gained his PhD. His dissertation was published as *God's People in God's Land* (Paternoster). His other publications include *Living as the People of God* (IVP). He is married, with four children.